Devolution

DEVOLUTION

SCOTTISH ANSWERS TO SCOTTISH QUESTIONS?

THE THIRD SCOTTISH SOCIAL ATTITUDES REPORT

EDITED BY CATHERINE BROMLEY, JOHN CURTICE,
KERSTIN HINDS AND ALISON PARK

EDINBURGH UNIVERSITY PRESS

Editorial arrangement © Catherine Bromley, John Curtice, Kerstin Hinds
and Alison Park, 2003. Other material © the contributors, 2003.

Edinburgh University Press Ltd
22 George Square, Edinburgh

Typeset in Goudy Old Style by
Hewer Text Ltd, Edinburgh, and
printed and bound in Great Britain by
MPG Books Ltd, Bodmin

A CIP record for this book is available from the British Library

ISBN 0 7486 1808 2 (paperback)

National Centre for Social Research

Scotland

Contents

List of Tables

Foreword

If you need convincing why you should read a volume like this, which, let's face it, contains an awful lot of statistics, then I suggest you cast your mind back briefly to the spring of the year 2000.

Then, if you believed the newspapers, Scotland was torn by ideological strife the like of which had not been seen since the Covenanting armies set forth to claim Christendom for the Kirk. Except this time Covenanters and Catholics were on the same side, crusading in favour of an obscure clause about teaching matters connected with homosexuality in schools. Scotland would be saved for the True Faith, the simple decencies and the missionary position.

Our cousins in England, preoccupied with such trivia as building a multicultural society and reforming the National Health Service, guffawed loudly. Not content with boring everyone to death with their vaunted 'national identity' and siphoning off the rest of the UK's money for their absurdly overfunded public services, now the Scots were wrapping themselves up in the sort of moral ardour one of their better-known shepherds had lampooned hundreds of years before in *Confessions of a Justified Sinner*. So much for devolution!

The reality was very different. We have long had the knockabout political argument against the caricature of Scotland above – when push came to shove the Scottish Parliament abolished Section 28, while Tony Blair backed off at the slightest whiff of trouble.

But the chapter on religion in this book has more profound implications. It implies that, far from being in thrall to the more intolerant varieties of Christianity, religious observance among Scots has now fallen so dramatically that it has reached a turning point. At the conference in Edinburgh which launched the findings explored in more detail here, Steve Bruce argued the real issue for Scotland was how to live in a society which, along with some others in Western Europe, had become post-religious. And, incidentally, he and Tony Glendinning are able to show that a majority of Scots think there is nothing wrong at all with school teachers explaining homosexuality to teenagers.

Their essay has similarly radical implications for our understanding of sectarianism. Of course, in certain areas of the country, sectarianism is alive and well, but the findings here suggest that across Scotland as a whole it is terminally ill.

That contradicts the 'common sense' view of Scotland, so much so that when the survey results were released initially, they were misreported as showing sectarianism is flourishing. Which points to a conclusion not dealt with systematically here: sometimes in Scotland we are keener to deal with our notions of reality rather than reality itself. Of course, 'Scots Relaxed About Religious Differences Shock' doesn't make much of a headline, but that is hardly the fault of the Scottish Social Attitudes (SSA) survey.

The survey results on religion are particularly enlightening, but there is much of interest in the rest of this volume. Perhaps we felt instinctively that contrary to Gordon Brown's views, people in Scotland believe that, as epitomised by the Scottish Parliament's legislation on care for the elderly, the welfare state should be universal, with no return to the means tests which haunted the Labour party in the past. Some of the figures here start to put flesh on those instincts. And to explore some new areas. It is interesting, for example, that younger Scots have more liberal views than their parents on matters of morality, but do not appear to have more libertarian views on the role of the state. One wonders how far that finding would be echoed across the European Union.

There is one question which, necessarily, this book cannot answer, although it may furnish some clues. This is the importance people in Scotland attach to elections to their new Parliament. The first Scottish parliamentary election was atypical simply by virtue of being the first. The next should be more 'normal' and in a sense it will be a double poll: an election about who should rule the country and an election about the status of elections to the Scottish Parliament. With regard to the latter, the turnout will be as important as the result. But there will be other indicators. If voters are more prepared to lodge protest votes than they would be at a Westminster election, for example, that might indicate they do not take Holyrood very seriously and thus don't much mind if the 'wrong' party runs it. A high turnout, on the other hand, might give some beef to the view, echoed by succeeding SSA surveys and other poll data, that people in Scotland want more power for the Parliament, even if they are not much enamoured of the present incumbents.

To say this book is part of a work in progress is, I know, something of a cliché. It's also a polite way of saying that to get the most from it you will have to buy the next edition. The principal value of the SSA is that it is building up a body of knowledge about Scottish attitudes that we simply did not have before and allowing changes in attitudes to be mapped over time.

So there is a strong case for continuing to collect the data and continuing to collect it on the same subjects. But there are also other areas to explore in that sometimes murky field which lies between straightforwardly party political opinion and views on society in general. And with Holyrood now sitting on a body of legislation which is in some respects significantly different from UK law, perhaps it is time to ask a few more questions.

Here are a few suggestions. Do people in Scotland accept the arguments of Tony Blair that while health services should be financed from general taxation, their provision should be through a variety of means, public, private and co-operative? Or do they believe the NHS should continue to run everything? Do people accept the consensual approach to helping substandard schools we have in Scotland? Or do they believe tougher options should be available on the English model – allowing failing schools to be taken over by more successful ones, for example, or closing entire education authorities? And what relationship do the answers to these questions have to the matter of Scottish identity, which too often simply boils down to whether people feel more Scottish than British?

So there remains plenty to be done. The SSA surveys have already provided us with a mirror of ourselves. And while policy should not necessarily be driven entirely by what we see there, it does seem sound sense to keep looking.

Gordon Brewer
Haddington, November 2002

Notes on the Contributors

Ross Bond is a Research Officer in the Institute for Governance, Edinburgh University.

Gordon Brewer is a presenter on BBC *Newsnight Scotland*.

Catherine Bromley is a Senior Researcher at the National Centre for Social Research Scotland and Co-Director of the Scottish Social Attitudes Survey.

Steve Bruce is Professor of Sociology at Aberdeen University.

John Curtice is Head of Research, National Centre for Social Research Scotland, Co-Director of the Scottish Social Attitudes Survey and Professor of Politics at Strathclyde University.

Lisa Curtice is Director of the Scottish Consortium for Learning Disability.

Maria Gannon is a Research Officer in the Centre for Drug Misuse Research.

Tony Glendinning is Senior Lecturer in Sociology and Anthropology, Aberdeen University.

Gordon Hay is a Research Officer in the Centre for Drug Misuse Research.

Kerstin Hinds is a Senior Researcher at the National Centre for Social Research Scotland and Co-Director of the Scottish Social Attitudes Survey.

Ade Kearns is Professor of Urban Studies at Glasgow University.

Neil McKeganey is Professor of Drug Misuse Research at Glasgow University.

Alison Park is a Research Director at the National Centre for Social Research and Co-Director of the Scottish Social Attitudes Survey.

Alison Parkes is a Research Officer in the Department of Urban Studies, Glasgow University.

Alison Petch is Professor of Community Care Studies at Glasgow University.

Michael Rosie is Lecturer in Sociology, Edinburgh University.

Paula Surridge is Lecturer in Sociology, Bristol University.

Introduction

The creation of the Scottish Parliament in 1999 has arguably been the biggest change to the government of Scotland since the Act of Union in 1707. A wide range of government policy in Scotland including health, education, criminal justice, agriculture and transport is now determined by an Executive located in Edinburgh and accountable to a parliament elected solely by the voters of Scotland. Subject to the financial constraints of the block grant it receives from London, the parliament has the freedom to decide the priorities for government action in Scotland and how those priorities should be tackled. If that means deviating from the policy of the UK government in London, so be it. Devolution means that Scottish answers can be given to Scottish questions.

No longer then should Scotland suffer the indignity of having foisted upon it policies designed to appeal to the average Conservative voter in the South of England – commonly alleged to have been its fate during the Conservative administration of 1979–97. But if the Scottish Parliament is to concern itself with the preferences of the average Scottish voter this raises an important question. How is the Parliament, or indeed anyone else, to know what the average Scottish voter considers to be the most important questions the government needs to address, let alone what they believe the answers might be? Of course, we can look at election results. But how voters decide to cast their ballots can give no more than the broadest indication of their policy preferences and priorities. It is certainly no substitute for asking voters themselves what they think about the various social and economic problems that face Scottish society.

The aim of this book is to provide a dispassionate and informed account of just what Scots do think about the major issues facing their country as they prepare to elect in May 2003 the second devolved Scottish Parliament.

In so doing we focus on two simple but important questions about devolution: What has it achieved so far? What challenges might it face in future? One way we can approach the first question is to examine how well the Scottish public thinks the new Parliament has performed. Has it met their expectations? How do they think it compares with Westminster? These issues are addressed in particular in Chapter 1. But we can also ask how far the policies that have been pursued by the Scottish Parliament are in tune with the opinions of the public that it seeks to serve. This perhaps is a particularly important question to ask of some of those policies that represent a departure from current UK government policy (such as the abolition of up-front tuition fees for university students and the introduction of so-called free personal care for older people). If such policies are not in line with Scottish public opinion we might have good reason to question whether devolution has indeed provided Scottish answers to Scottish questions. How representative Scottish public policy (or indeed UK government policy, where its scope extends north of the border) is of Scottish public opinion is a theme that recurs throughout the book but especially so in Chapters 2 to 4, which provide in-depth analyses of attitudes towards community care, housing and drugs.

It is of course naïve to believe that there is just one Scottish public opinion. Like any modern society, the country contains potentially divisive social differences. And divisions in public opinion within Scotland could present as much of a challenge to the success of devolution as its ability to reflect differences in public opinion between Scotland and the rest of the United Kingdom. If different communities in Scotland have sharply differing views then the Parliament may be faced with seemingly irreconcilable conflicts where any decision it might make is likely to be challenged, thereby posing a threat to the body's fledgling authority. The debate in the first year of the Parliament's life about the abolition of Clause 2A on the promotion of homosexuality by local councils, in which those of a religious persuasion were prominent amongst the opponents of change, appeared to illustrate the danger. Moreover, the creation of the Parliament might be thought to have exacerbated differences between those who feel Scottish and those who feel more British, perhaps raising doubts both about whether granting devolution is compatible with maintaining Scotland's membership of the United Kingdom as well as whether those who still feel British are comfortable with having a separate Scottish Parliament.

So the second half of the book, from Chapters 5 through to 8, examines some of the apparent social divisions in Scottish society. It asks how far those of different religious persuasions (and none), of different national identities, different classes or different generations have divergent views about the major social, moral and political issues that confront a devolved Scotland. Do they present sources of potential conflict that could undermine the ability of the Scottish Parliament to find any kind of acceptable answer? Do the attitudes of young people indicate possible changes in public attitudes up to which the Parliament will have to face in future? Or are some of the traditional divisions in Scottish society such as religion and class on the wane, thereby perhaps making Scotland an easier place to govern?

Between them these chapters provide a wealth of evidence about what Scotland thinks. In the Conclusion, we try to draw the strands back together and answer the two questions we have posed here: what has devolution achieved so far and what appear to be the challenges that it faces in future? Doubtless not all of our readers, let alone all of the individual contributors to this volume, will agree with our reading of the evidence. But we at least hope that the evidence presented in this book will help ensure that the debate about the successes and failures of devolution is a more informed one.

– DATA –

But what is the evidence upon which our analysis is based? It comes primarily from the 2001 Scottish Social Attitudes survey. In the summer and early autumn of that year, the National Centre for Social Research Scotland interviewed over 1,600 people aged 18 and over and asked them a set of standardised questions designed to elicit their views about topics as wide ranging as community care and churches, drugs and devolution, and education and ecstasy. In addition our respondents completed a short booklet of further questions. By asking everyone the same set of questions, by ensuring that as far as possible those whom we interviewed were representative of adults in Scotland as a whole, and by ensuring that all of the interviewing was conducted to the highest possible standards, our survey enables us to provide as accurate a picture as possible of what Scotland's adult population as a whole thinks. Further details about just how the survey was conducted can be found in the Technical Appendix at the back of this book.

Of course, one single survey conducted at one point in time cannot tell us how public opinion in Scotland has changed. Nor can it indicate whether public opinion in Scotland is different from that in the rest of the United Kingdom. However, our 2001 survey is part of a much larger enterprise. It was the third in what is intended to be an annual series of Scottish Social Attitudes surveys designed to provide both policy makers and students of Scottish society with high-quality evidence on the state of public opinion in post-devolution Scotland. So by comparing the results of our 2001 survey with its predecessors conducted in 1999 and 2000 (Paterson et al. 2001;

Curtice et al. 2002), we can begin to examine how public opinion may have changed during the course of the first Scottish Parliament. Luckily, we are also often able to provide a longer time perspective by comparing our results with those of earlier high-quality academic surveys conducted in Scotland, most notably the surveys in the Scottish Election Study series that were conducted after a number of UK general elections from 1979 onwards and many of which were undertaken by the National Centre for Social Research itself.

Equally important, however, are the links that our survey has with other surveys conducted elsewhere in the United Kingdom. Most important are our connections with the National Centre's annual British Social Attitudes survey which is designed and conducted in parallel with our Scottish survey, and which asked on its 2001 survey a large number of people in England many of the same questions included in our Scottish survey (Park et al. 2002).[1] This means that we can compare public opinion in Scotland with that in England and sometimes it helps us to compare how public opinion in the two countries has changed. In addition, some of the questions in our survey, particularly those about national identity and devolution, were also asked on surveys conducted in 2001 in Wales and Northern Ireland, that is the Welsh and the Northern Irish Life and Times surveys. So on occasion we are also able to compare public opinion in Scotland with that in the two other parts of the UK where devolution has recently been put in place.

In the next chapter, however, we begin by looking closer to home. Just what do the Scottish public think of their new parliament so far? Has devolution brought about some of the changes in public opinion that its advocates set out for it? And what appear to be the implications of the answers to those questions for what might happen when the Scottish public is invited to cast judgement on the performance of their devolved politicians when they are asked to vote in May 2003?

– ACKNOWLEDGEMENTS –

Any project as large as this incurs many debts. The biggest is to the 1,600 people who freely gave of their time to answer our questions. And of course the survey would not have been possible at all without the willingness of our interviewers to go out in all weathers and all times of the day and encourage our respondents to take part. In doing so they, and the researchers, were admirably supported by the National Centre's administrative staff. Equally, we should thank those who matched their faith in our work by providing the financial means to undertake it – the Economic and Social Research

Council (ESRC) and the Scottish Executive and Scottish Homes (now Communities Scotland). Our work has been enriched by our colleagues on the British Social Attitudes survey and the large number of fellow researchers with whom we are collaborating on a comparative study of devolution in all four corners of the UK as part of the ESRC's research programme on Devolution and Constitutional Change.

We would like to acknowledge too the invaluable support and encouragement provided by David McCrone and Lindsay Paterson of the University of Edinburgh in launching the Scottish Social Attitudes series successfully. Gordon Brewer kindly gave freely of his time to chair the conference held in March 2002 at which initial results of the survey were presented, while Pat Herd of the Centre for Scottish Public Policy was a tower of strength as organiser of that conference. Finally, we are grateful to Ann Mair of the Social Statistics Laboratory at the University of Strathclyde for her careful and detailed work in preparing the dataset on which we have so heavily relied.

– REFERENCES –

Curtice, J., McCrone, D., Park, A. and Paterson, L. (eds) (2002), *New Scotland, New Society? Are Social and Political Ties Fragmenting?*, Edinburgh: Polygon.

Park, A., Curtice J., Thomson K., Jarvis L., and Bromley C. (eds) (2002), *British Social Attitudes: the 19th report*, London: Sage.

Paterson, L., Brown A., Curtice J., Hinds K., McCrone D., Park A., Sproston K. and Surridge, P. (2001), *New Scotland, New Politics?*, Edinburgh: Polygon.

– NOTES –

1. The British Social Attitudes survey is conducted throughout Great Britain, but inevitably given the size of the Scottish population relative to the rest of Britain, its questions are asked of too few people in Scotland (currently a little over 300) to give robust estimates of Scottish opinion in any one year. (The same also applies to Wales.)

CHAPTER I

Devolution: Scorecard and Prospects

Catherine Bromley and John Curtice

– INTRODUCTION –

In the debate that raged prior to its creation, many claims were made about the benefits of having a Scottish Parliament. Now that the first parliamentary term of that body is coming to an end, we can begin to make first judgements about whether or not the expectations of devolution's advocates appear set to be fulfilled. In particular, has the Scottish Parliament lived up to its billing or is it, so far, a disappointment?

In this chapter we use the barometer of public opinion to assess whether three of the key claims made on behalf of devolution look as though they are being fulfilled (Paterson 1998). The first such claim concerns the policy-making process. Rule from Westminster, it was claimed, was both remote and insensitive. The House of Commons had little time for and even less interest in specifically Scottish matters. Decisions about Scotland were taken by ministers who spent much of their working week 400 or more miles away in London. And the authority of those ministers rested not upon their having secured electoral success in Scotland, but only across the United Kingdom as a whole. This led to the frequently uttered cry during the tenure of the 1979–97 Conservative government (which never won a plurality of the vote in Scotland) that Scottish policy was being determined by English votes, not least during the row about the introduction of the community charge or poll tax (Brown, McCrone and Paterson 1998: 64; Edwards 1989; Paterson 1994). It was argued that, under devolution, the picture would be very different. A Scottish parliament would devote its attention full time to specifically Scottish matters. Ministers would spend their working week in Scotland. Coupled with the introduction of more open and consultative decision-making procedures, these changes would ensure that those who made decisions were accessible to those ordinary citizens and pressure groups looking to promote their views (Scottish

Constitutional Convention 1995; Scottish Office 1999). Meanwhile, the mandate of Scottish ministers would depend only on Scottish votes. Consequently, they would have every incentive to follow the dictates of Scottish public opinion, even if that meant doing things differently from ministers in England. This argument was indeed at the heart of the cry that the Scottish Parliament would provide 'Scottish Answers to Scottish Questions'.

The second claim was about the consequences that devolution would have for the future of the Union between England and Scotland. The argument here was that devolution would strengthen that Union (Aughey 2001: chapter 7; Bogdanor 1999). Because, under the previous system, who ruled Scotland could well be determined by who was most popular in England, there was always a danger that Scotland's willingness to remain in the Union could be undermined by resentment about apparent rule from England. Certainly that system had provided an environment in which the pro-independence SNP had been able to become a significant player on the electoral stage over the last thirty years. But if a Scottish Parliament were created, one able to do things differently from England when Scottish public opinion required it, then it would be demonstrated that the Union was capable of accommodating Scottish distinctiveness. As a result, some thought that Scots' enthusiasm for independence would wane, and electoral support for the SNP would wither away.

But devolution was intended to do more than bolster support for the Union. Like much of the constitutional programme that Labour introduced after 1997, it was hoped that creating the Scottish Parliament would help reverse a loss of public confidence in politics and politicians that appeared to stem from the allegations of 'sleaze' that dogged the previous Conservative administration (Dewar 1998). Not the least of the reasons why this was thought important was that such declining confidence appeared to be eroding the public's willingness to vote for *anyone* at election time. So whether or not devolution has helped restore people's faith in their political system is the third and final claim that we examine.

– Improving the policy process –

The first claim that we consider is whether devolution has improved the policy-making process so far as the people of Scotland are concerned. We begin by assessing the evidence that people in Scotland have different policy preferences from those in England. If they do not, we might wonder why rule from Edinburgh should be more sensitive to Scottish needs than rule from London. Then we will consider what contribution the Scottish

Parliament is thought to have made, both to the way that decisions are made and to ensuring that the decisions that are made bring about successful outcomes. In doing so, we will also gain some insight into just how much power the Scottish Parliament is thought to have *vis-à-vis* Westminster.

– A distinctive Scottish voice –

There is perhaps no better place to start looking for different attitudes towards policy than education. After all, Scotland's educational system has always been distinct from that of England, leading us to anticipate that Scots might have particularly distinctive views. Certainly education policy provides one of the most high profile examples to date of the Scottish Executive using the freedom created by devolution to implement a different policy from London. That example, of course, is the decision that Scottish university students studying in Scotland should no longer have to pay tuition fees while they are studying, but instead should make a contribution to the cost of their education after they start earning.

To assess this, we asked two questions. First, we asked whether or not students and their families should contribute towards the costs of their tuition *while they are studying*. We suggested three possible answers:

All students or their families should pay towards their tuition costs while they are studying.
Some students or their families should pay towards their tuition costs while they are studying, depending on circumstances.
No students or their families should pay towards their tuition costs while they are studying.

We then asked a similar question, with similar possible answers, about whether students should be expected to pay back some of the costs of their tuition *after they have finished studying*. Table 1.1 shows the answers to both questions and compares the views of those who took part in our most recent Scottish survey to those of people in England asked the same question on the 2001 British Social Attitudes survey. It also shows the responses given to the same question, asked on the same two surveys, some twelve months earlier in 2000.

Despite what we might have expected, public opinion on tuition fees appears to be very similar in Scotland and England. In both countries, a majority believe that students should pay something towards the costs of a university education, either when they are studying or after they have started earning. Surprisingly, perhaps, neither public seems to distinguish particularly between asking students to pay while they are studying and requiring them to do so later when they have started earning. This would seem to cast some doubt on how much importance the public attaches to the Scottish Executive's decision to switch from the former option to the latter (but see Paterson et al. 2001). Meanwhile there is some evidence that opinion in Scotland (in contrast perhaps to that in England) is becoming even more accepting of the principle that students should have to pay at least something towards the cost of their tuition. For example, there was a seven point fall between 2000 and 2001 in the proportion in Scotland saying that *no* student or family should have to pay fees while they are studying. So, whatever attitudes might be as to the details of how and when students should pay, it appears that those who believe students should not pay at all have lost the argument so far as public opinion is concerned.

Table 1.1 Attitudes towards tuition fees in Scotland and England

	2000		2001	
	Scotland	England	Scotland	England
	%	%	%	%
Payment of fees while studying				
All students or their families should pay	5	8	4	7
Some students/families should pay,				
depending on circumstances	56	61	63	57
No students/families should pay	38	30	31	33
Payment of fees after studying				
All pay back some of the costs of their tuition	12	18	13	16
Some should pay, depending on circumstances	52	50	53	47
No students should pay back tuition costs	34	31	32	35
Sample size	*1663*	*969*	*1605*	*2761*

So there seems little evidence that the Scottish Executive's distinctive policy on tuition fees reflected a distinctively *Scottish* strand of public opinion, or indeed that it is any more popular with the Scottish public than the arrangements that preceded it. More recently, however, another less widely trumpeted (but perhaps more important) division has opened up between English and Scottish educational policy. In England, Tony Blair has signalled the end of the 'bog-standard comprehensive' and is increasingly encouraging secondary schools to become specialist schools with expertise in specific subject areas. One likely implication of this is, of course, that such schools will become particularly attractive to pupils who can demonstrate talent in their specialist area. By contrast, the Scottish

Executive has indicated its continuing faith in the principle of comprehensive secondary schools that have a remit to teach equally well across the full range of the curriculum.

On this matter, and in contrast to tuition fees, this difference between England and Scotland does seem to match rather different attitudes to secondary education north and south of the border. This can be seen in the answers given to the following question:

Which of the following statements comes closest to your views about what kind of secondary school children should go to?
Children should go to a different kind of secondary school, according to how well they do at primary school.
All children should go to the same kind of secondary school, no matter how well or badly they do at primary school.

In Scotland, support for the principle of comprehensive education, as embodied in the latter of these two statements, is substantially higher than it is in England. Nearly two-thirds (63 per cent) of people in Scotland back this option, while a third (34 per cent) think children should go to different kinds of secondary school. By contrast, in England opinion is almost equally divided, with 46 per cent backing the idea of children going to different kinds of school and 51 per cent favouring everyone attending the same kind of school. On secondary education, then, a distinctively Scottish policy does appear to reflect a distinctive strand of public opinion.

A second policy area where the Scottish Executive has pursued a notably distinctive policy is on so-called free personal care for the elderly. Under this system, and in contrast to England, older people in need of personal care have the costs of that care funded by government irrespective of their personal financial means. This subject is examined extensively in Chapter 2. Here we will simply note that the evidence suggests that, while the Scottish Executive's policy does appear to be in line with Scottish public opinion, it is not the case that public opinion in England is markedly different. Instead, it seems the Executive has fashioned a policy that has British-wide support, rather than followed a distinctively Scottish path.

But what do we find if we look beyond those issues that have recently been the subject of publicity and controversy? Is there any broader evidence that the Scottish and English public wish for markedly different public policies? And, if there is, do the differences relate to those matters that have been devolved to the Scottish Parliament, or do they instead still fall within the remit that has been reserved to Westminster?

In truth, on many key areas of public policy there appears to be little or no difference between attitudes in Scotland and those in England. People in Scotland are, at most, only marginally more likely than those in England to think that taxes should go up in order to fund higher levels of public spending, for example. As many as 63 per cent take that view in Scotland, as do 60 per cent in England (see also Chapter 7). There is also little difference between the two countries when it comes to nominating spending areas to receive increased funding. Just over a half (55 per cent) of people in Scotland say the National Health Service is the area most in need of more government spending, and a quarter say this of education. In England, the equivalent figures are 54 per cent and 29 per cent respectively. So it is perhaps little wonder that the Scottish Executive has largely followed the lead of the UK government in concentrating recent increases in government spending on those two areas. Equally, no less than 88 per cent of people in Scotland believe that it is the government's responsibility to ensure that the long-term sick and disabled have enough to live on – as do 86 per cent of people in England.

Moreover, where there are some signs of a difference of opinion between Scotland and England, they often appear to relate to policy areas that are reserved rather than those that have been devolved to the Scottish Parliament (see also Paterson 2002). For instance, no less than 45 per cent of people in Scotland say that benefits for unemployed people are 'too low and cause hardship', compared with only 36 per cent in England. And 85 per cent of people in Scotland say that the gap between those with high incomes and those with low incomes is 'too large', compared with 79 per cent in England. Indeed, as is discussed further in Chapter 7, people in Scotland tend consistently to be a little more left-wing than people in England on such issues as nationalisation, redistribution and trade unions. But, of course, all these are subjects where the relevant policy levers are primarily in the hands of the UK government at Westminster rather than with the Scottish Executive in Edinburgh.

So, in many respects, opinion in Scotland is similar to that in England. And, ironically, it differs more on reserved matters than devolved ones. Where the Scottish Executive has adopted policies in tune with Scottish public opinion (rather than just following the UK government's lead), these have tended to be issues where UK government policy is out of line with public opinion *everywhere* in Britain, rather than being examples of policy fashioned to reflect the divergent nature of Scottish opinion. It seems, therefore, that the potential for devolution to ensure that Scottish public policy is more sensitive to *distinctive* Scottish opinion is far more limited than advocates of devolution have suggested.

– Better decisions? Better outcomes? –

Pursuing a distinctive public policy that is more sensitive to Scottish public opinion is only one way in which devolution might have improved the policy process north of the border. Another possibility is that public policy has been *implemented* in a manner that takes more account of circumstances in Scotland, and is thus more likely to be effective and produce better outcomes.

One way in which we can address this question is to examine whether health, education and even the general standard of living in Scotland are thought to have improved over recent years. For, if the Scottish Parliament is thought to have produced better outcomes, we might anticipate that people would think these things have got better – or at least that they are *more* likely to think this than are their counterparts south of the border. Table 1.2 shows how people in England and Scotland perceive these matters since the election of the UK Labour government in 1997. This reveals that Scots are more likely to think that the standard of living in Scotland has risen than they are to think it has fallen, while the same is also true of education. Even so, they are *less* likely to think that either of these areas has improved than are people in England. Meanwhile, they are slightly *more* negative than people in England about recent trends in the health service. So it appears that having a Scottish Parliament has done nothing to improve the perceived outcome of public policy amongst the Scottish public.

Table 1.2 Evaluations of outcomes in Scotland and England

Perceived change since 1997	Scotland	England
	%	%
Standard of the NHS		
Increased a lot/a little	23	27
Stayed the same	29	32
Fallen a little/a lot	41	37
Quality of education		
Increased a lot/a little	27	34
Stayed the same	33	26
Fallen a little/a lot	21	29
General standard of living		
Increased a lot/a little	30	41
Stayed the same	45	36
Fallen a little/a lot	19	19
Sample size	*1605*	*2761*

Note: People in Scotland were asked about trends in Scotland, while those in England were asked about trends in England.

Of course, there are two quite different possible reasons for these results. One possibility is that the public believe that the Scottish Parliament has actually made things worse. But another is simply that it is not thought to have had much impact so far at all, and that the perhaps still insensitive hand of Westminster is seen as having remained primarily responsible for the shape of policy north of the border. All our evidence suggests that the second possibility is closer to the truth.

One clue is provided in table 1.3. This shows what people perceive as being mainly responsible for recent trends in the NHS's standards, the quality of education and the general standard of living – the policies of the UK government at Westminster or those of the Scottish Executive. This shows that the finger of credit, and blame, is clearly pointed at the UK government rather than the Executive. While this might be thought only reasonable so far as the general standard of living is concerned (given that macroeconomic policy remains a reserved matter), it seems rather surprising in the case of health and education, both of which are devolved responsibilities. Yet less than one in five think that the Scottish Executive is primarily responsible for what has happened to education over the last few years, and only one in eight think it is responsible for health.

Table 1.3 Perceived responsibility for outcomes since 1997

	Responsibility lies with	
	UK government	Scottish Executive
	%	%
Standard of the NHS	53	11
Quality of education	40	19
General standard of living	53	12

Note: Those answering 'both' or 'some other reason' not shown.

Intriguingly, the minority who see the Scottish Executive as primarily being responsible for recent trends have a rosier assessment than do those who think the UK government is responsible. For example, no less than half of those who think the Executive is primarily responsible for recent developments in education believe that the quality of education has improved, compared with only three in ten of those who say that the UK government is responsible. And there are similar differences in respect of the NHS and the general standard of living. In short, if the Scottish Executive is thought to have been responsible, things are generally thought to have gone well. To that extent, then, devolution is seen to have made a positive contribution to the success of public policy. The trouble is, however, that so few people think the devolved institutions have had as much influence as Westminster.

So the Scottish Executive does not seem to be seen as principally responsible for recent trends in devolved matters like health and education. Perhaps, then, we should not be surprised that the Parliament is not yet seen as the political crucible of the nation – or, indeed, that it is not believed to be as powerful as people thought it would be at the beginning of its life. In fact, as table 1.4 shows, only 15 per cent think that the Scottish Parliament has most influence on the way Scotland is run. As many as two thirds give that accolade to the UK government at Westminster. Yet, at the time of the first Scottish Parliament election in 1999, slightly more people thought that the Scottish Parliament would have most influence on Scotland than thought the UK government would.

Table 1.4 Who has most influence in Scotland?

	Which *will* have most influence?	Which *does* have most influence?	
	1999	2000	2001
	%	%	%
Scottish Parliament	41	13	15
UK government	39	66	66
Local councils	8	10	9
European Union	4	4	7
Sample size	*1482*	*1663*	*1605*

One further piece of evidence also suggests that the Scottish Parliament is simply thought not to be having much impact either way on policy outcomes in Scotland. We asked people whether they thought that the existence of the Scottish Parliament was improving the quality of education in Scotland, making things worse or making no difference either way. As table 1.5 shows, reality so far is not thought to have matched expectations. Just over one in four think that having a Parliament is increasing the standard of education in Scotland, whereas in 1999 well over a half thought that it would do so. Few, however, think the Scottish Parliament has reduced standards. Rather, the consensus now seems to be that it has simply not made any difference.

Of course, we must bear in mind that the Scottish Parliament is still in its relative infancy. Two years is not a long period of time in which to improve health and education. And, while expectations of what it will achieve in future are not as high now as they were at the time of the 1997 referendum (when nearly two in three thought having a Scottish Parliament would make the NHS and Scotland's economy better), optimists on this score still easily outnumber pessimists. Well over two in five Scots think that the NHS will improve as a result of having a Scottish Parliament; less than one in ten think the parliament will make matters worse. Similarly, 43 per cent think Scotland's economy will improve, and only ten per cent that it will suffer. So, while the parliament may not have lived up to its billing so far, a significant proportion of Scots evidently still have faith that it will eventually do so.[1]

Table 1.5 Perceived impact of the Scottish Parliament on education standards

Perceived impact on education	1999	2000	2001
	%	%	%
Increase standards	56	43	27
No difference	36	49	59
Reduce standards	3	3	5
Sample size	1482	1663	1605

Note: The wording of the introduction to the question in each year was as follows:
1999: As a result of having a Scottish Parliament will
2000: Is having a Scottish Parliament going to
2001: Do you think having a Scottish Parliament is

We noted earlier that one of the aspirations set out for the Scottish Parliament was not only that it would make better decisions, but also that it would improve the *process* of decision-making, by being more accessible and open than was possible under rule from Westminster. It appears that most Scots feel that this aspiration has yet to be realised. Just 38 per cent think that having a Scottish Parliament is giving ordinary people more say in how Scotland is governed, well down on the 64 per cent who thought in 1999 that this would be the case. But, while people are not sure that devolution has given them more say in what happens, they do at least seem to accept that the Parliament itself makes decisions in a different way from Westminster. For instance, one of the aspirations set out for the Scottish Parliament by the body that developed its standing orders was that power should be shared more widely amongst legislators in the Parliament, and between the Parliament and the Executive, an aspiration that was reflected in the creation of a relatively strong committee system on which all parties are represented (Scottish Office 1999). And, whereas only 29 per cent believe that MPs from different parties in the House of Commons work together to solve Britain's problems, no less than 51 per cent say the same of MSPs in the Scottish Parliament.

It appears that few Scots are convinced so far that having their own parliament has done much to improve policy outcomes north of the border. The reason for this is simple: Westminster is still thought to rule north of the border. This does not mean, of course, that a significant number of people think having a parliament will *never* make a difference. But, at present at least, it remains a body that has largely still to prove itself.

– Strengthening the Union –

The second aspiration for devolution to which we now turn is whether it has strengthened support for the Union. We start by considering whether support for Scotland's continued membership of the Union has declined over time, and whether the current constitutional settlement provides the degree of autonomy within the Union that Scots say they want. Then we will consider whether devolution has helped put the genie of political nationalism back in the bottle, or whether instead it has thrown the SNP a new political lifeline.

– Constitutional preferences –

We have already seen that, in practice, people see Westminster as still having the most influence on what happens in Scotland. But there is little sign that Scots have adjusted their hopes for the Parliament to this reality. As table 1.6 shows, Scots remain as keen as they were at the beginning of the Parliament's life that it (rather than the UK government in Westminster) should have most influence on the way that Scotland is run, with almost three in four taking that view. Comparing the figures in this table with those in table 1.4 above, we can see that a large gap has opened up between whom the public thinks should have most say in how Scotland is run and who actually does.

Table 1.6 Who should have most influence in Scotland?

	1999	2000	2001
	%	%	%
Scottish Parliament	74	72	74
UK government	13	13	14
Local councils	8	10	8
European Union	1	1	1
Sample size	1482	1663	1605

Given this gap between aspiration and perceived reality it would seem likely that people in Scotland would like their parliament to have more powers.

And, indeed, we find this consistently to be the case. Even in 1999, no less than 64 per cent said that they thought the Scottish Parliament should have more powers. Now that figure stands at 68 per cent. And six in ten (61 per cent) believe that the Scottish Parliament should decide levels of welfare benefits, while only 24 per cent agree that Westminster should continue to do so. Above all, there seems to be considerable support for the idea of 'fiscal autonomy' for the new parliament – as signified by agreement with the view that 'now that Scotland has its own parliament, it should pay for its services out of taxes collected in Scotland'. No less than 51 per cent agree with this proposition, while only 28 per cent disagree.

So there is then considerable public support for radical increases in the power of the Scottish Parliament of a kind that no political party other than the Scottish Nationalist Party (and the Scottish Socialist Party) would currently contemplate. This even includes acceptance of changes that might be thought to weaken Scotland's influence within the United Kingdom, but which critics of the current devolution settlement have suggested should be introduced as a quid pro quo for the creation of a Scottish Parliament. In particular, half (51 per cent) agree that Scottish MPs at Westminster should no longer be allowed to vote in the House of Commons on those laws that only affect England, while only 21 per cent disagree.

Do these findings suggest that the disappointments of devolution might well have served to undermine continued support for the Union? To gauge whether or not this is the case we can look at answers to a question that has been asked on a regular basis in Scotland in recent years. It runs as follows:

Which of these statements comes closest to your view?
Scotland should become independent, separate from the UK and the European Union.
Scotland should become independent, separate from the UK but part of the European Union.
Scotland should remain part of the UK, with its own elected parliament which has **some** *taxation powers.*
Scotland should remain part of the UK, with its own elected parliament which has **no** *taxation powers.*
Scotland should remain part of the UK **without** *an elected parliament.*

Table 1.7 shows which of these options people have chosen on each occasion that the question has been asked since 1997, with the answers to the two possible forms of independence combined.

Table 1.7 Constitutional preferences

	1997 general election	1997 referendum	1999	2000	2001
	%	%	%	%	%
Independence either in or outside the EU	26	37	28	30	27
Stay in UK, with parliament with taxation powers	42	32	50	47	54
Stay in UK, with parliament with *no* taxation powers	9	9	9	8	6
Stay in UK, with *no* parliament	17	17	10	12	9
Sample size	*841*	*676*	*1482*	*1663*	*1605*

It is clear that despite what we have seen so far, there is *no* evidence that support for independence has grown. Just over one in four favour independence either inside or outside the EU, almost exactly the same proportion that took that view at the time of the 1997 general election (and well below what appears to have been a temporary surge in favour of independence at the time of the 1997 referendum). Instead, ironically, there has been an increase in support for the option that is closest to the current devolution settlement – that is, a parliament within the Union that has some taxation powers. No less than 54 per cent now back that view, well up on the 42 per cent who did so in 1997. Much of this rise in support for devolution appears to have come at the expense of those who believe that there should be no separate Scottish Parliament. With less than one in ten taking that view, it appears that whatever are thought to be the limitations of the current Scottish Parliament, there is now no doubt that so far as the public is concerned, some form of parliament is here to stay.

Not only is there little sign of a growth in support for independence, but it also appears that the likely prospect of independence in the future has receded in the public mind too. As table 1.8 shows, the proportion who believe that having a Scottish Parliament will mean that Scotland will eventually leave the UK has fallen from 37 per cent in 1999 to 28 per cent in 2001. True, the proportion who think having a Scottish Parliament has helped cement Scotland's position in the Union has also declined somewhat (this is the view of slightly more than one in four). Echoing our earlier findings about the Parliament's impact, the most popular view is that it has not made any difference to the likelihood of independence. But evidently devolution is now less likely to be seen as a 'slippery slope' to independence in the way that some of its critics feared it would (Dalyell 1977). This is confirmed by the answers to a further question in which people were asked how likely or unlikely it was that Scotland will become completely independent from the UK within the next twenty years. Just 37 per cent now think that it is 'very' or 'quite' likely that this will happen, well down on the 51 per cent who thought so in 1999.

Table 1.8 Perceived impact of Scottish Parliament on independence

Having a Scottish Parliament will make it:	1999	2000	2001
More likely Scotland eventually leaves the UK	37	27	28
More likely Scotland stays in the UK	30	25	27
Will make no difference	27	43	41
Sample size	1482	1663	1605

Note: The wording of the introduction to the question in each year was as follows:
1999: A Scottish Parliament will
2000, 2001: Is having a Scottish Parliament going to

So we are left with a paradox. The Scottish Parliament is evidently not thought to be as powerful or as influential as a majority of Scots would prefer. Yet this does not mean that they have been persuaded of the merits of independence. Evidently, there is a widespread belief that a more powerful Scottish Parliament could be established which would remain part of the UK. Public support for Scotland's membership of the Union may not have been eroded by the advent of devolution, but that does not mean that Scots are happy with the current devolution settlement.

– Voting nationalist –

If, despite its disappointments, devolution has not lead to increased support for independence, what about support for the party that is most closely associated with that policy, the SNP? What impact has devolution had on its electoral support? Has the Parliament even begun to fulfil the hopes of those who wished that its introduction would erode nationalist support? Or has the call for independence been given a new opportunity to prosper?

At first glance, the outcome of the 2001 UK general election in Scotland would seem to give hope to those who believe devolution will bring about a decline in SNP support, with the party winning just 20.1 per cent of the vote. Not only was this nearly nine points down on the 28.7 per cent of the vote it won in the constituency contests in 1999, but it was the party's lowest share of the vote in a UK general election since 1987. So, even if it did relatively well in 1999, the party would now seem to be heading for a fall at the second Scottish Parliament election in 2003.

This, however, would be far too hasty a judgement. In our survey we not only asked our respondents how they voted in the 2001 UK general election, but also how they *would* have voted if it had been a Scottish Parliament election that day instead. Equally, in our 1999 survey we not only asked people how they had voted in the Scottish Parliament election, but also how they would have voted if it had been a Westminster contest. And, as table 1.9 shows, a similar pattern emerged on both occasions. In 1999, more people voted SNP in the Scottish election than said they would have done in a UK general election. And, in 2001, more people said they would have voted SNP in a Scottish election than said they did so in that year's UK election. The differences are not trivial: eight points in 1999 and ten in 2001.

Table 1.9 Difference between Scottish Parliament and Westminster vote

	1999	2001
	%	%
Conservative	–2	–1
Labour	–8	–6
Liberal Democrat	+1	–3
Nationalist	+8	+10
Others	+1	0
Sample size	1028/1239	1141/1043

Note: In 1999 this table shows for each party the difference between the proportion saying they had voted for that party on the constituency vote of the Scottish election and the proportion saying they would have done so in a UK general election. In 2001 it shows for each party the difference between the proportion saying they would have voted for that party on the constituency vote of a Scottish election and the proportion who said they did vote for that party in the UK general election. In each case the proportions in question have been calculated with those saying they did not/would not vote or who otherwise failed to name a party excluded from the denominator for that proportion.

So it seems the main reason for the SNP faring less well in 2001 than in 1999 is not because its support had been eroded, but because a different kind of contest was taking place. Put simply, people appear more willing to vote for the SNP in Scottish Parliament elections than they are in Westminster elections. Consequently, devolution seems to have given the nationalists a new political lifeline. Not only are Scottish elections held using a more proportional electoral system that makes it easier for the SNP to win seats, but voters are apparently more willing to give the party their vote in a Scottish election too.

Why does this happen (see also Curtice 2001; Curtice 2003; Paterson et al. 2001)? At least one important reason appears to be that voters have different considerations in mind when they vote in a Scottish election than when they participate in a Westminster one. Amongst those who voted in the Scottish elections in 1999, as many as 53 per cent said that they voted mostly according to what was going on in Scotland, whereas only 31 per cent said they said they voted mostly according to what was going on in Britain as a whole. By contrast, in the 2001 UK general election, the picture was very different. Only 34 per cent said they voted on the basis of what was happening in Scotland, while 44 per cent said their focus was on Britain as a whole. In short, when voters were being asked a Scottish question they did indeed give a Scottish answer. But, conversely, when they were asked a British question, they gave not surprisingly a British answer.

Whether voters think they are being asked a Scottish rather than a British question makes a significant difference to their propensity to support the SNP. For example, in the 1999 Scottish election, no less than 39 per cent of those who said they voted on the basis of what was happening in Scotland backed the SNP, compared with just 15 per cent of those who were voting on what was happening in Britain as a whole. In 2001, the equivalent figures were 33 per cent and 5 per cent respectively. Little wonder, then, that with more voters focusing their attention on Britain as a whole, SNP support dropped in the 2001 general election.

But why does asking voters a Scottish rather than a British question make them more inclined to vote SNP? One important clue can be gleaned from table 1.10, which shows how much voters trust each of the parties to look after the interests of people in Scotland. In the case of the Labour party we show separately people's views about 'New Labour at Westminster' and the 'Labour Party in Scotland'. We can see that people are far more likely to feel that the SNP looks 'very closely' after the interests of Scottish people in general than to think this about any other party. True, two in three people trust the Scottish Labour party to look after Scotland's interests, but they are not so sure about New Labour at Westminster. So, if voters are more likely in a Scottish election to ask 'Who is best for Scotland?', then it appears that they may well indeed reply with the answer, 'SNP'.[2]

Table 1.10 Who looks after Scotland?

% trust party to look after interests of Scottish people in general	New Labour at Westminster	Labour party in Scotland	SNP	Conservative party in Scotland
Very closely	3	8	21	2
Fairly closely	36	58	49	23
Not very closely	51	28	22	41
Not at all closely	8	3	6	32

Sample size = 1383

This provides us with a second paradox. People in Scotland are no keener on the idea of independence now than they were before the Scottish Parliament was created. But in creating that body, devolution has brought into being an institution in which the SNP is more likely to be electorally prosperous. As a result, political nationalism poses a greater challenge to the future of the Union than ever before. If they are to meet this challenge, it would appear that Scotland's other parties have to don the mantle of 'Scotland's champions' as effectively as hitherto have the SNP.

− RESTORING FAITH IN POLITICS −

The final claim made on behalf of devolution that we examine here is whether it has helped to reverse a decline in people's faith and confidence in the political system perceived to have occurred in the 1990s. To assess this we will first look at recent trends in a number of questions that tap people's attitudes towards the political system in general. We will then consider what lessons we might draw for the prospects for turnout in the 2003 Scottish parliamentary election.

− Political trust and efficacy −

Our survey included questions about two key features of people's attitudes towards politics and the political system. The first of these is political trust; that is, the degree to which people feel that they believe politicians and the apparatus of government can be trusted to act in the national interest. The second is political efficacy; that is, whether people feel that they have a reasonable chance of being able to influence a public policy they think should be changed. According to Almond and Verba (1963) ideally people should have an appropriate balance of both trust and efficacy.

Three of the questions we asked (one about political trust and two about political efficacy) were also included on a number of British Social Attitudes surveys in the 1980s and 1990s. By combining the results of these earlier surveys for more than one year (in order to achieve a respectable sample size in Scotland), we can provide reasonably robust estimates of the balance of opinion in Scotland during that period, and thus can establish whether faith in the political system did indeed decline in the 1990s, and whether or not matters have improved since then. In addition, as these questions have also been asked regularly on the British Social Attitudes survey in England, we can also examine whether trends in Scotland have been any different from those south of the border. If, for instance, the Scottish Parliament has helped restore people's faith in the political system then levels of trust and efficacy should have risen more in recent years in Scotland than they have in England.

Table 1.11 Trends in political trust and efficacy

	1986/87	1994/96	1997	2000	2001
% trust British governments of any party to place nation's needs first just about always/ most of the time					
Scotland	37	29	29	13	27
England	38	23	34	17	29
% strongly agree that parties are only interested in people's votes, not their opinions					
Scotland	11	29	16	24	21
England	18	26	16	26	26
% strongly agree that MPs lose touch with people pretty quickly					
Scotland	11	26	na	24	22
England	17	25	na	23	24
Sample size					
Scotland	276	216	760–882	1663	1605
England	2511	1972	2115–2492	1928	924

na: not asked

The first question in table 1.11 is our question on political trust. The table shows the proportion of people who trust governments of any party to place the needs of the nation above the interests of their own political party 'always' or 'most of the time'. The higher the figure, therefore, the higher the level of trust. Three important patterns emerge. First, there is no consistent evidence that in the 1980s and 1990s Scots trusted governments any less than did people in England. So, on this criterion at least, there is no evidence that the (then unfulfilled) demand for devolution festered disillusion with politics. Second, trust in government was lower on both sides of the border in the 1990s than it was in the 1980s. The allegations of sleaze in the 1990s do appear to have helped undermine faith in politics (Curtice and Jowell 1997; Bromley, Curtice and Seyd 2001). Third, trust in government fell to an all-time low in 2000 in the immediate wake of the introduction of the Scottish Parliament and, although it appears to have recovered somewhat subsequently, it has still not returned to the levels found in the 1980s. (Indeed the rise in 2001 is probably a temporary increase produced by a UK general election having just been held. See Bromley and Curtice 2002.) From this it follows that creating a Scottish Parliament has failed to restore trust in government. Rather, as recent trends in Scotland have continued to mirror those in England, it seems that the Scottish Parliament has not made much difference to the level of trust one way or another (see also Curtice 2002).

The remaining two questions in table 1.11 are our two measures of political efficacy. In both cases, respondents were asked to agree or disagree with an inefficacious proposition, so the more people that agree with the statement (and here we show the proportion that *strongly* agree) the *lower* the level of efficacy. The responses tell a similar story to that told previously about trust. In fact, levels of efficacy were if anything somewhat higher in Scotland than they were in England in the 1980s, but they declined on both sides of the border during the tenure of the last UK Conservative administration, and the advent of the Scottish Parliament does not seem to have helped bring about any particular recovery north of the border.

So, just as was the case when we examined the perceived impact of the Scottish Parliament on policy outcomes, it appears that the creation of the Scottish Parliament has simply not made any difference to public beliefs and attitudes. Consequently, trends in political trust and efficacy in Scotland continue largely to mirror those in England, suggesting that wider factors operating across Britain as a whole have primarily been responsible for what has happened. True, evidence from two other questions suggests that trust in the Scottish Parliament is much higher than it is in institutions of the British state. No less than 65 per cent say that they trust the Scottish Parliament to work in Scotland's interests 'always' or 'most of the time' while only 22 per cent say the same of the UK government (a figure similar to the 27 per cent we have seen believe British governments put the nation's interests first). But, with only 35 per cent saying that creating a Scottish Parliament has improved the way that Britain as a whole is run, and given the perceived relative weakness of the institution, we should not be surprised that, when asked about their faith in the political system as a whole, the advent of the Scottish Parliament should have made so little difference.

– Turnout –

This apparent failure of the creation of the Scottish Parliament to restore the public's faith in politics would seem potentially damaging to the prospects for a high turnout at the next Scottish election in 2003. A disillusioned electorate would seem unlikely to be one that is keen to go to the polls. Equally, there would seem little reason for the electorate to turn out and vote in a Scottish election if, as is apparently the case, they do not think the institution has much power. And there is perhaps even less reason for it to do so if the possibility of a major constitutional change in the form of independence is now regarded as a relatively remote prospect.

In fact, none of these arguments should be pushed too far. For example, only the minority (that is, less than one in five) who 'almost never' trust British governments to put the nation's interests first appear to have been particularly reluctant to vote in the 2001 UK election. Amongst this group, only 57 per cent claim to have voted in the 2001 election, 13 points lower than amongst those who say they trust them only 'some of the time'. But the turnout amongst the latter group was not much lower (only four points) than that found among those who trust governments 'just about always' or 'most of the time'. Meanwhile, in the 1999 Scottish Parliament election the turnout amongst those who said the Scottish Parliament would have most influence over what happened in Scotland was only seven points higher than it was amongst those who thought Westminster would remain the most powerful force in the land. And whether or not people thought independence was likely in the next twenty years seems to have made no difference at all to their chances of voting in 2001.

But there is one further trend that does raise doubts about the prospects for turnout in the 2003 Scottish election. This is that voters in Scotland are now even less likely to think that the outcome of a Scottish Parliament election matters than they did at the time of the first election in 1999. Then, 56 per cent thought that who won these elections would make 'a great deal' or 'quite a lot' of difference; now only 43 per cent take this view. Although there has been a similar decline in the perceived impact of the outcome of a UK general election (from 54 per cent to 45 per cent), this simply indicates that turnout in the next Scottish Parliament election could well be subject to the same adverse forces that in 2001 produced (in common with the rest of Great Britain) the lowest turnout in a UK general election since the beginning of the mass franchise in 1918 (58 per cent).

Table 1.12 shows that whether someone thinks it will make a difference who wins an election does make a clear and consistent difference to their chances of turning out to vote. Thus, in 1999, those who thought that the outcome of a Scottish Parliament election mattered a great deal were twice as likely to vote as were those who thought the outcome barely mattered at all. A similar gap is evident when we look at how the level of voting varied in the 2001 UK general election depending on whether the outcome of that election was thought to matter. So the decline in the perceived importance of the outcome of a Scottish election does not augur well for turnout in 2003, even if perhaps this perception could as much be a reflection of a lack of perceived differences between the offerings of the parties as it is a commentary on the lack of power that the Scottish Parliament is thought to have.

Table 1.12 Perceived importance of who wins and turnout, 1999 and 2001

How much does it matter who wins in elections to the (1999) Scottish Parliament/(2001) House of Commons?	1999	2001
	% who voted	
Great deal	86	84
Quite a lot	78	75
Some	64	69
Not very much	61	60
Not at all	43	38
Sample size	1482	1605

The failure of the 1999 Scottish election to secure the participation of as many as three in five voters came as a disappointment to those who thought that devolution would help rekindle Scots' faith in and commitment to their political system. It appears that there is a significant danger at least that turnout will fall further in 2003. If that does happen, then far from helping to connect Scots to their political system, devolution might have helped to create a new symbol of the apparent inability of politicians to persuade voters that getting involved in politics matters.

– CONCLUSION –

In many respects devolution is not turning out as its advocates had hoped. It is not thought to have contributed to better policy outcomes. The Scottish Parliament continues to be seen as playing second fiddle to Westminster. And many Scots do not think that the outcome of Scottish elections matter. It seems there is a serious danger that devolution could wither on the vine of public indifference.

Yet perhaps there is another story to tell too. It appears that Scots' reaction to the disappointments of devolution so far is to demand *better* devolution rather than abandon it altogether. In particular, they would like the Scottish Parliament to have more wide ranging powers than it has been given by the current constitutional settlement. And it seems that doing this would give the parliament more scope than the settlement for fashioning a Scottish public policy that is distinctive where Scottish public opinion is distinctive. In short, while most Scots still want to remain in the Union it seems they still have an appetite for a parliament that seems able to make a difference.

Of course, it may be that, given a few more years, the parliament will be able to persuade its public that it is worthy of their attention. But unless this happens in the not too distant future, advocates of devolution may have to face up to the fact that the current settlement does not provide an adequate basis for making the Scottish Parliament the political crucible of the nation while at the same time enabling Scotland to remain part of the Union. In short, the parliament could come to be seen as an irrelevance. Whether such an eventuality would persuade Scots to embrace independence, or alternatively persuade nationalists of the need to embrace a more powerful, but not formally independent, parliament, must at this stage remain mere speculation.

– References –

Almond, G. and Verba, S. (1963), *The Civic Culture: Political Attitudes and Democracy in Five Nations*, Princeton, NJ: Princeton University Press.

Aughey, A. (2001), *Nationalism, Devolution and the Challenge to the United Kingdom State*, London: Pluto Press.

Bogdanor, V. (1999), *Devolution in the United Kingdom*, Oxford: Oxford University Press.

Bromley, C., Curtice, J. and Seyd, B. (2001), 'Political engagement, trust and constitutional reform', in A. Park, J. Curtice, K. Thomson, L. Jarvis and C. Bromley (eds), *British Social Attitudes: the 18th report – Public Policy, Social Ties*, London: Sage.

Bromley, C. and Curtice, J. (2002), 'Where have all the voters gone?', in A. Park, J. Curtice, K. Thomson, L. Jarvis and C. Bromley (eds), *British Social Attitudes: the 19th report*, London: Sage.

Brown, A., McCrone, D., and Paterson, L. (1998), *Politics and Society in Scotland*, second edition, Basingstoke: Macmillan.

Curtice, J. (2001), 'Is devolution succouring nationalism?', *Contemporary Wales*, 14, pp. 80–103.

Curtice, J. (2002), 'Devolution and democracy: old trust or new cynicism?', in J. Curtice, D. McCrone, A. Park and L. Paterson (eds), *New Scotland, New Society*, Edinburgh: Polygon.

Curtice, J. (2003, forthcoming), 'Devolution meets the voters: the prospects for 2003', in R. Hazell (ed.), *The State of the Nations 2002*, Thorverton: Imprint Academic.

Curtice, J. and Jowell, R. (1997), 'Trust in the political system', in R. Jowell, J. Curtice, A. Park, L. Brook, K. Thomson and C. Bryson (eds), *British Social Attitudes: the 14th report – The End of Conservative Values?*, Aldershot: Ashgate.

Dalyell, T. (1977), *Devolution: The End of Britain?*, London: Jonathan Cape.

Dewar, D. (1998), 'The Scottish Parliament', *Scottish Affairs: Special Issue on Understanding Constitutional Change*, pp. 4–12.

Edwards, O. (ed.) (1989), *A Claim of Right for Scotland*, Edinburgh: Polygon.

Paterson, L. (1994), *The Autonomy of Modern Scotland*, Edinburgh: Edinburgh University Press.

Paterson, L. (1998), *A Diverse Assembly: The Debate on a Scottish Parliament*, Edinburgh: Edinburgh University Press.

Paterson, L. (2002), 'Governing from the centre: ideology and public policy', in J. Curtice, D. McCrone, A. Park and L. Paterson (eds), *New Scotland, New Society?*, Edinburgh: Polygon.

Paterson, L., Brown, A., Curtice, J., Hinds, K., McCrone, D., Park, A., Sproston, K. and Surridge, P. (2001), *New Scotland, New Politics?* Edinburgh: Polygon.

Scottish Constitutional Convention (1995), *Scotland's Parliament: Scotland's Right*, Edinburgh: COSLA.

Scottish Office (1999), *Shaping Scotland's Parliament: Report of the Consultative Steering Group on Scotland's Parliament*, Edinburgh: Stationery Office.

Scottish Parliament (2001), *Scottish Parliament Procedures Committee Official Report, Meeting 9 2001*, Edinburgh: Scottish Parliament. Available at http://www.scottish.parliament.uk/official_report/cttee/proced-01/pr02-0902.htm.

– Notes –

1. Even so, we might also note that despite the fact that no attempt has yet been made to use the parliament's tax varying powers, expectations that having a Scottish Parliament will result in higher taxes have not diminished as much as have expectations about its impact on health and the economy. As many as 53 per cent think that having the parliament will result in higher taxes, compared with 64 per cent in 1999. Evidently people's expectations that they will have to pay for devolution have declined less than their perceptions that they will benefit from it. We might speculate that one reason for this has been the unfavourable publicity that has surrounded the continually rising costs of building a permanent home for the parliament (Scottish Parliament 2001).

2. Further analysis reveals that indeed SNP support is particularly high amongst those who not only decide on the basis of what is happening in Scotland but who also think the SNP can be better trusted than Labour to look after Scotland's interests. See Curtice 2003.

CHAPTER 2

Does the Community Care?

Lisa Curtice and Alison Petch

– INTRODUCTION –

The decision by the Scottish Executive in January 2001 to fund, irrespective of an individual's financial means, the personal care costs of older people in need of long-term care (be they living in the community or in a residential or nursing home) has been one of the most distinctive as well as one of the most controversial policies to be introduced by the Scottish Executive since 1999. In England the UK Labour government rejected the majority recommendation of a Royal Commission on Long Term Care chaired by Sir Stewart Sutherland in March 1999 that such a policy should be introduced (Royal Commission on Long Term Care 1999). Moreover, the Scottish Executive itself announced a similar decision in October 2000. But when Henry McLeish succeeded Donald Dewar as First Minister in November 2000 he worked to reverse this decision. As a result since July 2002 the personal care costs of those assessed as needing long-term care have been funded in Scotland on a universal basis. In England they have been funded on a selective basis, that is taking into account a person's financial means.

The degree to which this eventual decision was in tune with Scottish public opinion (and indeed whether that opinion is different from England) is therefore important to any evaluation of the degree to which devolution has brought 'Scottish answers to Scottish questions'. But behind the headlines there are deeper issues at stake about our attitudes towards those who require some form of long-term care or support. This chapter examines these deeper issues about attitudes towards community care. It addresses two key questions. First, does the public believe that people should be enabled wherever possible to live in the community? In answering this question we shall examine how far people in Scotland believe that the government should be responsible for paying for care and whether their attitudes to this appear to be in any way different from those of people in England. Second, we consider who supports a policy of government-funded care in the community. Is there any evidence that those who might be likely to benefit from such a policy are the ones most likely to support it? And are those who believe that the government should supply the resources necessarily the same people as those who believe that people should be enabled to live in the community? Indeed, can we speak of such a thing as an 'attitude' towards community care policy and if there is such a stance, is it distinctive to Scotland?

– Does the community care? –

– What do we mean by support for community care policy? –

There are a number of dimensions to attitudes towards community care. These include attitudes to whether people should have the choice to live at home, who should receive support, who should pay for and provide that support and whether people who receive support services should be seen as responsible citizens. In the first place a defining feature of community care policy is that a person's need for support should not deprive them of their right to live at home in the community and they should not be forced to move because their needs increase (Scottish Office 1997 and 1998). Does the general public know about and agree with the policy that those in need of care should be enabled as far as possible to live at home in the community? It is far from clear that the underlying premises of community care are widely understood. Reinforced by stereotypical media representations (Philpot 1995), stigma and misunderstanding still surround, in particular, people with learning disabilities and those with mental illness. Thus the public may equate care in the community with risk to vulnerable individuals and themselves.

Second, do people think that all those whom the Government defines as community care service users (not only older people but also a range of other groups such as those with learning disabilities, those with mental health problems and those with various forms of physical and sensory impairment) have an equal claim to public support? Older people are undoubtedly widely regarded as deserving of extra government help and resources (Hills 2001). But does the public see it as society's responsibility as much to support a person with learning disabilities with everyday tasks as to support people during their old age? Even T. H. Marshall, the founder of social democratic citizenship, distinguished between the universal right to education and health care and the discretionary right to welfare support of those with disabilities, on the grounds that society would not suffer if the well-being of the latter were not maximised (Lewis 1998).

Third, does the general public think the government or the individual and their family should primarily pay for and provide the care and support that may be required? During the 1980s when Mrs Thatcher was Prime Minister, community care was presented as a means of reducing the role of the state and increasing the role of private provision and of informal support provided by family, friends and neighbours (Griffiths 1988 and Secretaries of State 1989). Yet, as part of its belief that citizens have 'responsibilities' as well as 'rights', the UK Labour government elected in 1997 has also emphasised the need for people to make adequate provision for their old age. So we cannot assume that people believe that community care equates with support provided by government rather than by families and friends.

Finally, does the general public share the aspiration that people who receive support because of long-term illness or disability should be regarded as citizens with rights and responsibilities within society? Government policy sees the goal of support in the community as greater social inclusion, enabling people to take an active part in their community and reducing the exclusion created by segregated services and limited opportunities (Scottish Executive 2000). In Scotland the emphasis on social inclusion, that is, having sufficient resources to be able to participate in society, is compatible with a wider theme of greater social justice that runs across many policy areas (Scottish Executive, Social Inclusion Division 2001). But it is not known whether the general public yet sees people who use support services as fellow citizens rather than as people in need of care.

– Methodological challenges –

There are two dangers when it comes to asking people about the kind of care that should be provided for different kinds of people. First, language that might once have been considered acceptable in referring to a particular group may now be considered discriminatory and offensive. Whilst it is desirable to avoid such language, newer terms that are deemed acceptable may not always be widely understood amongst the general population. Second, whatever term is used to describe a particular group, its use may simply elicit a reaction based on a stereotypical perception of that group rather than a judgement of the kinds of care and support they need. In order to avoid these dangers we tapped people's attitudes towards who should receive care in the community and who should provide that care by presenting our respondents with descriptions of four different people and for each one giving an indication of one particular aspect about their situation that might be thought to constitute a need for community care. Moreover, as respondents' reactions might depend on whether the person being described in each 'vignette' was male or female, half of the respondents were presented with versions where the person was female and half where he was male. Regrettably the space available did not allow us to represent every type of impairment so we concentrated on individuals whose circumstances led to a need for the main types of community care support – personal care, social support, the monitoring of a health need, and domestic help. The full wording of each vignette was as follows:

John (Susan) is 87 and lives alone. He often forgets things like leaving the gas on and has been found in the street in his night clothes. John needs to be checked on several times a day and needs help with bathing.

Alice (David) is 44 and moved out of a long-stay hospital two years ago. She cannot read or write, has limited speech and is not very aware of danger on the roads. She has trouble making friends and needs someone to take her to a club once a week.

Stuart (Pat) is 50. He has a mental illness and occasionally spends a few months in psychiatric hospitals. He often talks to himself in public. He takes medication that controls his illness but needs someone to check that he has taken it twice daily.

Sarah (Paul) is 90 and has recently had some falls at home. Last time she was not found for twelve hours. She is very independent and does not want to leave the family home where she has lived for 40 years. Sarah needs help with shopping and cooking.

For each of these four stories we asked questions designed to tap whether people believed that the person depicted should be enabled to live a full role in the community, who should provide the care and support that they need, and who should pay for that care.

– Living in the community –

Table 2.1 shows for our vignettes the answers given to three questions designed to ascertain whether people believe that the person depicted should be enabled to live in the community. In each case the answers for the male and female versions of the vignette are combined. The first question simply asked where it was best for the person to live. Three of the five possible answers that were offered were different forms of living in the community, that is, 'in own house with some help', 'with another family member', and 'in special housing with support in the community'. The other two possible answers were a care home (residential or nursing home) and 'in hospital'. The second question asked people how comfortable they would feel living next door to such a person. Finally, for two of the vignettes, where the person depicted was someone with learning disabilities and someone with a mental illness, we also asked whether that person should be considered for jury service, a role that might be considered central to what is meant by being a full citizen in society.

Table 2.1 Attitudes to community care

% who think	Should live in community	Very or fairly comfortable living next door to	Should serve on a jury
	%	%	%
S/P (50) has a mental illness	72	45	15
S/P (90) has had falls	74	73	na
J/S (87) often forgets things	58	42	na
A/D (44) can't read or write	88	61	25
Sample size	*1605*	*1605*	*1605*

Note: Should live in community – best place for person to live is one of 'in own house with some help', 'with another family member', or 'in special housing with support in the community'.
na: not asked

Some clear differences emerge between the different vignettes. For the most part there is widespread acceptance that both the person with learning disabilities and the frail older person should live in the community. Thus nearly three-quarters of our respondents say that the frail older person should live in the community, while a similar proportion also say that they would feel comfortable living next to such a person. And while only three in five accept that they would be comfortable living next door to the person with learning disabilities, nearly nine in ten accept that such a person should live in the community. However, people are less accepting that the person with a mental illness should live in the community. Although nearly three-quarters think they should live in a community setting, less than half say they would be comfortable having such a person as a neighbour. Meanwhile, less than three in five say that the older person with dementia should live in a community setting and only just over two in five that they would be comfortable living next door. Contrary to our expectations, however, whether the person described in the scenario was a man or woman does not make any significant difference to the pattern of response. The one exception to this is that women are less likely than men to say that they would feel comfortable living next door to the person with a mental illness if that person is described as male.

Even so, people draw some clear distinctions about the kind of person they believe should be enabled to live in the community. It appears possible that they are happy for someone to live in the community so long as they are not thought to be at risk of posing a danger to others, even if they might be at some risk of harm to themselves. Thus the right of the frail older person to live in the community is largely accepted even though they are at risk of being hurt in a fall, while the right of the older person with dementia who might leave the gas on is most likely to be questioned. But what is even more apparent is that acceptance of the right of someone to live in the community does not necessarily imply an acknowledgement that they can play a full role as citizens. Thus only one in four believe that the person with learning disabilities should be considered for jury service and just 15 per cent the person with a mental illness.

Table 2.2 Where would it be best for someone to live?

		Community		Residential		
	Own home	With family	Special housing	Care home	Hospital	Sample size
S/P (50) has a mental illness	% 24	6	42	19	7	1605
S/P (90) has had falls	% 50	6	17	25	*	1605
J/S (87) often forgets things	% 23	6	29	40	1	1605
A/D (44) can't read or write	% 29	9	50	10	1	1605

* Less than 0.5 per cent.

A more detailed breakdown of the answers to the question about where it is best for someone to live (see table 2.2) provides further insight into people's perceptions about who should be enabled to live in the community and how. Only in the case of the frail older person do at least half believe that they should live in their own home. Special housing is the most popular choice for both the person with learning disabilities and the person with mental illness. Two in five feel that the person with dementia should live in a residential or nursing home and another 29 per cent think that they should live in special housing. These responses may indicate a concern to ensure that people receive the support they need. Nonetheless they suggest that people believe that more support is capable of being provided outside a person's own home and that as a result they do not accept the ultimate logic of community care; that where someone lives should not depend on the type or level of support that they require.

– Providing care –

Further evidence that people see care at home as more appropriate for some than others comes from looking at the answers given when people were asked who would be the best person to provide the care and support that was needed in each vignette (see table 2.3). The person whom fewest people think should live in the community, that is the person with mental illness, is also the person whose care (in this case checking that they have taken their medication) is most likely to be thought to be best given by a formal carer, that is a nurse, a home help or a paid carer. Nearly three-quarters think this care is best delivered by a formal carer. In contrast, the person whom most people think should live in the community (the person with learning disabilities) is the one person where a majority think that their support (being taken to a club once a week) is best provided informally, that is by family, friends or a volunteer. Evidently the more formal the care that is thought to be necessary to meet a person's particular needs, the more it is thought that someone needs to live in a residential setting.

Table 2.3 Who should provide care?

	Informal			Formal		
	Family	Friend	Volunteer	Nurse	Home help	Sample size
S/P (50) has a mental illness %	19	5	1	39	35	1605
S/P (90) has had falls	29	13	2	2	53	1605
J/S (87) often forgets things %	21	4	1	15	58	1605
A/D (44) can't read or write %	31	19	25	1	22	1605

However, those who believe that care should be delivered in the community do not necessarily see this as a means of requiring families rather than the government to provide that care. This is perhaps best illustrated by looking at the frail older person, whom as many as half feel should live in their own home. While nearly three in ten believe that that person's care (in this case help with shopping and cooking) is best provided by their own family, over half say that it would best be provided by a home help. Even amongst those who actually feel that the frail older person should live in their own home, no less than 49 per cent believe that their care is best provided by a home help or other formal carer.

– Paying for care –

Equally, there is little sign that the provision of care in the community is seen as a means by which government could divest itself of the responsibility of paying for the cost of formal care. We asked our respondents:

Suppose that someone outside the family has to provide care for John/Susan, etc. Which of these statements comes closest to what you believe about who should pay for this? Bear in mind that under no circumstances would John/Susan, etc. have to sell the house that he lives in.
The government should pay, no matter how much money the person has.
The person should pay, no matter how much money he/she has.
Who pays should depend on how much money the person has.

This wording was intended to get at the heart of the recent debate about who should pay the cost of personal care while putting to one side the most emotive part of that debate, that is whether someone should be required to sell their own home in order to pay for their care costs. In fact, someone who is living in their own home (as opposed to a care home) would not be required by current policy to sell their home. Despite making this clear, table 2.4 shows that for all four scenarios roughly two in three believe the government should pay for care costs, while only around one in three say that who should pay should depend on how much money the person has. While belief that responsibility lies solely with the government is highest in respect of the person with mental illness (perhaps because of the greater risk that is thought to be involved or perhaps because the care they require is regarded as a medical rather than a personal need), what is most remarkable is the similarity of the response across all four scenarios.

Table 2.4 Who should pay for care?

		Government	Person	Depends on income	*Sample size*
S/P (50) has a mental illness	%	72	1	26	1605
S/P (90) has had falls	%	66	2	32	1605
J/S (87) often forgets things	%	62	2	35	1605
A/D (44) can't read or write	%	63	3	32	1605

The figures are similar if we just look at those who believe that the person should be able to live in their own home rather than in a care home. For example, in the case of the frail older person, 63 per cent of those who believe that it would be best for them to live at home believe that the government should pay for the cost of care irrespective of the person's financial means, only a little lower than the equivalent 73 per cent figure amongst those who thought it was best for them to live in a care home. For the older person with dementia, these figures are in fact almost identical at 63 and 65 per cent respectively.

There is other evidence that the public expects the government to meet the costs of community care for older people in particular and does not regard it as a way of reducing costs. Another question was designed to test how far people valued enabling someone to have the choice to continue to live in their own home by asking whether they felt that the government should pay for the costs of doing so even if it were to mean that it would cost more. It ran:

Imagine an elderly person who needs regular help and wants to stay in their own house. The help would be paid for by the government and would cost more than caring for them in a residential or nursing home. Which of these options comes closest to your view?
The person should be cared for in their own home because that is what they want.
They should be cared for in a residential or nursing home because that costs government less.

No less than 76 per cent opt for the first of these two options while just 12 per cent choose the second. Yet another question asked people whether they wanted more or less spending on a range of items. Respondents were reminded that if they said they wanted more spending it would probably mean they would have to pay higher taxes. Despite this warning, no less than 81 per cent say that they want more spending on 'help for elderly people so they can stay in their own homes', slightly higher than the 77 per cent who say the same for 'care for elderly people living in residential or nursing homes'. These figures are second only to those for health (on which 92 per cent said they wanted more spending) and are on a par with those for pensions (76 per cent).

So it appears then that in deciding to fund the personal care costs of those in need of long-term care the Scottish Executive has in fact implemented a policy that is in tune with majority public opinion north of the border. In this respect at least it appears that the Scottish Executive has provided a Scottish answer to a Scottish question. However, is there any evidence to suggest that opinion on this subject is different in Scotland to that in England and that as a result the devolution settlement has made it possible for a Scottish answer to be given to a *uniquely* Scottish question?

We have at least one clue that in fact opinion in Scotland is similar to that in England. Both our survey and the most recent British Social Attitudes survey asked:

Looking at this card, who do you think should be mainly responsible for paying for the care needs of elderly people living in residential and nursing homes?
Mainly the government.
Mainly a person themselves and their family.

This question asks who should pay for the costs of unspecified care in a residential setting rather than who should pay for the cost of specifically personal care, irrespective of setting. Moreover, those who might believe that the person themselves should make some contribution to the cost of their care if they have the means to do so but that the government should pay most of the cost may well answer 'mainly the government' in response to this question but 'depends' in response to our earlier questions. But in practice it appears that this question does tap a similar attitude towards the role of the government in funding the costs of care as do the questions we have been examining so far. Thus, for example, only 29 per cent of those who think that mainly the government should fund the costs of care in residential and nursing homes think that our frail older person should make any contribution to the costs of their care. In contrast as many as 53 per cent of those who say that most of the cost of residential and nursing home care should be paid by the person themselves and their family take that view.

Table 2.5 Attitudes towards the cost of care in England and Scotland

| | 1999 | | 2001 | |
	England	Scotland	England	Scotland
	%	%	%	%
Mainly the government	80	86	86	88
Mainly the person themselves and their family	16	11	12	9
Sample size	2722	1482	2786	1605

If people in England have different views from those in Scotland about who should pay the costs of personal care, we would expect to find a rather different pattern of response on the two sides of the border to our question about who should pay the care costs of those in residential and nursing homes. There is little evidence that this is so. As table 2.5 shows, the proportion saying that mainly the government should pay is only slightly higher in Scotland than it is in England. Moreover there is no evidence that opinion in the two countries has diverged in the wake of the different decisions made by the government in London and by the Executive in Edinburgh. In short, rather than responding to a specifically Scottish demand, the Scottish Executive's decision to fund the personal care costs of those in need of long-term care would appear to have implemented what would have been the more popular policy in England too.

– *Who supports community care?* –

We now turn to the second main question to be addressed in this chapter: who supports a policy of government-funded community care and what can this tell us about the attitudes underlying people's support?

The debate about whether or not the Scottish Executive should fund the long-term personal care costs of older people was in many respects an argument about the fundamental principles of the welfare state in Britain. Advocates of what has come to be known as 'free' personal care invoke the universal principle, arguing that all those who find themselves in need of personal care should receive that care for free in exactly the same way that all those who need the services of a doctor receive that help for free. In contrast, opponents of the policy argue that the policy simply provides a subsidy to those who are better off (Leontaridi and Bell 2001). In other words, as was recognised by the Care Development Group that was established by the Scottish Executive in January 2001 in order to identify the best way of delivering a free personal care policy, the two sides were emphasising two very different notions of 'equity'. The advocates of free personal care championed 'diagnostic equity', while its opponents emphasised 'income equity' (Care Development Group 2001).

The existence of this debate raises two important questions about who supports community care. First, who believes that the government should pay the costs of those in need of long-term care? Is it those sections of society that critics of the policy believe will be the principal beneficiaries, such as those in middle-class occupations and those with high incomes, as some previous research has suggested is the case (Deeming 2001). Or is it perhaps those groups who are usually regarded as more likely to favour more government spending, such as those on low incomes and those in working-class occupations? Similarly, is support for government spending on personal care primarily (as critics of the policy would expect) amongst those on the right of the political spectrum, or is it higher where support for more government spending is usually to be found, that is amongst those on the left?

Second, are those who believe in the government funding of care necessarily the same as those who believe in the provision of that care in the community and the values of social inclusion associated with that policy? We have already indicated one reason why this might not be so – that providing care in the community might be seen as a means by which the role of the state in the provision of care can be reduced. Another possibility, however, is that support for the idea that all sections of society should have the right to live as full a life as possible within the community may not have much to do with whether people generally hold 'left-' or 'right-wing' views at all. Rather it may have more to do with what previous research has suggested is a largely separate dimension of social attitudes, that is whether someone generally holds 'liberal' or 'authoritarian' views about social issues (Evans et al. 1996). Someone with liberal views largely accepts the right of individuals to determine their own lifestyle and as a result accepts that society will encompass a diversity of such lifestyles. Someone with authoritarian views, on the other hand, believes that it is important for society to uphold certain moral norms and as a result is less tolerant of diversity. An analysis of support for Third Way policies (Bromley and Curtice 1999) found that while attitudes to welfare and the role of the state varied by class, attitudes to lifestyle issues varied according to education and age. So it would appear quite likely that those who are keenest on the provision of care in the community are those with more liberal views and that this might matter more than whether they are on the 'left' or the 'right'.

– Self-interest or ideology? –

Who, then, supports government funding of community care costs irrespective of a person's financial means? Is it those who might be expected to benefit most from such a policy, or is it those who are traditionally most in favour of more government spending? One group that would be expected to benefit more from the policy comprises women, largely because they tend to live longer than men (Care Development Group 2001: 239). Yet as table 2.6 shows, women are slightly less likely than men to believe that the government should pay the costs of the care required in each of our four vignettes.

Table 2.6 Government should pay, by gender

% say government should pay	Men	Women
S/P (50) has a mental illness	73	70
S/P (90) has had falls	68	64
J/S (87) often forgets things	65	60
A/D (44) can't read or write	65	62
Sample size	*645*	*960*

Equally, those on higher incomes would be expected to benefit more from the policy than those on lower incomes. Yet, as table 2.7 shows, those on the highest incomes are least likely to say that the government should be solely responsible for the costs of care. Across the four vignettes those on the highest incomes are between seven and eleven points less likely to say that the government should pay than are those on the lowest incomes.

Table 2.7 Government should pay, by income

% say government should pay	Income quartile			
	Lowest	Low to middle	Middle to high	Highest
S/P (50) has a mental illness	75	70	73	65
S/P (90) has had falls	72	69	63	55
J/S (87) often forgets things	67	62	61	56
A/D (44) can't read or write	66	63	65	56
Sample size	*394*	*323*	*346*	*308*

Note:
Lowest income quartile: annual household income less than £8,000 pa.
Low to middle: £8,000 to £14,999.
Middle to high: £15,000 to £28,999.
High: £29,000 or more.

This picture is confirmed when we look at attitudes within each social class (for the definition of social class see the Technical Appendix at the end of this book). As table 2.8 shows, those most in favour of the policy are those in semi-routine and routine occupations who would be least expected to benefit from the policy of free care, while amongst those least in favour are managers and professionals who could expect to benefit most. Rather than reflecting self-interest, the pattern in table 2.8 conforms to what we would expect (as discussed further in Chapter 7) if attitudes towards who should pay for personal care are influenced by whether or not people are generally in favour of a greater role for government in the economy and society.

Perhaps, then, support for government funding of personal care has come to be seen as a 'left-wing' idea, more likely to be believed in by those who generally feel that government should have a large role, even though critics of the idea have argued that the policy is a regressive one that simply subsidises the better off.

Table 2.8 Government should pay, by social class

% say government should pay	Managers and professionals	Intermediate	Self-employed	Supervisory and technical	Semi-routine and routine
		Occupational class			
S/P (50) has a mental illness	66	73	65	74	75
S/P (90) has had falls	58	61	62	66	73
J/S (87) often forgets things	56	62	55	64	67
A/D (44) can't read or write	57	63	61	66	67
Sample size	460	170	70	161	587

We can test this proposition directly by looking at how beliefs about who should pay for care vary according to where someone stands on a scale of left–right attitudes that we included in our survey (for further details of this scale see the Technical Appendix). Table 2.9 shows that our expectation is upheld. For example, whereas less than three in five of those on the right of

Table 2.9 Government should pay, by left–right scale position

% say government should pay for care	Position on left–right scale			
	Left	Centre left	Centre right	Right
S/P (50) has a mental illness	77	72	69	67
S/P (90) has had falls	72	64	62	59
J/S (87) often forgets things	71	60	57	56
A/D (44) can't read or write	70	64	59	60
Sample size	295	477	304	287

Note:
Left: score of 2 or less on the left–right dimension.
Centre left: score between 2 and 2.5.
Centre right: score between 2.5 and 2.84.
Right: score greater than 2.84.

the political spectrum believe that the need of the 87-year-old who often forgets things for help with bathing should be funded solely by the government, over seven in ten of those on the left take that view. Critics of the Scottish Executive's policy on personal care appear to have failed to communicate their arguments to that section of the public that might have been expected to be most sympathetic to them.

As we suggested earlier, one of the problems faced by those critics is that their notion of what was equitable was not the only notion of equity being advanced in the debate. Their emphasis on 'income equity' had to compete with claims based on 'diagnostic equity'. And the potential power of the latter kind of argument is revealed by the answers we obtained to the following question:

Which of these views comes closest to your own about elderly people who need regular help looking after themselves?
All elderly people who need it should get the same quality of help.
Elderly people who can afford it should be able to pay for better-quality help.

No less than 74 per cent support the first of these two statements while only 21 per cent back the second. The idea that equality of need should be met with equality of support evidently has a strong hold on the public debate. And the influence that this idea has on people's views about who should pay for care is revealed by the fact that no less than 70 per cent of those who support the first statement say that the government should pay for the help needed by the frail 90-year-old, whereas only 45 per cent of those who back the second statement believe the government should pay. Similar differences are found if we look at the results for any of the other three vignettes. These views support universal rather than selective welfare responses; in other words, the Scottish and not the English answer to responsibility for the payment of personal care.

– The two faces of community care –

The view that government should fund care in the community is, then, an idea that is more common amongst those on the left than those on the right. But are those who believe that people should be enabled to live and participate in the community of a similar ideological disposition?

Table 2.10 reveals that in fact for all four vignettes, the proportion who say they would feel comfortable living next door to the person described bears little or no relation to whether someone has left- or right-wing views in general. In each case the proportion who say they are comfortable is almost

Table 2.10 Attitude to having a neighbour with needs, by left–right scale position

% very/fairly comfortable living next door to	Position on left–right scale			
	Left	Centre left	Centre right	Right
S/P (50) has a mental illness	50	46	42	46
S/J (90) has had falls	72	74	74	76
J/S (87) often forgets things	39	40	40	48
A/D (44) can't read or write	62	63	64	58
Sample size	295	477	304	287

Note: See table 2.9 for definition of left, centre left and so on.

exactly the same irrespective of where people stand on the left–right spectrum, and such differences as exist are not consistent from one vignette to the next. It seems that support for the idea that government should pay for community care does not necessarily go hand in hand with the idea that people should be enabled to live in the community.

Table 2.11 Attitude to having a neighbour, by liberal–authoritarian scale position

% very/fairly comfortable living next door to	Position on liberal–authoritarian scale			
	Liberal	Moderate liberal	Moderate authoritarian	Authoritarian
S/P (50) has a mental illness	50	47	45	41
S/J (90) has had falls	81	74	71	68
J/S (87) often forgets things	48	43	39	33
A/D (44) can't read or write	70	61	61	50
Sample size	334	430	280	320

Note:
Liberal: score of 3.2 or less on the liberal–authoritarian dimension.
Moderate liberal: score between 3.2 and 3.67.
Moderate authoritarian: score between 3.67 and 4.
Authoritarian: score greater than 4.

That those who support state responsibility for paying for care are not the same as those who support the principles of community care is revealed even more starkly by looking at how attitudes differ according to where people stand on a second liberal–authoritarian attitudinal scale. For more detail on this scale, see the Technical Appendix. Table 2.11 confirms our suspicion that that those who are most inclined to believe that people should be enabled to live in the community are those of a predominantly liberal disposition. For example, no less than 70 per cent of those at the liberal end of our scale say that they would be comfortable living next door to the person with learning disabilities, compared with only half of those at the authoritarian end. Similar differences also exist for each of the other three vignettes. On the other hand, if we look at whether or not people think the government should pay for the cost of care according to where they stand on the liberal–authoritarian scale, we find, as table 2.12 shows, a very different pattern. It is those on the authoritarian end of the scale who are most likely to believe that the government should pay, while those on the liberal end of the spectrum are least likely to take that view.

Table 2.12 Government should pay, by liberal–authoritarian scale position

% say government should pay	Position on liberal–authoritarian scale			
	Liberal	Moderate liberal	Moderate authoritarian	Authoritarian
S/P (50) has a mental illness	66	73	71	76
S/P (90) has had falls	59	66	62	71
J/S (87) often forgets things	57	61	59	66
A/D (44) can't read or write	59	65	60	70
Sample size	334	430	280	320

Note: See table 2.11 for definition of liberal, moderate liberal and so on.

There are, then, two faces to public support for a policy of community care. Those who are most likely to think that the government should pay are least likely to back a policy of enabling a diverse range of people to live in the community. Equally, those who believe in the latter policy are least likely to believe in government funding. A belief that government should pay is associated with a left-wing outlook, whereas caring for as many people as possible in the community is the product of a more liberal mind. Public support for government-funded community care depends on the support of two potentially diverse strands of opinion.

– CONCLUSION –

The Scottish Executive's decision to fund the long-term personal care costs of older people appears to have been in tune with the preferences of a majority of the public north of the border. On this issue at least devolution has resulted in public policy being more in line with the public's preferences than would otherwise have been the case. A Scottish answer was given to a Scottish question. But while devolution made it possible to accommodate Scottish public opinion, there is nothing apparently uniquely Scottish about that public opinion. From the evidence available to us, it looks as though a policy of 'free' personal care would be as popular in England as it is in Scotland.

We have also found that there is not a unified attitude towards community care in Scotland. Whereas there is widespread acceptance of public responsibility to meet the support needs of a wide range of individuals and to enable them to exercise their choice to live in the community, the acceptance of people who need support as full citizens, able, for example, to exercise the right and responsibility of jury service, is much more limited. And whereas support for state responsibility for funding is strongest amongst those on the political left, support for the principles of community care is more likely to be found amongst those who hold liberal rather than authoritarian views. There is little evidence that attitudes in Scotland on a range of issues are more or less liberal than those in England (Park 2002). The significance of these findings lies rather in their implications for New Labour's Third Way, in which a shared sense of rights and responsibilities is intended to provide the cement of social solidarity that will justify the continued public support of a reformed and more diverse welfare state (Giddens 2000). This analysis of attitudes to community care suggests that the connection between collective responsibility and social solidarity could still be fragile. Those who support collective responsibility for welfare (the vast majority) do not yet necessarily accept that the community is strengthened by the presence and contribution of all its members, whatever their needs.

– Acknowledgements –

The authors gratefully acknowledge funding from the Scottish Executive for the community care module as part of the Scottish Social Attitudes survey. Any opinions and errors are the authors' responsibility. A full report of the study is available from The Stationery Office (see Curtice and Petch 2002).

– References –

Bromley, C. and Curtice, J. (1999), 'Is there a Third Way?', in R. Jowell, J. Curtice, A. Park and K. Thomson (eds), *British Social Attitudes: the 16th report – Who Shares New Labour Values?*, Aldershot: Ashgate.

Care Development Group (2001), *Fair Care for Older People*, Edinburgh: The Stationery Office.

Curtice, L. and Petch, A. (2002), *How Does the Community Care? Public Attitudes to Community Care in Scotland*, Edinburgh: The Stationery Office.

Deeming, C. (2001), *A Fair Deal for Older People? Public Views on the Funding of Long-Term Care*, London: King's Fund.

Evans, G., Heath, A. and Lalljee, M. (1996), 'Measuring Left-Right and Libertarian-Authoritarian Values in the British Electorate', *British Journal of Sociology*, 47, pp. 93–112.

Giddens, A. (2000), *The Third Way and its Critics*, Oxford: Polity Press.

Griffiths, R. (1988), *Community Care: Agenda for Action*, London: HMSO.

Hills, J. (2001), 'Poverty and social security: What rights? Whose responsibilities?', in A. Park, J. Curtice, K. Thomson, L. Jarvis and C. Bromley (eds), *British Social Attitudes: the 18th report – Public Policy, Social Ties*, London: Sage.

Leontaridi, R. and Bell, D. (2001), *Informal Care of the Elderly in Scotland and the UK*, Health and Community Care Research Findings, no. 8, Edinburgh: Scottish Executive Central Research Unit.

Lewis, G. (1998), 'Citizenship' in G. Hughes (ed.), *Imagining Welfare Futures*, London: Routledge for the Open University.

Park, A. (2002), 'Scotland's morals', in J. Curtice, D. McCrone, A. Park and L. Paterson (eds), *New Scotland, New Society*, Edinburgh: Polygon.

Philpot, T. (1995), 'What the papers say: media images of people with learning difficulties', in T. Philpot and L. Ward (eds), *Values and Visions: Changing Ideas in Services for People with Learning Difficulties*, Oxford: Butterworth Heinemann.

Royal Commission on Long-Term Care (1999), *With Respect to Old Age: Long-Term Care – Rights and Responsibilities*, London: The Stationery Office.

Scottish Executive (2000), *The Same As You? Review of Services for People with Learning Disabilities in Scotland*, Edinburgh: The Stationery Office.

Scottish Executive, Social Inclusion Division (2001), *Social Justice Annual Report, Scotland 2001*, Edinburgh: The Stationery Office.

Scottish Office (1997), *A Framework for Mental Health Services in Scotland*, Edinburgh: The Stationery Office.

Scottish Office (1998), *Modernising Community Care – An Action Plan*, Edinburgh: The Stationery Office.

Secretaries of State for Health, Social Security, Wales & Scotland (1989), *Caring for People: Community Care in the Next Decade and Beyond*, cmn 849, London: HMSO.

CHAPTER 3

Housing, Neighbourhoods and Communities

Ade Kearns and Alison Parkes

INTRODUCTION: RESIDENTIAL POLICIES AND HOUSING CHANGE

The way housing is occupied and the way people live in their neighbourhoods are both central to the achievement of the Scottish Executive's aspirations for greater social justice. To quote the premise in the Executive's second report on Social Justice in Scotland: 'Where someone lives determines their quality of life and to a large extent their opportunities' (Scottish Executive 2001: 79).

Meanwhile, in laying out its plans for greater social justice, the Executive has identified three key housing and neighbourhood policies. These are:

- to reduce inequalities between communities;
- to increase residents' satisfaction with their neighbourhoods and communities; and
- to empower communities through extending participation, access to skills, knowledge and resources. (Scottish Executive 2001: 79–80)

In this chapter we analyse data from the 2001 Scottish Social Attitudes survey in order to assess the extent to which housing and neighbourhood policies can contribute to the fulfilment of the Scottish Executive's social justice objectives, and how much work it has to do 'to build the consensus [needed] in Scotland to deliver on social justice' (Baillie 2001: 3).

We focus on three policies in particular. The first, and so far most advanced, is so-called 'community empowerment' in housing. Nearly three years ago, the Scottish Executive declared its intention (which it shares with the UK government) to promote new forms of 'community ownership' for social rented housing. Local authorities were to be encouraged to seek tenants' support to transfer the ownership and management of their housing to new registered social landlords. It was argued that this would empower tenants, improve their rights and raise housing standards. Indeed, the policy has already resulted in the transfer of all of Glasgow City Council's stock to a new housing association.

Given the tradition of municipal socialism in Scotland, this policy is highly contentious. Supporters point to greater tenant involvement and empowerment as well as financial gains. The Executive itself has argued that community ownership will help revive deprived communities, attract private finance for housing investment, and provide greater certainty about rent levels for tenants (Communities Scotland 2002). On the other hand, opponents argue that local authority control of housing is more democratic and that further investment in rented housing could be achieved without altering the ownership arrangements if only the Treasury were more flexible about public expenditure rules (Hargrave 2002). Whilst in no way trying to adjudicate between these competing visions, we will ask whether this major tenet of the Scottish Executive's social rented housing policy has public support and consider whether tenants' assessments of their current situation lends any support to the claim that the policy is in their best interests.

The second policy on which we focus is the Executive's neighbourhood renewal strategy. In its recently published Community Regeneration Statement it argued in favour of 'closing the gap' between deprived and other areas, and 'turning round disadvantaged communities' through more effective public services and the development of social capital. In her introduction to the statement, the Minister said:

> We want to see a Scotland where every neighbourhood is a safe, attractive place to live, work and play, where public services meet the needs of people, not the demands of the organisations which deliver them, and where social justice is a right, not a privilege. (Scottish Executive 2002a: 1)

In so doing, the Executive closely echoed the argument of the UK government in its *Neighbourhood Renewal: National Strategy Action Plan* for England which stated that: 'It should no longer be accepted as routine that people on low incomes should suffer conditions and services that are failing and so sharply different from what the rest of the population receives' (Social Exclusion Unit 2001: 24).

This policy gives rise to several important questions. First, to what extent are people's lives played out within relatively small neighbourhood areas? Do neighbourhoods matter for those at whom the Executive's social justice policy is targeted? Second, to what extent are there currently perceived differences in the qualities of neighbourhoods? Are some kinds of people less likely than others to feel they live in a 'good' neighbourhood? Third, which aspects of the neighbourhood matter most, in terms of inequalities or their impact upon people's lives and behaviour?

These questions matter because they enable us to consider how neighbourhood renewal policy is related to the Scottish Executive's key policy of social justice. According to the Community Regeneration Statement, the intention of neighbourhood renewal policy is to 'provide better links between national, regional and neighbourhood priorities' (Scottish Executive 2002a: 11). However, in looking at how neighbourhood renewal might contribute to social justice, we need to be aware that social justice can be interpreted in at least three different ways (Goodlad et al. 2002). These are *egalitarian justice*, wherein everyone is given an equal start in life through equivalent resources, *distributional justice*, under which there is a just distribution of goods, benefits and rights, and *fair treatment* for all, which requires that decisions be made in accordance with the principles of justice but is relatively unconcerned about distributional outcomes. We return to these aspects of social justice in the conclusion to the chapter.

The third and final policy on which we focus has as yet to be officially promoted by the Executive, but is widely expected to feature in its Scottish Cities Review. This is that planning policy should encourage the creation of more mixed communities. The impetus for this comes from the report of Lord Rogers' Urban Task Force which argued: 'Whether we are talking about new settlements or expanding the capacity of existing urban areas, a good mix of incomes and tenures is important for a number of reasons' (Urban Task Force 1999: 65).

We ask three questions about this policy. Will mixed communities enhance neighbourhood quality and residential quality of life? When it comes to the question of where and how they wish to live, do the general public exhibit enthusiasm for the Government's declared values of diversity, tolerance and cohesion? And, lastly, does the policy of mixed communities have the necessary support of those in the majority housing tenure (owner occupation) for it to be realisable?

– HOUSING –

– Housing tenure and housing histories –

Scottish housing changed a great deal in the latter part of the twentieth century. Whereas in the 1960s, a little over a quarter of all dwellings in Scotland were owner occupied, by the mid-1990s three in five dwellings were owned. Conversely, public rented dwellings changed from being a

majority of the housing stock to being a minority. Our survey data show
that the country is now split 2:1 between owners and renters, closely
mirroring the results of the Scottish Household Survey, which reported that
61 per cent of households lived in owner-occupied housing and 37 per cent
in rented housing (Scottish Executive 2000). Local authorities are still the
biggest landlords, being responsible for 27 per cent of all dwellings, but it is
the housing association sub-sector which has been growing in recent years
and this now comprises five per cent of the Scottish housing market.

While most Scots no longer live in rented housing, it remains the case
that most Scots have had some experience of doing so. No less than 79 per
cent have lived in rented housing at some point in their adult lives, while no
less than 65 per cent grew up in rented housing, including 51 per cent in
council housing. So while, as table 3.1 shows, those whose parents owned a
home are themselves now more likely to be owner-occupiers, two-thirds
have some experience of renting. Meanwhile, although no less than three in
five of those who were brought up in rental accommodation have themselves become owner-occupiers, no less than 84 per cent have spent some
time as adults in rental accommodation.

Table 3.1 Housing histories

		Parental tenure	
		Owned	Rented
		%	%
Current tenure	Owned	75	61
	Rented	25	39
Renting experience	Yes	65	84
	No	35	15
Minimum sample size		*461*	*1065*

Yet if renting is an experience many Scots have in common, those who
are currently renting from a social landlord, that is a local authority or
housing association, have a very distinctive social profile. Social renters
are on lower incomes and are less likely to be in full-time employment
than those who are buying their own home (Scottish Executive 2002b).
They are also more likely to live in single-person households or in
households where the highest income earner is either permanently sick
or disabled. Evidently social renters are a relatively disadvantaged group
who might hope to be the beneficiaries of any policy designed to deliver
greater social justice.

– Knowledge and awareness of landlords –

If the aim of the Scottish Executive is to give those who rent a greater say in how their housing is provided and managed, then one might argue that its policy should be informed by the views of tenants themselves. On the other hand, uninformed views, based upon hearsay, inspired guesses or prejudices may not be very useful to policy-makers, even if they can be said to be democratic.

In our survey, respondents were asked to rate on the basis of *what you know or have heard* the three main types of landlord – councils, housing associations and private landlords – on six dimensions. These dimensions were:

- providing a good standard of repairs and maintenance in their homes;
- charging reasonable rents;
- allowing tenants to stay in their homes as long as they want to;
- providing housing in good neighbourhoods;
- providing housing quickly for those who need it;
- giving tenants a say in the way their houses are looked after.

In each case the landlord was rated on a five-point scale ranging from *nearly always good* to *nearly always bad*.

It appears that even those who rent their home feel they have limited information about different kinds of landlord. On average across the six dimensions, no less than 28 per cent felt unable to offer an opinion about the performance of housing associations and 27 per cent private landlords, though at 10 per cent people evidently feel more familiar with the work of local councils. Most importantly nearly a third of council tenants feel unable to rate the landlord that the Executive would like them to embrace, that is housing associations.

– Landlord performance –

In looking further at the answers to these questions, it is useful to draw a distinction between landlord performance and landlord reputation. Landlord performance, which we look at first, consists of the views of a landlord type by people who currently reside in that sector, for example council tenants' views on councils as landlords. Landlord reputation, on the other hand, comprises the views of a landlord type held by tenants who rent in a different sector, for example the views of housing association and private sector tenants on councils as landlords. (Although not shown here, owner-occupiers' relative perceptions of the three types of landlords are in fact similar to those of tenants.)

Table 3.2 shows for each dimension the proportion of those who rent from a particular type of landlord who think that that type of landlord is either *nearly always* or *often* good. Given the relatively small number housing association and private rental tenants in our sample, not all of the differences in the table are statistically significant. But both council tenants and housing associations were significantly more likely than those renting from a private landlord to think that their kind of landlord was good at providing repairs, charging reasonable rents and allowing tenants to stay in their homes for as long as they want. However, there was no dimension on which councils were rated significantly more highly than were housing associations, although there is clearly a hint in our data that councils are, relatively speaking, most highly valued for their willingness to allow tenants to stay and for charging reasonable rents. Most importantly, however, housing associations were significantly more likely than local councils to be regarded as good at giving a tenants a say in how their homes are looked after, just as those who regard such associations as a means of community empowerment would argue they are. Even so, one might be surprised that more housing association tenants did not regard housing associations as good at giving them a say, given the strong claims made by the advocates of community empowerment about the performance of housing associations in this area. It appears that in practice housing associations need to do better if the Executive's aim to 'ensure that there is effective tenant involvement in key decisions' under new community ownership arrangements (Scottish Office 1999) is to be achieved.

Table 3.2 Landlord performance

Service dimension	Councils	Housing associations	Private landlords
	% current tenants saying 'nearly always' or 'often' good		
Give tenants a say	26	40	18
Provide housing quickly	29	40	30
Provide housing in good neighbourhoods	33	41	39
Provide good standard of repairs	44	51	23
Charge reasonable rents	48	44	13
Allow tenants to stay in their home as long as they want	70	58	21
Sample size	*374*	*71*	*82*

Of course the merit of the Executive's policy also depends on how much difference being given a say makes to tenants' satisfaction with their housing. Indeed, how much difference any of the dimensions in table 3.2 makes to tenants' satisfaction is thrown into doubt by the fact that even though private landlords had the lowest ratings in the table, their tenants are most likely to be satisfied with their housing. As many as 36 per cent of private tenants are 'very satisfied' and a further 39 per cent 'quite satisfied'. In contrast, only around one in five council and housing association tenants are 'very satisfied' while a half are 'quite satisfied'.

In fact, it appears that just two of our dimensions matter. In table 3.3 we model the probability that a tenant is 'satisfied' with their current landlord. It shows that the odds that someone is either 'very' or 'quite' satisfied with their current landlord are more than doubled if they consider that their landlord provides housing in good neighbourhoods and provides a good repairs service. Thus, to make tenants happy, landlords have to provide a good repair service, improve the neighbourhoods around their housing and manage those neighbourhoods well. In contrast, giving tenants a say in how their housing is run, the ideological core of the community empowerment proposals, is not in itself a significant predictor of tenant satisfaction. Thus, community empowerment in and of itself does not appear to produce happier tenants, though obviously it may be a route to improving the performance of landlords in other ways.

Table 3.3 Predictors of tenant satisfaction

Variable	Odds ratio for probability that tenant is satisfied with landlord
Good (vs. not good/can't choose) at:	
Providing repairs	2.4[**]
Providing housing in good neighbourhoods	2.0[*]
Charging reasonable rents	1.6
Giving tenants a say	1.5
Providing housing quickly	1.1
Allowing tenants to stay	1.0
Landlord type (compared with council)	
Private landlord	1.9
Housing association	0.9
Sample size	*524*

* $p < 0.05$
** $p < 0.01$
Note: An odds ratio of greater than 1 indicates that the group in question is more likely to exhibit the response than the comparison group, while an odds ratio of less than 1 indicates that the group is less likely to exhibit the response.

– Landlord reputations –

We now turn to consider what tenants think of *other* types of landlord. Table 3.4 shows how each type of landlord is regarded by those tenants who do not rent from that sector. The low perceived performance of private landlords is matched by their reputation, which is significantly lower than that of both housing associations and councils on all our dimensions except for providing accommodation quickly, on which there are no significant differences between any of the types of landlord.

In contrast, the reputation of councils and housing associations differs rather more than does their perceived performance. Housing associations have a significantly higher reputation for providing housing in good neighbourhoods, even though there was no significant difference between their perceived performance. And as we found for landlord performance, housing associations also have a significantly higher reputation for tenant empowerment than other types of landlord. On the other hand, housing associations have a significantly worse reputation for charging reasonable rents and allowing tenants to stay as long as they want, again despite the absence of performance differences on these dimensions.

Table 3.4 Landlord reputations

Service dimension	Councils	Housing associations	Private landlords
	% tenants in other tenures saying 'nearly always' or 'often' 'good'		
Provide housing in good neighbourhoods	13	34	18
Give tenants a say	16	27	12
Provide housing quickly	20	24	19
Provide good standard of repairs	24	35	15
Charge reasonable rents	47	30	10
Allow tenants to stay in their home as long as they want	54	38	12
Sample size	*153*	*456*	*445*

It would appear then that despite their generally favourable performance and reputation, housing associations, the Executive's preferred type of social landlord, have an image of being relatively expensive and also tougher landlords (thus offering less security in the long-term). Moreover, table 3.5 indicates that this picture is particularly true for council tenants. Current council tenants see councils as far better than housing associations for, first, allowing people to stay as long as they want and, second, charging reasonable rents. They also regard councils as slightly better for providing repairs and providing housing quickly, while they see no difference at all between them when it comes to providing houses in good neighbourhoods and, most notably, giving tenants a say. Evidently the biggest barriers to tenants welcoming a transfer to the housing association sector are concerns about future levels of rents and about whether housing associations can be relied upon to be fair landlords who will allow them to continue renting their current home for as long as they want. Meanwhile, as yet at least the idea that housing associations would empower citizens by giving them more say is not proving to be a particularly attractive feature of housing associations in the eyes of council tenants.

Table 3.5 Council tenants' ratings of councils and housing associations

Service dimension	Council	Housing associations	Difference (council–housing association)
	% council tenants saying 'nearly always' or 'often' 'good'		
Allow tenants to stay in their home as long as they want	70	37	33
Charge reasonable rents	48	28	20
Provide good standard of repairs	44	35	9
Provide housing quickly	29	26	3
Provide housing in good neighbourhoods	33	35	-2
Give tenants a say	26	28	-2
Sample size	*374*	*374*	

– Preferred landlords –

The apparent continued popularity of council housing seems to be confirmed when tenants are asked from whom they would prefer to rent. No less than two out of three said they would prefer to rent from a public landlord (that is a local council or Scottish Homes), only just under one in five would prefer to rent from a housing association, while only one in ten favour a private landlord. However, these figures suggest that there may have been a decline in the popularity of council housing over the last half dozen years or so. According to the combined results of the second and third consumer preference surveys in housing (Pieda 1995: table 6.4; Pieda 1996: table 5.4), in the mid-1990s 87 per cent of those renters who preferred to rent favoured doing so from a public sector landlord whilst only 7 per cent favoured renting from a housing association.[1] This suggests that there has been a 20-point drop in the proportion favouring public renting while the proportion who prefer to rent from a housing association has risen by 11 points. Equally, comparison with the results of a survey carried out in 1993 suggests that the proportion of current renters who prefer to rent privately has also risen (Scottish Homes 1994: 52).

Moreover, one possible reason why councils remain the most popular kind of landlord is that people simply tend to be loyal to whatever landlord they currently have, perhaps because of emotional allegiance, a fear of change, or because they align their expectations with their current experience. Loyalty is certainly high in practice, with four-fifths of renters preferring to rent from the type of landlord they presently have. As table 3.6 shows, this is particularly true of council tenants, nine out of ten of whom say they prefer to rent from a council. Two out of three housing association tenants are also loyal to their current landlord, though in the case of private sector tenants this figure falls to a half. Older council and housing association tenants are particularly likely to be loyal. Otherwise, the only other factor that appears to be associated with a wish to swap landlords is a perception that their current landlord does not provide a good repairs service.

Table 3.6 Landlord preferences, by current tenure

| | Current tenure | | |
Preferred landlord	Council	Housing association	Private landlord
	%	%	%
Council or Scottish Homes	**89**	21	21
Housing association	8	**64**	20
Private landlord	2	4	**50**
Other/don't know	1	11	9
Sample size	*450*	*83*	*106*

– NEIGHBOURHOODS –

The Scottish Executive stated in its report *Social Justice . . . A Scotland Where Everyone Matters* that 'The strength and wellbeing of communities and neighbourhoods is vital because this is where we live together' (Scottish Executive 1999: 16). As well as declaring its belief that neighbourhoods matter to people's well-being, the Scottish Executive also committed itself in the same document to the fulfilment of a long-term target to 'increase residents' satisfaction with their neighbourhoods and communities' (Scottish Executive 1999: 17). Our survey enables us to shed light on both what relevance neighbourhood has to people's lives and on what they think of their neighbourhoods.

– Neighbourhood size –

What is meant by a neighbourhood is ill-defined. It is well known that different people can have widely different views on what constitutes their local area. Our survey provides two ways of assessing what people consider to be the size of their neighbourhood and the nature of their attachment to their local area. First, respondents were asked what they thought of as their 'local area' and then, second, if they had moved into their present home within the last ten years, they were asked from how far away they had moved.

Table 3.7 shows the answers to both these questions broken down by their current housing tenure. Clearly those in living in different tenures have different conceptions of a neighbourhood and vary in their degree of attachment. No less than three in five of those in social housing had last moved house over a distance of a mile or less, whereas this is true of only two in five owner-occupiers. Meanwhile, as we might expect, those living in the private rental sector had on average moved the greatest distance of all, with 37 per cent having moved over 30 miles to their present home.

Table 3.7 Neighbourhood size, by current housing tenure

	Owner-occupier	Council	Housing association	Private rental	All
	%	%	%	%	%
Distance moved to current home					
Up to 1 mile	40	61	60	24	45
Up to 2 miles	11	13	7	9	11
Up to 5 miles	14	11	3	8	11
Up to 10 miles	9	5	19	4	8
Over 10 miles	26	11	10	56	24
Sample size	*455*	*258*	*63*	*91*	*833*
Area thought of as 'local area'					
Within 1 mile	45	57	55	34	47
Within 2 miles	20	22	27	23	21
Within 5 miles	19	14	7	14	17
Within 10 miles	10	5	8	19	9
Wider than 10 miles	6	3	3	10	6
Sample size	*949*	*450*	*83*	*106*	*1606*

Equally, those living in social housing also have the narrowest definition of what constitutes their local area. No less than four in five of those renting social housing feel that their local area extends to no more than two miles from their home compared with two in three owner-occupiers. More generally, despite the policy emphasis upon local neighbourhoods, we should recognise that not everyone operates their private life at such a scale: nearly a third of the population considers that their local area covers a distance of more than two miles.

One reason for this is perhaps unsurprising. Those living in rural areas are less likely to regard their neighbourhood as covering a small area. As table 3.8 shows, only 40 per cent of those living in the lowest population density (and thus most rural) parts of Scotland regard their local area as being within two miles or less of their home, whereas over twice as many do so in the mostly densely populated urban parts of the country. We also find that those on low incomes also tend to have a smaller definition of their neighbourhood, perhaps both because they are less able to afford the costs of travelling and have had less opportunity to become familiar with a wider area. People on lower incomes were also less likely than those on higher incomes to have moved house over a distance of more than two miles.

Table 3.8 Neighbourhood size, by population density and income

	Population density				
	Low	Low to medium	Medium	Medium to high	High
	%	%	%	%	%
Think of 'local area' as within 2 miles	40	61	76	79	86
Sample size	293	317	339	316	338
		Income Band			
		‹ £10k	£10–20k	£20–35k	›£35k
		%	%	%	%
Think of 'local area' as within 2 miles		80	67	67	61
Sample size		506	359	79	310

Note: Population density is based on postcode sector information at the time of the 1991 census. The cut-off points divide respondents into quintiles. Low density=0.04–0.5 persons per hectare; low to medium=0.55–3.48; medium=3.89–15.71; medium to high=16.78–35.71; high=37.31–103.65.

The unemployed were also more likely to have a narrower definition of their local area. As many as 57 per cent defined their local area as being within a mile of their home and 77 per cent within two miles. In addition, nearly two-thirds of the unemployed had also moved house over a distance of a mile or less. So while a significant proportion of people in Scotland may feel that they live out their lives over quite a wide geographical area, the immediate local area does matter most to those who might be considered the principal targets of any social justice policy, that is the unemployed, those on low incomes, and those in social housing. And evidently one reason why the unemployed and those on low incomes suffer from social exclusion is likely to be because they have a more limited and more spatially constrained range of people and facilities with whom they have contact.

– Neighbourhood quality –

But what do people in Scotland think of their neighbourhoods? The quality of Scottish neighbourhoods is pertinent to Executive policy both because the Executive wishes to 'close the gap' between poor areas and the rest of the country, and because New Labour views the local neighbourhood as an arena of social, economic and political resources through which people's quality of life, social outcomes and social inclusion can be enhanced. Even though new technology and greater prosperity might make it easier for people to communicate over long distances, 'place' is still thought to matter. As one of the UK government's influential policy advisers put it:

> Yet even in the most technologically advanced societies, there is still a role for connections based on place. Proximity matters because humans are unavoidably physical: our well-being depends on the quality of the immediate environment, its safety, the cleanness of its air. It matters because so much communication is non-verbal, and face to face communications have an intensity that no technologies can match. (Mulgan 1997: 98)

However, many sociologists have argued that community- and neighbourhood-based relationships have become less important in Britain and that we now live in a society dominated by looser, 'friend-like' relationships which constitute 'social convoys' which we mobilise to achieve given ends (Pahl and Spencer 1997). As a result, it is argued that we can no longer rely upon traditional community relations as a solution to modern social problems, especially given the greater exposure of modern societies to risk and social change. Our evidence, however, suggests that traditional community values and relationships have not yet disappeared in Scotland. One in three people say that they live in an area where 'people do things together to try to help each other' while only one in four say that in their area 'people mostly go their own way' (25 per cent). Meanwhile, nearly two in five say they live in an area characterised by both types of behaviour.

Table 3.9 Predictors of poor neighbourhood quality

Independent variables	People go their own way	No good shops	Bad reputation	Area will get worse
	Odds ratios for probability of taking a negative view			
Respondent characteristics				
Age	0.99**	1.00	0.97***	1.00
Income	1.12	0.98	0.84	1.05
Unemployed	1.30	1.25	1.02	0.88
Dwelling type				
Flat	1.29*	0.78**	0.77**	1.10
Rented	0.97	1.01	1.06	1.12
Area type				
Mostly owners	1.19	1.20	0.15***	0.76
Mostly renters	2.01**	1.68	2.14**	2.31**
Mixed	0.80	1.07	1.05	0.98
Urban area	1.10	0.75***	1.05	0.87
Poor area	0.96	1.09	1.92***	1.25*

* $p < 0.05$
** $p < 0.01$
*** $p < 0.001$

Note: Whether a respondent is classified as living in an area of 'mostly owners', 'mostly renters' or a 'mixed' area is based on respondents' own description of their area. Those living in urban areas comprise those living in postcode sectors with more than 9 persons per hectare. Those living in poor areas are those living in areas classified by Acorn as types 47–54 (estates with high unemployment, and council flats with high unemployment, lone parents and overcrowding). For further details of the Acorn classification, see *ACORN: the complete classification*, available at http://www.caci.co.uk.

Odds ratios for age and income show the effect of increasing age and income on the dependent variables. For all other variables, odds ratios are based on deviation coefficients and show the effect of the variable category compared with the population average.

But experience of 'neighbourliness' evidently varies. As table 3.9 shows, someone living in an area of mostly rented housing (though not necessarily those renting themselves) is twice as likely as the average person to say that local people 'go their own way' rather than 'help each other'. Those living in a flat are also more likely to say that people tend to go their own way. Flats are of course most common in high-density urban areas, and that people living in such areas tend to have more independent lifestyles was recognised as long ago as 1938 by Wirth in his classic essay *Urbanism as a Way of Life*

(Wirth 1938). Younger people are also more likely to feel that people tend to go their own way (one in three 18- to 24-year-olds), a reflection perhaps of the fact that they are more likely to live in areas with a high level of residential turnover.

However, neighbourliness is only one aspect of the quality of a local area. Another is the quality of shops, which continues to be important in the twenty-first century. A study of attitudes to urban living conducted for the Urban Task Force reported that city dwellers 'liked access to shops and facilities' even if they also disliked the accompanying noise and congestion (Urbed, Mori and SPS 1999: 20). Furthermore, another British study argued that 'Local shopping centres . . . are at the social and physical heart of neighbourhoods. This is especially true in regeneration areas' and that bearing in mind that 60,000 local shops disappear every decade in Britain, 'The decline of local retailing needs to be countered' (Carley, Kirk and McIntosh 2001). Our survey too finds that those living in an urban area are less likely to feel that their area lacks good local shops. So also are those living in flats rather than houses. This latter finding may echo concerns that have recently been expressed in England that there has recently been a decline in the number of retail outlets in established, suburban residential areas (Gwilliam et al. 1998).

But differences between areas in their level of neighbourliness and the availability of good shops are far less marked than are differences in the reputations of areas. Those living in an area where mostly people rent are twice as likely as the average respondent to feel that they live in an area with a bad reputation, while living in a poor neighbourhood also nearly doubles the odds that an area is felt to have a bad reputation. Previous research has shown that the problem of a poor area reputation can prove both to be intractable (Dean and Hastings 2000) and to have wide-ranging conse-quences. One such consequence is that people are less likely to be satisfied with their housing. If we re-run the analysis in table 3.3 and include each of our indicators of neighbourhood quality, we find that the chances of someone being satisfied with their landlord are halved if they live in an area with a bad reputation.

One of the effects of a poor reputation and of neighbourhood decline is a residential pessimism in which people come to believe that neither the local authority nor other stakeholders have any commitment to the future of their area and that the area will be allowed to 'die' (Kearns 2000). While only one in six people in our survey said that they expect their local area to get worse over the next two years; the odds of someone holding that view are more than doubled if they live in an area where most people rent. So once again those living in a area where most people rent are more likely to have a negative evaluation of their area. Living in a poor area also increased the chances of pessimism about the future, though to a lesser extent.

So those who live in areas where most people rent are significantly more likely to have a negative evaluation of their area on three of our four indicators of neighbourhood quality. Therefore, any policy designed to achieve greater social justice for those living in socially rented housing needs to address the quality of the areas in which people live.

– Neighbourhoods and housing behaviour –

One common diagnosis of the problems facing towns and cities across Britain, including those in Scotland, is that people leave to live elsewhere in order to escape decaying, unattractive environments. If this flow is to be reversed and towns and cities made attractive places to live once more, then it is argued that neighbourhood conditions, amongst other things, need to be 'rebuilt' (Power and Mumford 1999). Our survey collected two pieces of

Table 3.10 Reasons for moving home

	Reasons for needing to move home	Reasons for last moving home
	%	%
Accommodation reasons		
Want larger/smaller home	45	32
To move to a preferred home	20	11
Problems with landlords/tenants	11	5
Home in poor condition	10	4
Any accommodation reason	70	47
Area reasons		
To move to a better area	26	12
To be close to work	10	9
Any area reason	39	22
Personal reasons		
To be nearer family/friends	8	10
Marriage/cohabitation	5	10
Moving out of parents' home	3	8
Divorce/separation	1	7
Any personal reason	21	37
Financial reasons		
Want to buy	10	10
Any financial reason	10	12
Sample size	*174*	*87*

Note: Only the most commonly given reasons are shown.

information that enable us to examine how much the kind of area in which someone lives influences whether or not they prefer to stay or leave. First we asked all those who had moved house in the last ten years why they had moved. Second, we asked our respondents whether they needed to move from their present home (one in six said they did) and, if so, why. The results are summarised in table 3.10.

The three most common reasons both for having moved house in the past and for needing to move now are to move to a larger or smaller home, to move to a better area, and simply to move to a house that was better liked. Overall, reasons to do with accommodation are more prevalent than area, personal or financial reasons. However, area reasons are the second most common group of reasons given for needing to move home, albeit that they are overtaken by personal reasons when it comes to having moved home in the past.

Moreover, as table 3.11 shows, those living in an area with a bad reputation are particularly likely both to feel the need to move and to do so in order to move to a better area. Nearly three in ten of those living in such areas felt they needed to move home and no less than three in five of these wanted to do so in order to move to a better area. But at the same time nearly three in ten of those living in stigmatised areas consider that it would be very difficult for them to move home. Thus a significant number of people living in areas with a poor reputation feel 'stuck' in their present residential circumstances.

Table 3.11 Area reputation and moving behaviour

	Reputation of area as perceived by respondent	
	Good reputation	Bad reputation
	%	%
Currently need to move home	12	29
(of which, give need to move to		
a better area as reason)[a]	(8)	(60)
Would be very difficult to move home	10	29
Sample size	886	146

a. Sample sizes are 104 and 48 respectively.

Indeed, a multivariate analysis of perceived need to move home indicates that it is pessimism about the future of an area that matters most in giving people reason to want to leave (see table 3.12). The odds that someone feels the need to move are almost tripled if they feel that their area is going to become a worse place to live. Those living in poor areas were also rather more likely to feel the need to move, and indeed also to cite reasons for wanting to do so (see table 3.11). People often wish to flee what they see as an undesirable neighbourhood even if they do not always have the means to do so.

Table 3.12 Predictors of the need to move home

Dimension	Variable	Odds ratio for probability that respondent needs to move home
Age	18–24	2.10[***]
	25–44	1.18
	45–59	0.55[***]
	60+	0.74
Dwelling type	Flat	1.30[**]
Housing Tenure	Owner-occupier	0.52[*]
	Rents from local authority	0.61
	Rents from housing association	0.50
	Rents from private landlord	1.47
Area type	Poor area	1.54[***]
Future of area	Area will get worse in next 2 years	2.81[***]
Sample size		*1259*

* $p < 0.05$
** $p < 0.01$
*** $p < 0.001$

Note: For definition of a poor area, see table 3.9. Odds ratios are based on deviation coefficients and show the effect of being in that category compared with the population average. The following were also included in the analysis but are not shown because there was no significant association: income; economic status; whether most people in the area rent or own; and area reputation.

– Communities –

We noted in the introduction that one of the key features of New Labour's urban policy, albeit one yet to be adopted officially in Scotland, is to promote mixed communities. A key influence on the development of this policy was the work of the think-tank Demos, whose 'Richness of Cities' study carried out in conjunction with Comedia argued that 'the celebration of cultural diversity and a respect for difference constitute two of the most important values of urban life in Britain today' (Worpole and Greenhaulgh 1999: 15). Demos pointed the finger at the housing industry in particular for not encouraging diversity and not offering more choice in housing types and settlement forms. However, advocates of this policy do not simply want to encourage the creation of communities with a mixture of housing tenures, but also ones that are mixed in respect of other characteristics.

> Mixed communities are not simply a matter of mixed tenure . . . Communities can also be mixed by age, religion or ethnic origin. This will include people with physical or mental disabilities, and land use may be mixed so that residents can work close to their homes. (Birch 1999: 3)

Those in favour of mixed communities put forward two arguments as to why they are desirable. First they claim that across a city as a whole social and cultural diversity can foster understanding and learning and thereby 'affect a city's creative capacity' (Landry 2000: 111). Meanwhile, so far as individual communities are concerned it is argued that diversity can combat social exclusion and segregation. Certainly, this vision of twenty-first-century urbanism is the dominant one today. For example, the environmentalist Schoon, who calls the policy Mixed Use Higher Density (MUHD) urbanism, says 'MUHD's time may have come' (Schoon 2001: 236).

But there are those who, while supporting this approach, also urge a dose of realism. The National Housing Forum, while supporting the principle of mixed communities also declares that Aneurin Bevan's notion of 'the living tapestry of a mixed community' may not be possible or desirable today (Birch 1999). Cole et al. after studying housing developments in the North East conclude that a 'balanced community' is difficult to achieve; that diversity does not necessarily produce a stronger sense of community; enforced balancing may produce conflict, and that 'tenure mix is no panacea'. Even so, they still state categorically that 'Mixed tenure schemes should be the rule rather than the exception . . . for new developments' (Cole et al. 1997: 66).

How much support is there in Scotland for the idea of mixed communities? Respondents were asked their views both about the desirability of mixed tenure communities and also about those that were socially diverse more generally. The two questions we asked were:

Mixed tenure:
Would you rather live in an area where most people own their own homes, or where most people rent, or where there is a mixture?

and

Social diversity:
Would you rather live in an area with lots of different kinds of people or where most people are similar to you?

Overall, there is more support for the idea of socially diverse communities than for mixed-tenure communities. As many as a half favour the former but only a third support the latter. Support for socially diverse communities was highest amongst those aged 18 to 24 (59 per cent in favour), the unemployed (61 per cent in favour), and people educated to degree level (62 per cent in favour). The fact that the unemployed strongly support social diversity suggests that this group may concur with the claims made by advocates of social capital theory who argue that the unemployed need access to more diverse social networks that can help them find routes out of poverty and exclusion (for example, Perri 6 1997). However, in the short-term at least, there may be difficulties achieving social diversity as older (over 60 years) and less educated people are less likely to prefer living in areas containing a mixture of people. But we might expect public support for mixed communities to rise as this group is replaced by new, more highly educated younger generations.

The prospects for developing a consensus in favour of mixed-tenure communities are, however, clearly less good. Overall, only a third are in favour, and owner-occupiers are particularly opposed. Only 26 per cent of owner-occupiers prefer mixed-tenure communities compared with 44 per cent of renters. An equally stark divide is apparent when we compare the attitudes of those who live in predominantly owner-occupied areas and those who live in predominantly rental ones (see table 3.13). A majority of those who live in predominantly owner-occupied areas are in fact entirely happy to live alongside fellow owner-occupiers. In contrast, even amongst those who live in predominantly rented areas, only nine per cent actually prefer to do so. It seems as though those who rent would be happy to see the creation of more mixed-tenure communities but their feelings are not reciprocated by owner-occupiers. Yet of course members of both tenures need to favour the idea of mixed tenure communities if in practice they are going to be widely achieved.

Table 3.13 Support for mixed-tenure neighbourhoods, by current tenure mix

Preferred tenure mix	Current tenure mix		
	Mostly owned	Mostly rented	Equal
	%	%	%
Mostly owned	56	20	18
Mostly rented	0	9	3
Mixture	20	40	45
Don't mind/can't choose	25	30	34
Sample size	576	308	436

Note: For definition of current tenure mix, see table 3.9.

On the other hand there is some reason to believe that mixed-tenure communities are favourably regarded by their members. Mixed-tenure neighbourhoods are rated more highly than 'mostly rented' areas on all four of our measures of neighbourhood quality (see table 3.14). They even also perform better than 'mostly owned' areas in respect of reciprocity and shopping facilities. And as we have already seen in table 3.9, these findings also hold true in statistical modelling in which respondents' background, dwelling and locational characteristics are controlled for. The fact that mixed-tenure areas have a much lower incidence of problems of a bad reputation and of a bleak future than 'mostly rented' areas constitutes perhaps the strongest reason for pursuing this type of residential structure instead of continuing with the existence of areas segregated by housing tenure.

Table 3.14 Poor neighbourhood quality, by current tenure mix

	Current tenure mix		
% say (in) their area:	Mostly owned	Mostly rented	Equal
People mostly go their own way	24	29	21
No good local shop	24	34	19
Has bad reputation	1	25	10
Will get worse	12	33	16
Sample size	*576*	*308*	*436*

Note: For definition of current tenure mix, see table 3.9.

– CONCLUSION –

In this chapter we have examined three aspects of contemporary residential policy. First we considered the policy of community empowerment, namely 'the transfer of existing public sector rented housing to alternative community landlords' (Scottish Office 1999). We found that most tenants prefer to rent from the type of landlord from which they already rent their home, be it public, voluntary or private. However, councils were particularly popular with their current tenants, suggesting that Scotland's tradition of municipal socialism still appears to be strong.

Even so, the Scottish Executive's community empowerment policy could be considered to be appropriate rather than misguided, for two reasons. First, the popularity of councils as landlords appears to have declined over the last decade while at the same time that of housing associations seems to have risen. So community empowerment policy appears at least to be in line with the trend in public opinion. Second, according to current tenants themselves, housing associations outperform other types of landlord on many aspects of housing management. So current policy can perhaps be justified as being in the best interests of residents. However, we should also note that what has most influence on people's satisfaction with their housing is not who is their landlord or whether they have a say in how their housing is managed – the issue on which advocates of community empowerment focus – but rather the quality of the repairs service and of the neighbourhoods in which they have to live.

Our analysis also shows that council tenants need to be reassured on two issues if they are to be persuaded to opt for alternative landlords. These are, first, the level and affordability of rents charged by alternative landlords and, second, their right to remain in a rented dwelling for as long as they want. The latter finding might well indicate a concern about the severity (or 'fairness') of the housing management policies of alternative landlords. Clearly the Scottish Executive still has more work to do both to persuade council tenants of the merits of community empowerment, and thereafter to regulate alternative landlords in order to give the public reassurance.

The second policy we considered was neighbourhood renewal, particularly as part of the Executive's social justice agenda. We found that low income groups in particular, but also the unemployed and those in social rented housing, were more likely to identify with smaller 'local areas' and to have moved house over smaller distances. Although having a strong attachment to place may have its advantages, our findings also raise the question – relevant to social justice – of whether this is due to feelings of belonging or to constrained mobility. Equally, perhaps people's opportunities are being restricted through having smaller local worlds. If this is so, then policy-makers need to be aware that by emphasising the need to improve neighbourhoods, public policy could simply reinforce rather than dilute these circumstances.

At the same time we also found that those who live in areas of predominantly rented housing were more likely to have a negative evaluation of their area. One feature relevant to an egalitarian view of social justice (that is that citizens should have equal resources for an equal start in life) was that people in 'mostly rented' areas were more likely to think that 'people go their own way', though this was also a perception shared by those living in flats, a form of accommodation most common in areas of high population density. Evidently researchers and policy-makers need to establish whether this form of social behaviour simply matches people's expectations and needs, or whether social independence adversely affects quality of life and life chances for residents in such areas. If the latter holds true, then action to promote community activism and neighbourliness may be warranted.

So far as social justice as fair treatment is concerned, we found that those people living in predominantly rented areas were more likely to believe that their area both had a poor reputation and that it was likely to become a worse place to live in the near future. As a result they felt a greater need to move home. So here at least it seems clear that improving neighbourhoods is a means to promoting social justice, and that the Executive is right to focus its holistic renewal programmes on poor and rented-housing neighbourhoods. However, much more effort needs to go into considering how to counter the incidence and effects of poor area reputation – many of which arise outside of the area itself – and into ensuring that people in all Scotland's neighbourhoods have optimism about their area's future. Doing so could help reduce the incidence of people feeling the need to move home and achieve greater residential stability

In contrast, our findings of relevance to questions of distributional justice suggest that the absence of 'good local shops' is a widespread issue rather than limited to poor areas. Rural areas and areas of residential housing are the ones most likely to suffer this problem. Given the importance of shops to daily and community life, the extent of their apparent shortfall needs to be properly identified and quantified and its amelioration promoted by policies designed to work across Scotland as a whole rather than by targeted neighbourhood renewal programmes.

The third policy that we have considered is the promotion of mixed communities. Our evidence suggests that as judged by those who live in them, such communities appear to be attractive. They are also thought desirable by those who currently live in rental housing and by those living in predominantly rented neighbourhoods. However, their vision is not shared by the majority of owner-occupiers. It is perhaps no accident that to date the main ways in which mixed-tenure neighbourhoods have been developed in the UK have been ones that promote the dilution rather than the dispersal of rented tenures, namely the right-to-buy for council housing tenants and the development of private housing on council estates (Kearns 2002).

Our analysis indicates that there are a number of challenges facing policy-makers seeking to find Scottish answers to Scottish questions. Firstly, there is a tension between addressing current policy issues and constructing policies that are in line with current public preferences. In social rented housing, the policy of housing stock transfer can be justified in terms of tenants' own assessment of landlord performance, but it does not yet match tenants' current landlord preferences. This leaves the policy-maker out on a limb, even if trying to act in people's best interests.

Secondly, we have identified both the necessity and the dangers of spatially targeted policies. Community regeneration policy as it is known in Scotland focuses much of its attention on improving public services in deprived areas. Doing so is consistent with the fact that, as we have seen, many aspects of neighbourhood quality are worse in areas of mostly rented housing. However, we have also seen that some apparent problems, such as poor shopping facilities and unhelpful neighbours, are much more widespread than this. Thus policies targeted at socially deprived areas will not necessarily resolve all of the problems in Scotland's communities. And there is an additional danger that spatially targeted policies could further entrench the geographically narrower horizons of those living in deprived areas, either because low income and unemployed people are not encouraged to widen their horizons beyond their immediate home area, or because the area will retain its relative isolation and poor reputation. Policies which operate beyond the immediate confines of deprived areas will also be required.

Lastly, our analysis suggests that a bolder approach is required in the future if substantial progress is to be made towards achieving mixed communities in Scotland. If mixed communities are to be achieved with public support rather than in the face of public conflict, policy-makers, planners and developers have to find better ways of both widening access to affordable owner-occupied housing and developing more integrated forms of social rented housing. In short, a combination of boldness of vision and effective implementation is essential if Scotland is to overcome the social divisions and polarisation exhibited by much of urban Britain (Pacione 1997) and make progress towards sustainable housing, neighbourhoods and communities in the near future.

– REFERENCES –

Baillie, J. (2001), 'Foreword: A fair, caring and tolerant Scotland where everyone matters', in Scottish Executive (2001), *Social Justice . . . A Scotland Where Everyone Matters Annual Report 2001*, Edinburgh: Scottish Executive.

Birch, J. (1999), *Mixed Communities. One More than Housing*, East Hanney: National Housing Forum.

Carley, M., Kirk, K. and McIntosh, S. (2001), *Retailing, Sustainability and Neighbourhood Regeneration*, York: YPS/JRF.

Cole, I., Gidley, G., Ritchie, C., Simpson, D. and Wishart, B. (1997), *Creating Communities or Welfare Housing? A Study of New Housing Association Developments in Yorkshire/Humberside*, Coventry: Chartered Institute of Housing.

Communities Scotland (2002), *Housing Market Context Statement. Clydeside*, Edinburgh: Communities Scotland.

Dean, J. and Hastings, A. (2000), *Challenging Images. Housing Estates, Stigma and Regeneration*, Bristol: The Policy Press.

Goodlad, R., Sterling, R. and Bailey, N. (2002), 'Social justice in Scotland: a draft conceptual framework', mimeo., Glasgow: Scottish Centre for Research on Social Justice.

Gwilliam, M., Bourne, C., Swain, C. and Prat, A. (1998), *Sustainable Renewal of Suburban Areas*, York: YPS/JRF.

Hargrave, I. (2002), 'Ground control', *Housing*, Dec./Jan., 40.

Kearns, A. (2000), 'What's the problem? Patterns, processes and perceptions', in J. Low. (ed.), *Regeneration in the 21st Century. Policies into Practice*, Bristol: The Policy Press.

Kearns, A. (2002), 'Response: From residential disadvantage to opportunity? Reflections on British and European policy and research', *Housing Studies*, 17, pp. 145–50.

Landry, C. (2000), *The Creative City. A Toolkit for Urban Innovators*, London: Earthscan.

Mulgan, G. (1997), *Connexity: Responsibility, Freedom, Business and Power in the New Century*, London: Vintage.

Pacione, M. (1997), *Britain's Cities. Geographies of Division in Urban Britain*, London: Routledge.

Pahl, R. and Spencer, L. (1997), 'The politics of friendship', *Renewal*, pp. 100–7.

Perri 6 (1997), *Escaping Poverty. From Safety Nets to Networks of Opportunity*, London: Demos.

Pieda (1995), *Second Survey of Consumer Preference in Housing*, Research Report 43, Edinburgh: Scottish Homes.

Pieda (1996), *Third Survey of Consumer Preference in Housing*, Research Report 51, Edinburgh: Scottish Homes.

Power, A. and Mumford, K. (1999), *The Slow Death of Great Cities? Urban Abandonment or Urban Renaissance*, York: YPS/JRF.

Ravetz, A. (2001), *Council Housing and Culture. The History of a Social Experiment*, London: Routledge.

Schoon, N. (2001), *The Chosen City*, London: Spon Press.

Scottish Executive (1999), *Social Justice . . . A Scotland Where Everyone Matters*, Edinburgh: Scottish Executive.

Scottish Executive (2000), *Scottish Household Survey Bulletin 4*, Edinburgh: Scottish Executive.

Scottish Executive (2001), *Social Justice . . . A Scotland Where Everyone Matters Annual Report 2001*, Edinburgh: Scottish Executive.

Scottish Executive (2002a), *Better Communities in Scotland: Closing the Gap. The Scottish Executive's Community Regeneration Statement*, Edinburgh: Scottish Executive.

Scottish Executive (2002b), *Scottish Household Survey Bulletin 8*, Edinburgh: Scottish Executive.

Scottish Homes (1994), *Consumer Preference in Housing*, Edinburgh: Scottish Homes.

Scottish Office (1999), *Investing in Modernisation – An Agenda for Scotland's Housing*, Edinburgh: Scottish Office.

Social Exclusion Unit (2001), *A New Commitment to Neighbourhood Renewal. National Strategy Action Plan*, London: Cabinet Office.

Urban Task Force (1999), *Towards an Urban Renaissance. Final Report of the Urban Task Force*, London: Spon Press.

Urbed, Mori and SPS (1999), *But Would You Live There? Shaping Attitudes to Urban Living*, London: Urban Task Force.

Wirth, L. (1938), 'Urbanism as a way of life', reprinted in P. Kasinitz (ed.) (1995), *Metropolis. Centre and Symbol of Our Times*, 58–82, London: Macmillan.

Worpole, K. and Greenhaulgh, L. (1999), *The Richness of Cities. Urban Policy in a New Landscape*, London: Comedia/Demos.

– Note –

1. The second and third surveys of consumer preference in housing, conducted in 1994 and 1995, comprised a national random sample of adults in Scotland and included samples of 430 and 819 renters respectively, who were asked, 'If you had a choice, realistically which tenure would you most like to achieve?' We have combined the responses from the two surveys and examined the distribution of preferences amongst those respondents who gave an answer other than 'owner-occupation'.

CHAPTER 4

Attitudes Towards Illegal Drugs Use

Maria Gannon, Neil McKeganey, Gordon Hay and Kerstin Hinds

– INTRODUCTION –

We are half way through the period covered by the UK government's ten-year drug strategy as set out in *Tackling Drugs to Build a Better Britain* (Stationery Office 1998) and its Scottish equivalent *Tackling Drugs in Scotland: Action in Partnership* (Scottish Office 1999). Influential as these documents have been, all of the recent discussions about illegal drugs have been concerned with changes that are not even mentioned in these documents. In the last twelve months the Home Secretary has announced his decision to seek parliamentary approval for rescheduling cannabis from class B to class C within the Misuse of Drugs Act, thereby making possession of small amounts of cannabis a non-arrestable offence. The former minister, Dr Mo Mowlam, who was once responsible for UK drug strategy, has called for the legalisation of all drugs (Mowlam 2002). The Home Affairs Select Committee of the House of Commons has called for a radical overhaul of UK drug policies, recommending that treatment rather than punishment should be at the heart of UK drug policies, that ecstasy should be reclassified from class A to class B, and that pilot injecting rooms should be developed for heroin addicts to inject under supervised conditions (Home Affairs Select Committee 2002). At the same time the Metropolitan Police have been running their much heralded programme of cautioning rather than arresting individuals found in possession of small amounts of cannabis in Lambeth.

Within Scotland the drugs policy climate has been no less volatile. Currently, the right to legislate on illegal drugs is reserved to the Westminster parliament and it is not possible for the devolved Scottish Parliament to initiate changes to the UK drug laws. Nevertheless, over the last twelve months the whole tenor of Scottish government policy on illegal drugs has changed. Instead of the stridently anti-drugs line closely associated with the 'Scotland Against Drugs' campaign that was launched with cross party political support in 1996, the recently announced 'Know the Score' campaign has an explicitly harm reduction focus that emphasises the importance of providing young people with factual information about illegal drugs, avoiding the 'just say no' approach to drug education and reducing the harms associated with drug misuse.

In this chapter we look at how far these developments and suggested changes are in line with public opinion in Scotland. We consider whether Scots are in favour of the Home Secretary's policy of softening the policing of cannabis or whether Scots would wish to see all drugs legalised in the manner suggested by Mo Mowlam. We look at attitudes towards those who are using cannabis, heroin and ecstasy and towards those who are selling these drugs. We also consider how much support there is in Scotland for the harm reduction approaches of providing drug users with sterile injecting equipment, educating young people about how to use drugs safely and allowing doctors to prescribe drugs to addicts. We consider whether attitudes towards changes in cannabis legislation and the promotion of a harm reduction perspective are similar to or at variance with attitudes and developments in England, and thus ultimately whether a Westminster-based drug policy that is attuned to public opinion in England can also find favour in Scotland or is likely to be rejected by Scots. We look first at Scottish attitudes towards cannabis, heroin and ecstasy.

– Attitudes towards cannabis, heroin and ecstasy –

We begin with the drug on which UK government policy has recently changed, cannabis. Does the change that is being made reflect a change in public opinion? Because the Scottish Social Attitudes survey only began in 1999 and as attitudes towards drugs were not asked about on previous Scottish Election Surveys, we have to rely on the findings of the relatively small samples obtained in Scotland by the British Social Attitudes survey in order to look at attitudes before 1999. Fortunately, as can be seen from table 4.1, the results are unambiguous.

Support for the legalisation of cannabis has risen from 15 per cent in 1983 to 37 per cent in 2001. Moreover, this trend is almost identical to what has happened in the rest of Britain (Gould and Stratford 2002). On this question, however, the current level of support in Scotland for legalising cannabis is still slightly lower than it is in England where 41 per cent favour legalisation.

Table 4.1 Attitudes towards the legalisation of cannabis 1993–2001

Smoking cannabis should be legalised	1983	1993	1995	2001
	%	%	%	%
Agree	15	19	29	37
Neither agree or disagree	12	21	14	16
Disagree	71	59	55	45
Sample size	*166*	*123*	*96*	*1383*

The trend is confirmed by the answers to a second question that has also been asked on a regular basis on the British Social Attitudes surveys. As can be seen from table 4.2, when faced with a choice between cannabis being legal without restrictions, legal but only available in licensed shops, and remaining illegal, in 1993 over two in three Scots believed it should remain illegal. Now only a little under half do so. Moreover, on this measure the level of support for some form of legalisation is as high as it is in England. However, faced with the choice between allowing cannabis to be available without restrictions or only in licensed shops, only 4 per cent opt for the former.

Table 4.2 Attitudes towards the legal status of cannabis 1993–2001

% agree that:	1993	1995	2000	2001
Taking cannabis should be legal, without restrictions	4	4	5	4
Taking cannabis should be legal, but it should only be available from licensed shops	26	33	44	46
Taking cannabis should remain illegal	68	58	50	47
Sample size	*146*	*108*	*166*	*1605*

This change in attitudes has further been matched by a change of behaviour (or at least a willingness to report behaviour). Now no less than 28 per cent of people in Scotland say they have tried cannabis themselves. In 1993 only 10 per cent claimed to have done so and in 1995, 16 per cent. Even more dramatically, over half (56 per cent) of people aged under 35 now admit to having taken the drug.

But who is in favour of legalising cannabis? As one might expect, and can be seen in table 4.3, the strongest support for legalisation is to be found among those who have tried cannabis; no less than seven in ten of them are in favour. Of course, which comes first, support for legalisation or experience of using cannabis, is difficult to say. A clear majority in favour also exists among those who report having either a friend or a family member who has used illegal drugs. Meanwhile, the younger someone is, the more likely they are to be in favour of legalisation. Over half of under-35s back legalisation, suggesting that as older generations are replaced by younger ones, support for legalisation could yet grow further. Table 4.3 also looks at whether the level of support for legalising cannabis in Scotland differs between rural and non-rural areas. And as one might expect, whereas in rural areas only 30 per cent are in favour of legalising cannabis, as many as 41 per cent of those living in more urban areas are so.

Table 4.3 Who favours legalising cannabis?

Smoking cannabis should be legalised	% agree	Sample size
Cannabis experience		
Ever tried cannabis	70	375
Friend/family member ever used illegal drugs	58	562
Council area		
Rural	30	561
Urban	41	948
Age group		
16–24	63	118
25–34	51	232
35–44	43	283
45–54	37	233
55–64	21	197
65+	17	320
All	37	1383

Note: Rural council area: respondent living in a local authority with a population density of less than one person per hectare.

While there is clearly considerable if not yet majority support for legalising cannabis in Scotland, this does not mean that the same view is taken of heroin and ecstasy. As table 4.4 shows, people draw a clear distinction between cannabis on the one hand and heroin and ecstasy on the other. So while nearly a half feel that cannabis should remain illegal, nearly nine in ten believe that heroin and ecstasy should do so. There seems to be very little support in Scotland for Mo Mowlam's position of legalising all drugs.

Table 4.4 Attitudes towards the legal status of cannabis, heroin and ecstasy

Taking cannabis, heroin or ecstasy:	Cannabis	Heroin	Ecstasy
	%	%	%
Should be legal without restrictions	4	1	1
Should be legal but only available from licensed shops	46	8	8
Should remain illegal	47	89	89
Sample size	1605	1605	1605

As we would expect, cannabis users are overwhelmingly in favour of the legalisation of cannabis on this measure too – though strikingly little more than one in ten believe that it should be available without restrictions. Moreover, just as many Scots draw a clear distinction between cannabis and other drugs, so also do most cannabis users. True, as table 4.5 shows, nearly one in five of cannabis users favours some form of legalisation of ecstasy compared with only one in twenty of non-users. Equally, cannabis users are nearly twice as likely to be in favour of the legalisation of heroin. But even so the level of support for the legalisation of these two drugs among cannabis users remains very low.

Table 4.5 Attitudes towards the legal status of cannabis, heroin and ecstasy, by cannabis use

	Ever tried cannabis	Never tried cannabis
Taking cannabis		
Should be legal without restrictions	11	2
Should be legal but only available from licensed shops	71	36
Should remain illegal	6	60
Taking heroin		
Should be legal without restrictions	2	1
Should be legal but only available from licensed shops	12	7
Should remain illegal	85	91
Taking ecstasy		
Should be legal without restrictions	1	*
Should be legal but only available from licensed shops	18	5
Should remain illegal	80	92
Sample size	430	1168

* Less than 0.5 per cent.

Table 4.6 Attitudes towards possession of cannabis, heroin and ecstasy for personal use

	People should be prosecuted for possession of		
	Cannabis	Heroin	Ecstasy
	%	%	%
Agree	36	77	75
Neither agree nor disagree	9	6	6
Disagree	52	15	16
Sample size	1605	1605	1605

In discussions about how the government should respond to illegal drugs, a distinction is often drawn between those who are in possession of an illegal drug for personal use and those who supply drugs to others. First of all in table 4.6 we look at Scots' attitudes towards the prosecution of individuals for possessing cannabis, heroin or ecstasy for reasons of personal use. We will then examine attitudes towards drug dealers.

Only just over one in three agrees that people should be prosecuted for possession of cannabis for personal use, whereas around three in four favour prosecution in cases of possession for personal use of heroin and ecstasy. So again a clear distinction is drawn between cannabis and other drugs. But this is far less true of drug dealing. Even in the case of cannabis, no less than 70 per cent say that drug dealers should always be prosecuted. Meanwhile, in the case of ecstasy the figure is 91 per cent, and for heroin 96 per cent. Nothing could illustrate more clearly how negatively drug dealing is regarded by Scots in general.

Table 4.7 Attitudes towards the prosecution of drug dealers, by cannabis use

Dealers should always be prosecuted for selling	Ever tried cannabis	Never tried cannabis
	%	%
Cannabis		
Agree	48	79
Neither agree nor disagree	16	8
Disagree	36	11
Heroin		
Agree	93	97
Neither agree nor disagree	2	1
Disagree	5	2
Ecstasy		
Agree	85	93
Neither agree nor disagree	8	*
Disagree	4	3
Sample size	*430*	*1168*

* Less than 0.5 per cent.

However, as table 4.7 shows, those who have ever tried cannabis are more likely to adopt a more liberal line towards drug dealers. Indeed slightly under half believe that those who deal in cannabis should be prosecuted, though perhaps this might still be considered high given that at some point they have, through their own use of cannabis, given a drug dealer some trade. Cannabis users are also somewhat more likely not to support the blanket prosecution of dealers in heroin and ecstasy.

To sum up, there is clear evidence of rising support, though not yet majority support, for the legalisation of cannabis. Many Scots (although again nowhere near a majority) are in favour of cannabis being made available from licensed premises. But the vast majority wish to see heroin and ecstasy remain illegal. And at the same time large majorities take the hardline view that drug dealers, including dealers in cannabis, should always be prosecuted. Given these results it seems there is considerable support in Scotland for the Home Secretary's proposal to make the possession of cannabis for personal use a non-arrestable offence and at the same time widespread approval of the UK government's rejection of appeals to legalise all drugs. It also appears there is relatively little support for the calls from the Home Affairs Select Committee for a softening in the approach to ecstasy, a drug which continues to be seen in similar terms to heroin.

– ATTITUDES TOWARDS HARM REDUCTION –

In the second half of this chapter we look at attitudes towards harm reduction approaches. Harm reduction approaches arose in Scotland in the mid- to late 1980s as a result of concerns about the spread of HIV infection. In 1986 an influential committee of the then Scottish Home Office and Health Department published a report, *HIV Infection in Scotland*, which underlined the importance of tackling the then growing problem of HIV amongst injecting drug users within Scotland.

> Injecting drug misusers who cannot or will not abstain from misuse must be educated in safer drug taking practices. It is of the utmost importance that those who continue to inject are persuaded to use clean equipment and never to share it. Clean equipment should therefore not be denied to those who cannot be dissuaded from injecting. In this connection authorities should be reminded that the threat to life of HIV infection is greater than that of drug misuse. On balance the prevention of spread should take priority over any perceived risk of increased drug misuse. (Scottish Committee on HIV Infection and Intravenous Drug Use 1986: 12)

The views expressed in this report were further underlined by the Advisory Council for the Misuse of Drugs, which emphasised that 'the spread of HIV is a greater danger to individual and public health than drug misuse' (ACMD 1988: 5). Needle and syringe exchange were seen as crucial in reducing the need for injectors to share injecting equipment. Education, the second element of a harm reduction approach, was felt to be important in its role of informing injectors about the main routes of HIV transmission. Finally, prescribing methadone, the third element of a harm reduction approach, was felt to be an important means of reducing drug injectors' HIV-related risk behaviour and allowing drug treatment services to maintain contact with drug users.

By the mid-1990s, however, concern about the spread of HIV had receded substantially and government policy shifted to perceiving drug misuse itself as a greater threat than HIV. In 1994, a Ministerial Drugs Task Force published its report, *Drugs in Scotland: Meeting the Challenge*, in which it stated that:

> Drug misuse is a serious and escalating problem in Scotland. For the individual drugs can provide a quick boost but at the risk of prosecution, damage to health, a drift into destitution, and in a significant and worrying number of cases even death. For the families of misusers (their parents, spouses, and children) drugs can mean anguish, social conflict, break-up and poverty. For the wider community drug misuse imposes heavy demands on services, is a major contributor to crime levels, gives rise to public health hazards, and in relation to drug trafficking is closely associated with organised crime, intimidation and violence. (Scottish Office Ministerial Drugs Task Force 1994: 11)

This report more than any other signalled that drug misuse rather than HIV was seen as the bigger threat to Scottish society. In turn the Scottish Office set up a national anti-drugs movement with cross party political support and the resulting 'Scotland Against Drugs' campaign came to symbolise the government's principal message on drugs throughout much of the mid- to late 1990s. In 2002, however, official policy on illegal drugs in Scotland changed again and harm reduction was promoted once more by the 'Know the Score' campaign. Championed by a drugs minister with medical training, this approach emphasised the provision of factual information about drugs, the rejection of a so-called 'just say no approach' to drug education, a commitment to reduce the harms associated with drug use, and a vigorous promotion of the merits of prescribing methadone to drug users.

But how much public support is there for the three key elements of the harm reduction approach, namely whether drug users should be provided with sterile injecting equipment, whether young people should be educated about how to use drugs more safely, and finally whether doctors should be allowed to prescribe drugs to addicts? No less than 62 per cent of Scots agree with the idea of supplying drug users with clean needles. As one might have anticipated, the level of support for needle and syringe exchange is even higher among those who report having used cannabis or who know someone who has. But as table 4.8 shows, there is rather less support for the second element of the harm reduction approach, namely the suggestion that young people should be provided with information on how to use illegal drugs more safely, which a little under half favour.

Meanwhile, there is relatively little support for the third element of the harm reduction approach, namely allowing doctors to prescribe drugs to addicts, a practice that only one in four endorses. This is perhaps understandable given that many Scots feel the overall goal of treatment is to get people off drugs altogether. Indeed, in response to a further question no less than 48 per cent agree that 'the best way to treat people who are addicted to drugs is to stop them from using drugs altogether'. Nevertheless, this is an important finding since over the last few years there has been a massive expansion in the provision of methadone to drug users in Scotland. In contrast, at present there are very few drug treatment services within Scotland that have an explicitly abstinence-orientated therapeutic programme.

Table 4.8 Attitudes towards harm reduction

% agree that:	Ever tried cannabis	Friend/family ever used illegal drugs	All
Drug users should be given clean needles to stop them getting diseases	72	67	62
Young people should be given information about how to use drugs safely	62	55	47
Doctors must be allowed to prescribe drugs for those addicted to them	33	30	25
Sample size	*375*	*562*	*1383*

However, this mixture of attitudes towards harm reduction is not unique to Scotland. It is to be found in England too. Almost identical proportions of people in England and Scotland are in favour of drug users being given clean needles and allowing doctors to prescribe to addicts. However, people in England appear to be slightly keener than Scots on educating young people about how to use drugs safely, as south of the border 54 per cent are in favour.

– CONCLUSIONS –

Our survey provides a rare opportunity to look not at what government ministers, the media, academics and other social commentators feel about illegal drugs but instead at the views of people in general. As we have shown there is considerable support in Scotland for changing the legal position of cannabis. Some of that support appears to go well beyond the current proposal to reschedule cannabis from class B to class C within the Misuse of

Drugs Act, as fully 37 per cent favour legalisation. When our respondents were questioned further, however, we see a more cautious attitude emerging, with only four per cent feeling that cannabis should be legalised without any restrictions.

There are clear indications that people in Scotland view cannabis in very different terms from heroin or ecstasy. Only a tiny minority are in favour of legalising either heroin or ecstasy. A clear distinction is also drawn between drug possession and drug dealing. Only just over one in three Scots is in favour of prosecuting individuals found in possession of cannabis for personal use, while 70 per cent are in favour of prosecuting individuals found to be selling cannabis. Somewhat surprisingly even among those who report having used cannabis (a fair proportion of whom will presumably have bought the drug), nearly half are in favour of prosecuting those found selling the drug.

Of the three components of the harm reduction approach so central to current Scottish Executive policies on illegal drugs (needle and syringe exchange, education and prescribing), the one with the highest level of public support is the provision of clean needles, backed by over three in five. By contrast, only one in four supports doctors being allowed to prescribe to addicts and even somewhat less than a majority favour informing young people about how to use illegal drugs more safely. There is evidently only limited support among Scots for the Scottish Executive's current harm reduction policy.

Crafting a drugs policy that is in tune with public opinion is a difficult task for any politician. The law on drugs is reserved to the Westminster parliament and in that sense it is politicians south of the border, rather more than those in Edinburgh, who have the difficult task of balancing their own views about illegal drugs with those of their constituents. However, there does appear to be considerable support in Scotland for the Home Secretary's proposed rescheduling of cannabis and for his refusal to adopt a softer line in relation to the policing of ecstasy and heroin. But there is only limited acceptance of the merits of the harm reduction approach to illegal drugs. The arguments in support of providing drug users with access to sterile injecting equipment, perceived by many critics in the 1980s as equivalent to condoning drug use, have come to be widely accepted. But the public are by no means as convinced of the merits either of educating young people about how to use drugs more safely or allowing doctors to prescribe to addicts. So far as the latter is concerned, the view remains widespread that the aim of drug treatment should be to get people off drugs altogether rather than to provide addicts with a medicalised source of drugs.

Still, despite these differences between the public's views and current harm reduction practice, drug policy appears to be one area where the current devolution settlement is not under strain. Scottish attitudes towards the legal status of drugs mirror those of people in England. So the fact that the law on drugs in Scotland is still made in London does not mean that Scotland is being foisted with English answers to English questions. Indeed, given the level of shared views about illegal drugs north and south of the border, many of Scotland's politicians may feel that it is a topic they can safely leave in Westminster's hands.

– REFERENCES –

Advisory Council on the Misuse of Drugs (1988), *Aids and Drugs Misuse*, part 1, London: HMSO.

Gould, A. and Stratford, N. (2002), 'Illegal drugs: highs and lows', in A. Park, J. Curtice, K. Thomson, L. Jarvis, and C. Bromley (eds), *British Social Attitudes: the 19th report*, London: Sage.

Home Affairs Select Committee (2002), *The Government's Drugs Policy: Is It Working?* Third Report of the Home Affairs Select Committee of the House of Commons, Session 2001-2, HC 318, London: House of Commons.

McKeganey, N. (1998), 'Drug misuse in Scotland: policy, prevalence, and public health', *Journal of Drug Issues*, 28, pp. 91–107.

Mowlam, M (2002), *Momentum: The Struggle for Peace Politics and the People*, London: Hodder and Stoughton.

Scottish Committee on HIV Infection and Intravenous Drug Misuse (1986), *HIV Infection in Scotland*, Edinburgh: Scottish Home Office and Health Department.

Scottish Office Ministerial Drugs Task Force (1994), *Drugs in Scotland: Meeting the Challenge*, Edinburgh: HMSO.

Scottish Office (1999), *Tackling Drugs in Scotland: Action in Partnership*, Edinburgh: Scottish Office.

Stationery Office (1998), *Tackling Drugs to Build a Better Britain: the Government's 10-Year Anti-Drugs Strategy*, Cm 3945, London: The Stationery Office.

CHAPTER 5

Religious Beliefs and Differences
Steve Bruce and Tony Glendinning

– INTRODUCTION –

The People's Friend, a magazine from Dundee's D. C. Thomson organisation, often features a country church on its cover. In one popular self-image, Scotland is a land of small burghs populated by couthy monarchist and church-going Presbyterian folk who farm and fish. In another, exemplified by Billy Connolly's bitter-sweet recollections of his Glasgow childhood, religion again plays an important part, this time in the form of the Catholic priest whose piety casts a long shadow on a matriarchal working-class culture.

It is common for a state's peripheries to be more devout than its centre. In part this is a natural consequence of the social changes that undermine religion, changes that appear first and most strikingly in the industrial heartlands. But the supposed difference is then taken up by the peripheries as a badge of pride. For most of the twentieth century, the Scots (along with the Welsh and Northern Irish) have seen themselves, and have been seen, as markedly more church-going than the English.

This chapter examines how far and in what ways religion still matters in Scotland. In the second half we will consider the extent to which Scotland is divided by religious identity. But first we describe the basic contours of today's Scottish religious landscape.

– RELIGIOUS IDENTITIES –

We asked, 'Do you regard yourself as belonging to any particular religion?'[1] Not surprisingly given it is the national church, the most commonly chosen religious identity was Church of Scotland (36 per cent). Next came Roman Catholic (14 per cent), followed by 'Christian, but of no specific denomination' (five per cent) and Episcopalian (three per cent). As we would expect, these estimates are higher than the membership figures which religious organisations derive from their own records (Brierley 1999, 2000, 2001) but the order of relative size is the same. What is surprising is that more than a third decline to nominate any religion; the 'no religion' option (37 per cent) even outstripped belonging to the national church. The popularity of 'no religion' is relatively new. Such a response was rare in surveys before the 1960s. By 1974, it was the choice of 24 per cent (Field 2001). Its present level thus represents a growth of 50 per cent in twenty-five years. No other religious identity is claimed by more than one per cent, and all non-Christian religions together amount to just over one per cent.[2] Strictly speaking, Scotland is not a multi-faith or multicultural society. It is a formerly Christian society with a large minority of active Christians and very small representations of other faiths.

Another way to see the decline of the Christian churches is to compare what people say they are now with how they answered, 'In what religion, if any, were you brought up?' By creating a table with present religious identity on one axis and religion of upbringing on the other we can map a pattern of change.

Table 5.1 Current religion, by religious upbringing

Current religion	Religious upbringing				
	No religion	Christian of no specific denomination	Catholic	Mainstream Protestant	Conservative Protestant
	%	%	%	%	%
No religion	89	54	20	31	35
No denomination	3	44	2	3	4
Catholic	*	2	75	2	–
Mainstream Protestant	6	–	2	63	28
Conservative Protestant	1	–	*	*	32
Other religions	*	–	*	*	1
Sample size	190	55	286	993	54

* Less than 0.5 per cent.
– None.
Note: 'Other religions' includes other Christian denominations as well as non-Christian religions.

Each column in table 5.1 represents the fate of that group. Very few people who were not raised in a religion have subsequently acquired one; very few have moved from the religion in which they were raised to other alternatives, such as non-Christian religions, while there is no significant movement from identifying with the Kirk to identifying with conservative Protestant alternatives.[3] The most important point is that the flows are very much in one direction: towards the secular.

When interpreting such figures we should note that some changes may represent changes in willingness to describe oneself in certain ways rather than major changes in belief. The largest shift in the flow chart is from 'Christian of no specific denomination' to 'no religion'. Doubtless some of this reflects a real difference between what the respondent now believes and how he or she was raised but the scale of the change suggests something else. The general decline of the churches has reduced the value of 'Christian' as a general mark of respectability and made it easier for those people who actually have very little connection with or interest in religion bluntly to say just that.

Our results confirm what the clergy see every Sunday: religion is more popular with the old than with the young. Just over a third of our sample were aged 55 or over, but, as can be seen from table 5.2, more than half of those who describe themselves as Church of Scotland fall into that age bracket (and the imbalance was even greater among church-goers, with approaching two-thirds aged 55 or over). This might be seen as evidence of an ageing effect: as people get older (perhaps because they are confronted with their own mortality) they become more religious. This is unlikely, as the overwhelming majority of those who were not raised in a religion have not subsequently become religious. Hence if older people are more likely to be church-going now, this is almost certainly because they always were. There is no obvious reason why those young people who now say they have no religion should be unlike their predecessors. We are seeing a cohort rather than an ageing effect.

Table 5.2 Current religious identification and age

Age group	Religious identity				
	No religion	Christian of no specific denomination	Catholic	Mainstream Protestant	Conservative Protestant
	%	%	%	%	%
18–34 years	40	38	32	14	8
5–54 years	40	42	38	33	42
55+ years	20	20	30	53	50
Sample size	592	73	225	662	27

– Religious involvement –

From the fact that more than a third identify with the Church of Scotland while its rolls claim less than 10 per cent of the adult population, it is clear that claimed religious identities do not tell us much about behaviour or belief. So we also asked:

'Apart from such special occasions such as weddings, funerals and baptisms, how often nowadays do you attend services or meetings connected with your religion?'

Half of Church of Scotland identifiers go to church less than once a year and only a third say they attend regularly, that is once a month or more often. And given the tendency for survey respondents to exaggerate the positive, the real attendance rate is almost certainly lower.

These figures represent a major fall over the last three decades (Field 2001). The proportion of Scots attending a religious service weekly has declined from 24 per cent in 1972 to 15 per cent. Over the same period the proportion who rarely or never attend church has steadily increased. In 1972 it was 43 per cent, in 1982 the figure was 50 per cent, and now it is over 60 per cent. Put bluntly, most Scots now have no connection with the churches.

To get some idea of just how distanced people are from organised religion, we asked those who had once attended church regularly but no longer do so if they had ever considered going back. Three-quarters say they have not. We also wished to find out why they had stopped going. Given the constraints of a survey we could not pursue this directly but instead asked at what age they had stopped. Among the 37 per cent of our sample who had once attended church regularly but then given it up, the most popular ages for stopping were

Table 5.3 Disaffiliation and birth cohort

	Birth cohort		
	1930–9	1940–9	1950–9
% stopped attending			
Out of those who ever went regularly to services	44	63	65
Sample size	*152*	*147*	*186*
% stopped attending			
Before the age of 21 out of all who stopped	34	48	61
Sample size	*68*	*93*	*122*

Note: Earlier and later birth cohorts where the data are 'incomplete' are excluded.

between 12 and 16. Well over half had stopped by the age of 20. This early age of defection is important because it suggests that much of it results not from adult dissatisfaction with the churches but from family dynamics. That we know the age of the respondents and the date at which they gave up church-going allows us to identify the patterns for specific age cohorts (divided into decade groups) to give a historical picture of defection. As table 5.3 shows, there is a difference between the pattern for the oldest cohort (that is, those born in the 1930s) and that for subsequent cohorts. Among Scots born in the early 1940s and later, a higher proportion appear to have stopped attending at an earlier age. With the most popular ages for disaffiliation being 11/12 and 15/16, this means that the Scottish churches must have been deprived of a significant number of new members in the 1950s and the 1960s. This fits fairly well with the date for the onset of decline that Callum Brown calculates from membership data (Brown 2001). Brown himself supposes that the causes of decline are to be found in the same period as the decline itself. For him, the strength of Christianity was undermined by the permissive culture of the 1960s. There is doubtless much to this but two elements of our data suggest that at least part of the explanation of decline must be found earlier.

First, the period when a significant proportion of Scots *never* attended church appears to predate those who came of age in the 1960s. Of the respondents who were born between the early 1930s and the early 1940s (who would have reached age 16 before the 1960s), 28 per cent had never attended church regularly. The corresponding figure for those who reached age 16 in the 1960s is little different at 30 per cent. Thus what we might think of as the Scottish churches' failure to reproduce themselves may well predate the 1960s.[4]

The second point concerns the implications of the pattern of early teenage defection. Stopping going to church at age 12 is presumably more of a family matter than is stopping at, say, 25 or 45. The post-1940 pattern of defection suggests that the parents of that and subsequent birth cohorts either lost the power to ensure their children maintained family traditions or that those parents were themselves lacking the religious commitment of previous generations. There are obviously limits to what we can deduce from survey data but we are able to compare the church-going behaviour of respondents whose parents were both of the same religion with those whose parents 'married out'.

Table 5.4 shows that, especially for the oldest age groups, the likelihood of a respondent being a regular church-goer varies considerably according to whether his or her parents were of the same or a different religious denomination. There is considerable debate about exactly why parents of different denominations should be less successful in reproducing their faith than families which are united in their church allegiance (Bruce 1999: 54–7; Iannaccone 1990), but it seems reasonable to suppose that, whatever changes occur to the nature of people's religious beliefs once they are wedded to someone who does not share them, there is a prior factor involved. Those who take their religion very seriously are unlikely to view those of a different faith (or none) as suitable marriage partners. In any event, among our oldest birth cohort those whose parents were of a different denomination are 15 or 16 percentage points less likely to be currently a regular church-goer than are those whose parents were of the same denomination. But among our three youngest cohorts who were born into a more secular age there is no more than a six- or seven-point gap. Evidently, as church-going becomes less popular (and presumably as the social pressure to attend decreases) so the impact of parental marrying out declines.

Table 5.4 Church-going, parental religion and birth-cohort

| Birth cohort | % currently attend services regularly if: | | |
	Both parents no specific religion	Parents different religion	Parents same religion
1930s	–	29	45
Sample size	5	26	151
1940s	–	14	29
Sample size	8	25	146
1950s	4	19	24
Sample size	23	58	154
1960s	7	13	20
Sample size	55	50	168
1970s	5	13	15
Sample size	39	54	78

Note: 'Parents different religion' includes those cases where one of the parents had no specific religion as well as where they had different religions.

Much more could be said about this but our conclusion is that significant changes in Scottish church life can be traced back from the first birth cohort (that of the 1940s) that started to leave church in large numbers in their teens to the religious attitudes of their parents. Unfortunately we cannot be more precise about timing because we do not know when the parents of people in that cohort married but most marriages would have been in the late 1930s and early 1940s. In brief, while Brown is surely right to point to the abrupt cultural changes of the 1960s as significant in the decline of authority and tradition, our analysis suggests that major changes associated with the period of the Second World War had already weakened the foundations of religious adherence.[5]

– BELIEVING BUT NOT BELONGING? –

Many who study church decline suppose that what needs to be explained is a decline in the plausibility of Christian ideas; that is, it is supposed people stop going to church because they no longer believe the things the churches profess. There is an alternative. It could be that people have retained their religious beliefs and have lost only faith in religious institutions or in institutions more generally.[6] To use the distinction made by Davie (1994), believing and belonging may not be the same. Is there evidence of Christian beliefs remaining strong despite the decline in attendance? A large majority of our respondents say they believe in God (72 per cent), but as table 5.5 shows, more detailed questioning shows that the conventional Christian view has now been overtaken by much vaguer formulations, and the notions that 'there is some sort of spirit or life force' or that 'there is something there' are as popular as belief in God.

Table 5.5 Belief in God

% saying statement is closest to their beliefs	Scotland 2001	Britain 2000
There is some sort of spirit or life force	28	21
There is a personal, creator God	25	26
There is something there	24	23
I don't really know what to think	11	12
I don't think there's any sort of God, spirit, or life force	6	15
None of the above	6	3
Sample size	*1598*	*1000*

Source (Britain 2000): BBC 'Soul of Britain' Survey, Opinion Research Business, 25/4–7/5/00.

To pursue the Davie thesis further, we analysed those respondents who assented to the conventional Christian view by religious practice. Regular church-goers are much more likely than others to believe in a personal God. Interestingly, the data show the value of asking those who had once regularly attended but since stopped if they had ever seriously considered going back. There is a marked difference of belief between those who have *not* considered going back (16 per cent say they believe in a personal God) and those who have (40 per cent continue to believe). That the latter group is much closer to the regular attenders in their beliefs suggests that they could rightly be described by Davie's 'believing but not belonging' slogan. However, at one in ten of the sample, this is a small group. Few of those who were not raised in a religion, who never attended regularly, or who stopped and have never considered going back, hold a theistic view.

It is also notable that around a half of regular church-goers do not believe in a personal creator God, preferring more the general idea of spirit or life force. We do not have the scope to pursue this further here but it is worth pointing out that stability in religious behaviour can co-exist with considerable change in the significance of that behaviour and its underlying ideological justifications. As we have argued elsewhere (Bruce 2002), many liberal Christians remain loyal to the outward expressions of nineteenth-century Christianity while significantly re-interpreting their faith in a 'this-worldly' and 'human-centred' direction.

The other major factor in religious belief, as in so much else, is age. For example, there are clear age differences among those who once attended church regularly but stopped and have not considered going back: 20 per cent of those over the age of 55 continue to believe in a personal God compared to 10 per cent of those under 35. In combination with many other age-related data in the survey, these figures suggest that it would be a mistake to suppose that, because indices of religious belief are higher than indices of religious behaviour, belief is independent of behaviour (and hence that a Christian culture can endure without active church-going Christians). Rather, those people who grew up in a church-going culture, even though not personally socialised into religious beliefs, nonetheless acquire a familiarity with them and hence find some religious beliefs more plausible than do younger people. Nowadays, unless young people have a strong family connection, they will not acquire any familiarity with religious ideas.

– New Age spirituality –

From a wide variety of different presumptions, the case has been made that humans are in some sense 'essentially' religious. Hence as one religious tradition declines, something else should rise to take its place. In the 1970s there was much talk of new religious movements such as the Unification Church or Scientology filling the gap. When they failed to acquire more than a handful of adherents attention turned to the more amorphous phenomenon of 'New Age' spirituality (Heelas 1996). Because what characterises the New Age is the ability of any individual to select an idiosyncratic mix of religious philosophies, religious disciplines, techniques for divining the future, therapies and quasi-medical practices from a now genuinely global cafeteria of influences, it is notoriously difficult to estimate the size or importance of the phenomenon. From the fact that Findhorn, Europe's oldest New Age centre, is based in Morayshire, one might suppose that Scotland is particularly receptive to New Age ideas. It is certainly the case that New Agers are fond of imputing a native spirituality to indigenous 'Celts' but acquaintance with Findhorn makes it clear that most residents are incomers, usually from the south of England or further afield (Bruce 2002). So what can we detect of Scotland's receptivity?

We asked our respondents if they had ever tried a variety of arguably New Age activities, such as tarot, fortune telling, or astrology, yoga or meditation, alternative medicines or therapies, and horoscopes, and if they had, how important were these in their lives. Table 5.6 summarises the replies.

Table 5.6 Experience and importance of New Age practices

	Horoscopes	Divination	Yoga or meditation	Alternative medicine
	%	%	%	%
Tried and considered:				
Very important	1	2	3	5
Quite important	4	4	7	15
Not very important	21	13	9	20
Not at all important	15	11	4	5
Never tried	59	70	78	55
Sample size	*1605*	*1605*	*1605*	*1605*

Note: 'Horoscopes' refers to consulting horoscopes in newspapers and magazines. 'Divination' means consulting a tarot-card reader, fortune teller or astrologer (other than reading horoscopes in newspapers and magazines). 'Alternative medicine' is defined as 'alternative or complementary medicine, such as herbal remedies, homeopathy or aromatherapy'.

Most Scots have not tried these things, particularly those that represent a significant commitment, and of those who have tried them, most do not think them very important. The questions are perhaps too blunt to make too much of the answers but there is a clear pattern that fits well with the findings of a study of New Age providers and consumers in Kendal, Cumbria.[7] Rather than seeing the New Age as compensating for a decline in Christianity, we should see it as an extension of the surgery, the clinic, the gym or the beauty salon. Trying to divine the future is much less popular than herbal medicine, homeopathy and aromatherapy. The Kendal researchers found that while most of the providers of aromatherapy or Shiatsu massage, for example, saw their activity as spiritual, most consumers did not. They saw it in 'this-worldly' terms, as a way to improved well-being.

We might add that interest in any of these things varies strongly by age, gender and education. Older people are less likely to have experimented with any of these things, or to see them as important, and certainly most men express little interest. Among women education is a strong consideration. Younger generations of women who have not continued with their education beyond school-level are more likely to have tried divination and horoscopes, and to regard these as equally important as alternative medicine and yoga. Nonetheless, without much exaggeration (and this fits perfectly the profile emerging from the Kendal research) we can say that the typical person seriously interested in yoga or alternative medicine is a university-educated woman under 55.

– Sympathy for religion –

In the nineteenth century many continental European countries became deeply divided over religion with the upper classes and rural people remaining loyal to a conservative Catholic Church and the rising middle class and urban working classes becoming aggressively anti-clerical; a pattern that resulted in France, Italy, Spain and Portugal both retaining a strong conservative Catholic culture and generating powerful and popular communist parties. Secularisation in Britain has taken a very different course. Organised atheism is trivial. Hostility to the Christian churches is almost unknown. The rather different matter of opposition to one particular church will be discussed below. It is indifference, not hostility, that is killing the British churches. However, at the same time what is very clear from our survey is that most Scots, despite themselves being indifferent to Christianity, have a considerable sympathy for religion. We asked our respondents if they were in favour of daily prayers in state schools. As we see in table 5.7, almost half are in favour; 40 per cent are against. Again age makes a difference: a clear majority of younger people are opposed to school prayers while a clear majority of older people are in favour.

Equally revealing are the responses to a question about religious broadcasting. As a condition of their licences, British television companies are required to produce religious programmes, a reflection of the power of the vision of John Reith, the founder of the BBC. We explained this requirement and asked if it should be continued or phased out. Just over half the respondents do not mind either way, 40 per cent are in favour and only 6 per cent against. Younger Scots are most indifferent, while the majority of older Scots are in favour. However, unlike the school prayer issue, few people of any age are opposed to television companies being forced to air religious programmes. When we put this preference for religious television next to the audiences for such programmes (which are tiny, hence the desire of broadcasters to be rid of the requirement) we come to an appreciation of how most Scots feel about religion generally – that it is something of little personal relevance.

Table 5.7 Sympathy for religion

		Yes	No	Don't mind/ can't choose	Sample size
There should be daily prayers in state schools					
18–34	%	24	62	14	347
35–54	%	41	48	11	515
55 and over	%	70	30	10	515
The BBC and ITV should be legally required to show religious programmes[a]					
18–34	%	21	10	69	411
35–54	%	36	7	57	573
55 and over	%	55	3	42	615

a. For this item, 'Yes' means 'should continue' and 'No' means 'should be phased out'.

It is conventional in surveys of religious beliefs to ask people whether they feel it is appropriate for religious leaders to speak out on this or that matter. One reason is to assess ideas about the appropriate reach of religion. This is an important matter in modern societies that have responded to the potential for conflict inherent in competing religions by confining religion to the home and hearth, making it a leisure activity and a matter of personal preference. Another purpose is to see to what extent even committed members of religious communities are willing to accept the authority of their leaders. The general supposition is that increased prosperity has resulted in declining willingness, even among believers, to accept the authority of religious institutions (Inglehart 1997: 284).

So, we asked our respondents if they thought it right for religious leaders to speak out on a variety of issues. In one sense the responses are counter-intuitive. A large majority are happy for church leaders speak out on such large abstractions as world poverty and the environment, whereas views on education were more divided, and only a minority think it proper for church leaders to pronounce on abortion or personal sexual behaviour. Yet the churches spend a great deal of their time instructing us on personal sexuality: the late Cardinal Winning, for example, was a vocal opponent of abortion and homosexuality and promoted these as the Catholic Church's main policy interests.

As to why some topics are thought more suitable for religious direction than others, we suspect that the explanation lies in the apparent paradox of considerable sympathy for religion as a notion and popular indifference to its substance. We guess that most people outside or on the fringes of organised religion see it not as a matter of bodies of doctrine, liturgies, rituals and a concern for a right relationship with a Creator God, but as largely a matter of morality. Especially given current public concern about crime and incivility, religion is regarded as a good thing because it teaches people about right and wrong. So on the one hand we have a widely shared perception that religion is in some sense a good thing; on the other we have the fact that most Scots are not themselves religious. The resolution of this tension is to approve of organised religion provided it inhabits some vague social space some distance from the respondent. Though most Scots are generally sympathetic to the idea of religion, that might be qualified by adding that our sympathies extend only to liberal, denominational, tolerant and ecumenical religion.

– A divided society? –

Irrespective of levels of popular religiosity, modern liberal democracies are secular in the sense that they allocate rights to individuals irrespective of religious identities. Though it was commonplace 200 ago, we now regard it as unacceptable to employ only one's co-religionists, to deny the vote to those who worship the wrong God, or to allocate such public goods as council houses on the grounds of religious affiliation. That is now discrimination. Though generally we regard marriage as a private matter, even to insist that one's children should marry co-religionists is regarded with suspicion, as offending against the egalitarian ethos of the modern world.

To a far greater extent than England (where it was largely confined to the north-west), Scotland has had a recent history of sectarian conflict. The Reformation was popular and successful, and with the exception of small pockets of Catholicism in some of the Western Isles and in Aberdeenshire, early modern Scotland became a Protestant country. Most Scots Catholics are descendants of Irish immigrants who settled in the second half of the nineteenth century. Lacking both capital and the skills required for industrial work, the Catholic Irish came into the labour market at the bottom and there were many native Scots who wished to keep them there. The guilds of skilled tradesmen and the labour unions saw them as an economic threat; committed Protestants saw their religion as a cultural threat. Initially the Irish formed relatively insulated clusters, drawn inwards by the Catholic Church, which was as fearful of losing its people as evangelical Protestants were of losing their cultural dominance.[8]

Commentators agree that sectarian divisions in Scotland declined in salience over the twentieth century. What is at issue is the extent of change. More particularly what exercises analysts is the significance of occasional episodes of sectarian violence (such as those associated with football rivalry) and the occasional expression of sectarian animosity. In the 1930s when anti-Catholic parties briefly flourished in Glasgow and Edinburgh, the outward expressions were the tip of an iceberg of major social conflict. Are they still? Is sectarianism still a major problem or is it now confined to hooliganism?

– Party politics –

It is typical of deeply divided societies that religio-ethnic groups pursue competing politics, either to further their own interests as a 'bloc' or to promote the interests of members of the religio-ethnic bloc in another state. When the Irish first moved to Scotland in significant numbers they exhibited both patterns. Irish politics were repeated in a minor key in Scotland. There were branches of various Irish parties active in central Scotland (Gallagher 1987) but once the Irish problem was resolved (temporarily as it turned out) with the formation of the Irish Free State in the early 1920s, the Irish in Scotland turned to local issues. Unlike the model of continental Europe, where Catholics formed sectional, often clergy-led, parties that were antithetical to the left, Scotland's Catholics became involved through the trade unions in the organisations that became the Labour party. Once the labour movement had conceded the main Catholic Church demand – control over its own schools – and once it became clear that Scottish labourism was neither communist nor particularly socialist, the Catholic Church dropped its opposition. Gradually Catholic strength in the manual working class, and hence in the large trade unions, came to be reflected in large numbers of Labour party local councillors, and members of parliament. Such was the hegemony in Glasgow that during the lifetime of Strathclyde Regional Council (1975–95) every leader of the Labour party and every Lord Provost was a Catholic. In the early 1990s more than half of Scotland's Labour MPs in the industrial heartlands were Catholic.

There was a corresponding preference on the other side. In the late nineteenth century, Gladstone's support for Irish home rule split the Scottish Liberals, who until then had been strongly supported by evangelical Presbyterians. The Presbyterians became Liberal 'Unionists'. They were defined by their support for the continued union of Great Britain and Ireland; their support for the union of Scotland and England was taken for granted. The Liberal Unionists eventually merged with the

Conservatives to form what until 1965 was called the Scottish Unionist party.

Hence for the first part of the twentieth century religious and political identities tended to overlap: Catholics were pro-Labour and anti-Conservative while Protestants were more likely to vote Conservative. It is not our place to say how people should vote but a simple way of expressing the connection is to say that significant numbers of Catholics and Protestants voted against what elsewhere would have been their class interests. Many working-class Protestants voted Conservative (Seawright 1999) and many middle-class Catholics voted Labour.

Does this pattern still hold? Table 5.8 shows that Catholics do have a distinctly strong preference for Labour.[9] They are overwhelmingly Labour voters. More importantly, they remain so when we control for social class (see table 5.9): a half of middle-class Catholics voted for Labour in the 2001 UK general election. They are less likely than Protestants to support the Scottish Nationalists, or come to that the Liberal Democrats, and are even more distinctive in their hostility to the Conservatives. Almost none voted Conservative in 2001. Or to put it another way, although only a small minority vote Conservative, Scottish Protestants remain much more likely to do so than others.

Table 5.8 Vote in the 2001 general election and religious identification

	No religion	Protestant	Catholic	Other religion
	%	%	%	%
Did not vote	41	22	34	33
Conservativ	5	12	*	5
Labour	28	36	51	29
Liberal Democrat	9	14	4	19
Scottish National Party	11	12	5	7
Other	3	1	3	5
Sample size	592	689	229	92

* Less than 0.5 per cent.

In table 5.8, we have identified respondents simply by the religious label they selected. We also undertook the same analysis looking at only those who attend church regularly. Church-going Catholics are much more likely to vote Labour (65 per cent) than nominal Catholics (35 per cent), although there is no difference between church-going and nominal Protestants (36 and 37 per cent respectively). Moreover, church-going Catholics are distinctive in their support for Labour irrespective of their class background. On the other side of the divide, it is middle-class church-going Protestants who are most distinctive in their support for the Conservative party in Scotland, but even so only 23 per cent voted that way in 2001.

Table 5.9 Labour voting in the 2001 general election, by religion and age/class

	Age group			Social class		
	18–34	35–54	55+	Non-manual	Manual	All
% voting Labour in 2001 election among:						
Catholics	29	52	73	50	52	51
Sample size	69	77	79	88	117	225
Other respondents	22	35	36	29	37	32
Sample size	341	495	537	684	554	1373

Note: 'Non-manual': those in NS-SEC classes 'employers and managers', 'intermediate occupations' and 'small employers'. 'Manual': those in NS-SEC classes 'lower supervisory and technical occupations' and 'semi-routine and routine occupations'. For further details, see the Technical Appendix.

This much continues the patterns of the past. However, a new pattern is revealed once we divide the sample into three age bands (see table 5.9).[10] Whereas more than two in three older Catholics voted Labour in 2001, less than one in three younger ones did so. Put simply, only for an older generation of Scots do traditional religious loyalties still matter; for a younger generation they do not. The most popular choice of Scots under the age of 35 was not to vote at all in the 2001 general election, irrespective of whether or not they were Catholic, Protestant or neither. Scottish Catholics are becoming much like the rest of the country. Seen in that light, talk about continuing Catholic support for Labour is irrelevant.

Yet seen in another light, and in apparent continuity with the past, younger committed church-going Catholics do vote (three-quarters voted in 2001) and they vote Labour (two-thirds of those who voted chose Labour) and, such has been the decline of Protestantism in Scotland, younger Catholics now represent more than half of all younger church-going Scots. On the other side of the divide, the Conservative party is less deeply unpopular with younger church-going Protestants than with other younger Scots. Thus, religion and politics continue to be intertwined, but even so, the reach of religion has been so diminished in Scottish life that the same general conclusion can be drawn: for most younger Scots religion does not matter (and apparently, for many, neither does the political process in Westminster). For only 6 per cent of all Scots under the age of 35 are church-going Catholics, a mere 3 per cent are church-going Protestants, and only a further 2 per cent of younger Scots regularly attend the services of other religions or faiths.[11]

One might carelessly suppose that any sign of difference between Catholics and Protestants is evidence of a divided society. The matter is more complicated. When we compare Catholic and Protestant voting in Northern Ireland we see two radically separated populations pulling in competing directions. In Scottish politics, whatever Catholic distinctiveness that does exist is not in that sense divisive. There are not separate Catholic and Protestant parties and Catholics are unusual only in being more likely than other Scots to support the political party that a plurality of Scots supports. Labour is the most popular party among all Scots who vote. More importantly it is also the most preferred party among Protestant Scots taken as a bloc: 46 per cent of those Protestants who voted chose Labour, more than twice the number who voted for the next most popular choice. The minority Catholic population is not un-Scottish; it is now hyper-Scottish. It is not Catholics who are unusual: it is that very small number of traditional Scottish Protestants who vote Conservative.

– Socio-economic status –

Deeply divided societies are rarely 'separate but equal', as the public relations slogan of apartheid South Africa had it. Separation is usually a product of structured inequality and reinforces it. We know that most Scots Catholics (especially those descended from Irish migrants) were once in a subordinate position (Handley 1945). We also know that most legal disabilities against Catholics were removed in the nineteenth century. But legal disabilities do not exhaust discrimination. As the fate of US blacks shows, it is quite possible for informal obstacles to social progress effectively to replace formal law.

There is plenty of evidence that Scottish Catholics, particularly in the western industrial lowlands, were long disadvantaged by informal recruitment systems. Skilled industrial workers would use their contacts to give preferential access to apprenticeships and the like to kin and friends and, when intermarriage was rare, that meant to co-religionists. Over the twentieth century one major change disrupted such systems and another made them less relevant. First, small locally owned and locally controlled firms were taken over by British, then American and then international concerns, and the role of informal recruitment was much reduced. Second, there was a huge growth in the number of white-collar occupations for which one needed educational and professional qualifications and where people answered to national rather than local reference groups. Hence we would expect to find that both the experience of job discrimination[12] and differences in the socio-economic status of Catholics and Protestants have declined.

We first explored Scots' perceptions of discrimination by asking if our respondents believed that 'being a Catholic limits employment or promotion opportunities in present-day Scotland'. Catholics are more likely than non-Catholics to think that being a Catholic remains a disadvantage. One half of those raised as Catholics feel their religion still matters while a third of other respondents feel that being Catholic matters. However, when we asked our respondents if they had experienced discrimination themselves because of their religious identity, only 18 per cent of Catholics said this had happened, though this is far higher than the 3 per cent reported by other respondents. This reminds us of the power of shared perceptions. Two-thirds of those who think discrimination is a problem nevertheless do not feel that they have suffered it themselves. And when we further break down responses (as in table 5.10) we find it is older Catholics and men who are mostly likely to think they have been discriminated against.

Table 5.10 Experience of discrimination among Catholics, by age and gender

	Age group			Gender	
	18–34	35–54	55 and over	Women	Men
% Catholics who have experience of religious beliefs limiting employment or promotion opportunities	11	20	22	10	31
Sample size	69	77	79	147	78

Before considering the current relative socio-economic status of Catholics and Protestants it is worth looking at educational qualifications. Although credentials are not the only influence on employment prospects, they are important and any difference we may find could help explain any differences that might exist. In so doing we have of course to bear in mind that older people have considerably lower levels of educational attainment. Once we do so we find that differences in the educational attainment of Protestants and Catholics seem to be declining. Among older Scots, Protestants are much more likely than Catholics to have advanced, post-school qualifications (20 per cent compared to 8 per cent). But among middle-aged and younger Scots, Protestants are only better qualified in so far as they are more likely to hold some sort of qualification. Among middle-aged Scots, 81 per cent of Protestants and 72 per cent of Catholics have some sort of qualification; for the youngest cohort, these figures are 94 per cent and 84 per cent. But younger and middle-aged Catholics are no less likely than Protestants to have advanced qualifications.

These results largely confirm the view that Paterson (2000) derived from a detailed analysis of the 1997 Scottish Election survey. A major change seems to have come with the ending of academic selection for secondary schools in 1965. Until then Catholics had been at a disadvantage because, though they made up 19 per cent of the secondary school population, only 5 per cent of academic secondary schools were Catholic. Hence the difference in the incidence of post-school qualifications in our oldest age cohort. Under the post-1965 comprehensive system, sectarian differences in educational attainment have largely disappeared, although we have provided some evidence to suggest that younger Protestants are still least likely to end up with nothing.

What then of socio-economic status? There are a number of apparent connections between religion of upbringing and occupation. People raised with no religion are more likely than Catholics who are more likely than Protestants to work in lower-status semi-routine or routine jobs. As for managerial and professional positions, the relationship is precisely reversed. However, given that respondents' claims of discrimination vary considerably with age, it is important to divide the survey sample into age cohorts.[13] As table 5.11 shows, the greatest differences in socio-economic status are found among older Catholics (particularly men). Among those aged 55 and over, only 26 per cent of respondents raised as Catholics but 46 per cent of those raised as Protestants were in non-manual occupations (a difference of twenty points).[14] Among younger respondents the difference was only five points, confirming the impression derived from our analysis of educational qualifications. What was once a major sectarian divide has been reduced markedly.

It is important to know if such figures should be read as religion influencing social class or as social class influencing religion. Because our data are only a one-off 'snapshot' we cannot properly follow the fate of a single group over time and thus get a better idea of what causes what. There is an element of questionable extrapolation in our use of the three age groups to talk about change over time. Nonetheless it is worth trying to eliminate one possible explanation of the correlation between religion and social class. It could be that as some Catholics enjoy upward social mobility, they cease to be religious, move away from the areas in which they were brought up, and stop thinking of themselves as 'Catholic'. Hence data showing that Catholics are more likely to be of a lower social class than non-

Catholics could illustrate the fate, not of individual Catholics, but of 'Catholic' as a nominal identity: something to be shed by the person who moves out as he or she moves upward.

Table 5.11 Class, by religious upbringing and age

	Religious upbringing	
	Protestant	Catholic
	%	%
18–34		
Non-manual	61	56
Manual	30	38
Sample size	*166*	*82*
35–54		
Non-manual	55	48
Manual	36	42
Sample size	*385*	*111*
55 and over		
Non-manual	46	26
Manual	45	58
Sample size	*496*	*93*

Note: For definitions of 'Manual' and 'Non-manual', see table 5.9.

In the analysis above we have eliminated this explanation by using religious upbringing rather than current religious identity as our measure of religion. But we also tested it directly by comparing the social class with that of those who have abandoned a Catholic identity and those who have retained it. There is no significant difference. Although it does not finally settle the matter, our analysis suggests that in the correlation between having been raised as a Catholic and having a lower than typical socio-economic profile, we are seeing the effects of 'being a Catholic' (whatever those are) rather than the effects of some self-selecting process in which those who do well abandon their Catholic identity.

That any group has a distinctive occupational profile is not in itself proof of discrimination. We need to remember that the group with the lowest social profile is that of people raised in no religion and it is difficult to imagine this population being systematically victimised as the characteristic its members share is not at all visible. Irrespective of the attitudes of others towards them, members of a particular population may simply share characteristics that disadvantage them in the labour market. Older Catholics may have been the victims of discrimination, but they may also have suffered from poorer schooling, and from a lack of opportunities in the regions in which they are concentrated.

We might add that this class profile is mirrored in a number of other observations. Those from Catholic backgrounds tend to be poorer and are more likely to rent housing, particularly from a local authority, while Protestants are more likely to own their home. Such differences have consequences – for example, in comparison to Scots who were raised in other religions, Catholic respondents are less likely to say that they are 'living comfortably' and they are more likely to say that they find it 'difficult' on their present income. However, as with the data on class position, the significant differences are to be found among older age cohorts.

Table 5.12 Class, by religious upbringing, age and region

	South-west of Scotland		Other regions	
	Protestant	Catholic	Protestant	Catholic
	%	%	%	%
18–54				
Non-manual	65	52	55	51
Manual	21	39	37	40
Sample size	98	70	453	123
55 and over				
Non-manual	58	12	43	36
Manual	37	72	47	50
Sample size	90	40	406	53

Note: Some percentage pairs do not total 100 because not all respondents could be assigned a class. For definition of class, see table 5.9.

But is it sensible to make comparisons between Catholic and other older respondents across the whole of Scotland? Less than one in twenty Scots in the north of the country come from Catholic families. And many Catholics, particularly older Catholics, live in the ageing industrial heartlands of Scotland, in areas that are often characterised by poor socio-economic profiles.[15] It may be that their situation is entirely similar to that of other Scots who live in these areas, irrespective of religious background. The answer appears to be not.[16] Table 5.12 compares the occupational profiles of older Catholics and Protestants separately for those who live in the south-west of Scotland and those elsewhere. It appears that class differences between Catholics and Protestants are relatively small in most of Scotland but remain significant in the south-west of Scotland, particularly for older respondents. In summary, what our findings suggest is that although Catholic relative disadvantage has not entirely disappeared, it has been markedly eroded. We now turn to what is possibly a cause and is certainly a consequence of that change.

– Intermarriage –

The extent to which two populations intermarry is important both as a symptom and as a cause of integration. It is symptomatic because the willingness to marry someone of another race, nation, ethnic group or religion shows the importance of those characteristics as against personal emotional attachment. Given that whom we marry is itself influenced by whom we meet, the extent of intermarriage is also a good measure of the extent of mixing as equals. But it is also a cause of further integration. For bigots to maintain a culture or a structure of discrimination they must be able to divide those they wish to advance ('oor ain folk') from those they wish to deprive of opportunities ('them'). The more that 'we' marry 'them' and produce children who cannot easily be labelled, the harder it is to discriminate and the more likely it is that religious or ethnic preferences will be overridden by other considerations. As populations mix, being a good uncle or brother-in-law competes with being a loyal Catholic or Protestant, and in stable affluent societies that are not divided by competing political agendas, family loyalties trump loyalty to religio-ethnic group.[17]

What does our survey tell us about intermarriage? First, it tells us that the vast majority of Scots have no objection to a relative marrying someone of a different religion. Only 3 per cent 'mind a great deal'; a further 7 per cent mind 'slightly'. Over two-thirds do not mind at all. Almost all of those who mind a great deal are committed evangelical Protestants and we would suggest this is based less on a generalised dislike for other religions and more on the fear that people who marry out lose their faith. Because they have the sectarian's certainty that their religion is essential for salvation they are fearful that if a son or daughter marries out they will not see them again in heaven.

The general tolerance expressed in answers to the hypothetical question is matched by behaviour. Put simply, it was once the norm for Catholics to marry other Catholics. Among Catholic respondents aged between 65 and 74, 94 per cent are married to a Catholic. Of those aged between 55 and 64, the figure is 86 per cent and it gradually falls with age until among those aged 25 to 34 no more than half of Catholics are married to non-Catholics. To put these figures in context, we can note that in Northern Ireland in 1991 only 2 per cent of marriages were religiously mixed (Morgan et al.

1996).[18] The point is compelling and simple. Young Scots no longer regard religion (or more precisely religio-ethnic identity) as an important consideration in the most important decision they make.

– National identity –

Joseph Bradley (1995) has suggested that, although the main objective differences between the heirs to the Irish and other Scots have been largely eroded, there is still a degree of cultural exclusion. Phrases such as 'a cold house for Catholics' are used to suggest that the ex-Irish do not feel at home in Britain (Hickman 1995).

Our survey data offer little support for such claims. As table 5.13 shows, Catholics are more likely than Protestants to describe themselves as 'Scottish not British'. This sentiment is strongest among younger Catholics: more than half see themselves as 'Scottish not British'. The relative lack of Catholic sympathy for British identity may also reflect some politically inspired anti-Westminster feeling. However, the 'other description' row in the table is also significant. It was open to those who felt 'Irish' rather than Scottish or British to say that. They did not.[19]

Table 5.13 Religious identity and national identity

National identity	No religion	Catholic	Other religion
	%	%	%
Scottish not British	38	40	32
More Scottish than British	30	34	29
Equally Scottish and British	20	19	28
More British than Scottish	3	1	4
British not Scottish	3	1	4
Other description	5	3	2
Sample size	592	225	880

Another place we might find evidence of Catholic alienation is in attitudes towards devolution. In the 1970s there was some reluctance among Catholics to support devolution because they feared that an autonomous Scotland would be a more robustly Protestant country than one run from London (Kellas 1975). In the run-up to the referendum on the Scottish Parliament, the late Cardinal Winning announced very publicly that Catholics had nothing to fear from a Scottish parliament. Whether he led or merely represented a change is not clear but the pattern of voting suggests there is no Catholic hostility to devolution. Catholics were as likely as Protestants to vote for a parliament in the 1997 referendum.

– Socio-moral values –

Given the way that the reach of religion in modern societies is typically reduced so that it applies primarily to personal relationships and morality (rather than, say, to the operations of the economy or the polity), one area in which we might expect to find major differences between Protestants and Catholics is in attitudes to sexuality.

On the whole, as illustrated in table 5.14, our survey suggests Scots hold liberal views about sexual intimacy before marriage: two-thirds think it is not wrong at all. Despite the fierce debate in 2000 about the abolition or retention of Clause 2A, the majority support the idea that homosexuality should be explained to teenagers by teachers in school: just over half think it is not wrong at all to do so. There might also be said to be an acceptance of abortion: just over a third feel it is wrong only sometimes while just under a third feel it is not wrong at all. These figures suggest an increasingly liberal and tolerant society. The most succinct way to summarise them would be to say that only about one in five Scots believes such things to be wrong most of the time, and at the extreme, just around one in ten sees them as absolutely wrong. Nonetheless, the picture appears quite different for homosexual intimacy: on this Scots are evenly divided between those who feel it is mostly wrong and those who do not. And Scots claim to frown on adultery: 59 per cent see it as always wrong, and a further 26 per cent almost always wrong.

Table 5.14 Attitudes towards personal morality

Do you personally think it is wrong or not wrong for:		Always wrong	Almost always wrong	Wrong sometime	Not wrong at all	Can't choose	Sample size
A man or woman to have sexual relations before marriage	%	10	5	11	65	7	1381
School teachers to explain homosexuality to teenagers	%	14	8	13	51	13	1381
A woman to have an abortion	%	11	12	37	29	10	1381
Adults of the same sex to have sexual relations	%	38	7	10	30	14	1381
A married person to have sex with someone other than their spouse	%	59	26	8	2	3	1381

But how far does religion influence such attitudes? Does religion only matter for the older generation and ceased to be a moral guide for the young? As can be seen from table 5.15 on homosexuality, age is important but religion is not. Most of the older generation think homosexuality is wrong irrespective of their religious identity. For the youngest cohort of all religious persuasions, homosexuality is not wrong. Despite the positions taken by the church hierarchy, the influence of religion is weak even for Catholics. It is only in the case of two very small populations (church-going conservative Protestants and non-Christians) that religion makes a big difference and that is a reflection of the distinct culture maintained by evangelicals and, for example, Muslims.

Table 5.15 Views on homosexuality, by age and religious identity

% think homosexuality is always wrong	No religion	Catholic	Other religion
18–34	17	19	13
Sample size	214	53	81
35–54	31	34	37
Sample size	236	70	208
55 and over	58	62	60
Sample size	118	66	332

We can extend this analysis by looking at attitudes to sex education in schools. Here we find that religion does have some influence on attitudes to whether or not teachers should explain homosexuality to teenagers. Older Catholics stand out as least supportive: almost half disapprove.[20] But even so the influence of religion exercises little apparent influence on younger Catholics.

Table 5.16 Views on abortion, by age and religious identity

% think abortion is always wrong	No religion	Other religion	Catholic
18–34	7	6	6
Sample size	214	81	53
35–54	5	7	21
Sample size	236	208	70
55 and over	14	14	50
Sample size	118	332	66

As can be seen from table 5.16, religion influences views on abortion among middle-aged and older respondents. In general, only a minority think abortion is wrong but older Catholic respondents are much more likely to feel that way. And more than half of older working-class church-goers disapprove, particularly older Catholics who go regularly to mass.[21] Again, older church-goers are the most disapproving of adultery, but there is little to choose between different religions. At well over 90 per cent, most church-goers simply see adultery as wrong in almost all circumstances.

In sum, religion remains an influence on socio-moral values but much less so among the young than the old. Religion no longer determines culture. Only among the oldest generation of church-going Catholics do we find attitudes that conform to the Church's conservative teachings. Otherwise there are not big differences between Catholics and mainstream Protestants. The great divide is not between Catholics and Protestants but between the Christian mainstream and the small number of evangelical Protestants and non-Christians.

– Conclusions –

It is commonplace for observers to draw parallels between the sectarian divide in Scotland and in Northern Ireland. Our interpretation of the history, which we find reinforced by our survey data, is quite different. The model is not Northern Ireland, where competing political interests caused religio-ethnic divisions to become firmly entrenched in a zero-sum game. There are far stronger parallels with the USA, New Zealand and Australia. Catholic immigrants entered the labour market at the bottom and initially formed a quite distinct community. However, as the immigrants prospered they became less distinctive, the barriers came down, intermarriage increased. Instead of forming a Catholic party, Scottish Catholics worked with Scottish Protestants in the secular labour movement. In Northern Ireland the political conflict has ensured that religious affiliation remains central to most of life and in a number of roundabout ways (such as preventing cross-religious intermarriage) the Troubles have protected religion from many of the secularising influences that have eroded it in other modern industrial societies. Religion in Scotland enjoyed no such protection and has declined considerably.

As religion has declined in popularity it has lost its ability to define an 'ethos'. A century ago, when most of those labelled 'Protestant' or 'Catholic' had some real connection with those faiths, the committed believers could overlook the imperfections of those whose adherence to the defining faith was at best nominal. As the proportion of church adherents has declined so has the plausibility of community identities. For example, organisations such as the Orange Order and the Ancient Order of Hibernians, that sustained a religio-ethnic identity and channelled it for political purposes, have declined. Little more than one in twenty Scots still belong to such organisations, and these are mostly older, working-class men who were raised in a Protestant tradition by Protestant parents, but who themselves are now neither necessarily devout nor church-going. And although Catholic church attendance began to decline much later than it did among mainstream Protestants, the Catholic Church's loss of 24 per cent of attenders between 1980 and 2000 is similar to the Church of Scotland's 27-per-cent fall over the same period (Brierley 2000: table 2.14.2). Put simply, the Catholic Church can no longer think of itself as having 'a people'. Instead it is a voluntary association providing services for individual consumers.

To return to the rhetorical question with which we introduced this analysis, it is clear to us that Scotland is no longer deeply divided by religio-ethnic or sectarian identities. Differences between Catholics and Protestants can be found in demographic characteristics and in attitudes but that these are strongest among our oldest respondents and weakest among our youngest confirms our impression that the social sources of division have been weakening since the Second World War. Although Catholic-Protestant divisions were never as deep in Scotland as in Northern Ireland, it is reasonable to suppose that had Scotland had its own democratically elected polity in the 1930s, then sectarianism would have been a more significant force. As Bruce (1998) has argued, the concentration of political power in the Westminster parliament prevented a rivalry, potent in the west of Scotland but of little relevance in the UK as a whole, becoming embedded in the preferences of the major political parties. The political impotence of the small number of Scottish bigots was a major cause of their marginalisation. Scottish Catholics achieved considerable upward social mobility and at the same time lost a great deal of their personal piety. This combined with the general secularisation of Scottish Protestants to ensure that by the time Scotland regained its parliament at the end of the century religion was of pressing importance to very few Scots.

In this chapter we have only scratched the surface of what can be inferred from our survey data. In one sense the findings reported are no surprise. Although a few US scholars insist that secularisation is a myth dreamt up by atheistic sociologists and assert that there has been no major change in the religious lives of European societies, those of us familiar with Scotland's religious landscape know that there has been a major decline in the popularity and importance of Christianity in Scotland over the twentieth century. The landscape reference is not an idle metaphor; the countryside is littered with churches converted into private houses, carpet warehouses, restaurants, pubs and clubs. This and other recent surveys confirm what we know from studies of churches' membership figures and from censuses of church attendance: most Scots are no longer involved in Christian organisations. In trying to evaluate competing explanations of that change it is important that we notice the recurrent references to age. In part this shows the extent of secularisation. Irrespective of personal faith, age matters because our oldest respondents grew up in a world in which religious ideas and institutions were sufficiently powerful to permeate the general culture. But the age relationship also points to an important fact about the way in which secularisation occurs. The problem is not one of adults giving up their faith; it is a matter of young people never acquiring one. Decline mainly occurs because churches fail to recruit the next generation in sufficient numbers to replace natural attrition.

Many of the questions we asked in our survey were designed to get some sense of what, if anything, was replacing the fading Christian heritage. Put simply, the answer is not much. A national representative sample survey is not a terribly sensitive tool for identifying underground currents or spotting the next big thing but it is significant that no non-Christian religion is sufficiently popular to appear in the lists of claimed identities of those who have given up Christianity. New religious movements of the 1970s (such as Scientology, the Unification Church or 'Moonies', and Hare Krishna) attracted a great deal of media attention but very few adherents. Activities which might signify an interest in non-Christian spirituality (meditation, for example) are not at all popular and there is little evidence of any strong sense of the sacred beyond those who are conventionally involved in orthodox religion.

The difference between a religious and a secular world is not the possibility of imagining religious ideas. Anything can be imagined by someone. It is the likelihood of them catching on. Our explanation of the decline of religion does not rest on specific secular ideas or challenges having disproved or displaced religious tenets. Instead it concentrates on the role of social circumstances in maintaining the plausibility of a religious culture. If everyone believes the same things, then parents and wider kinship networks can co-operate in indoctrinating children and schools can reinforce conviction. When everyone worships the same God then the trivia of everyday interaction, as when two farmers mutter their appreciation of God's rainfall, provides the threads which carry the significance of such grand rituals as Harvest Thanksgiving down into the minds of the laity. Then the mass media reinforces the same messages. We can see how a culture remains strong and we explain its decline by pointing to the many small ways in which the supports for Christianity gradually collapsed. This 'removal-of-supports' approach to secularisation does not project an end-point. Rather it explains why shared ideas are no longer as persuasive as they once were. It does not rule out the possibility of someone putting together strange claims about space travel, the likelihood of life on other planets and the unlikelihood of people having built the pyramids, marinating these with a large dose of wishful thinking and coming up with a flying-saucer cult. What it does rule out is the possibility of any such theories becoming very widely accepted, under the political, social and economic circumstances that we can presently imagine.

– REFERENCES –

Bradley, J. (1995), *Ethnic and Religious Identity in Scotland: Culture, Politics and Football*, Aldershot: Gower.

Brierley, P. (1999), *Religious Trends No. 1: 1999/2000*, London: Christian Research Association.

Brierley, P. (2000), *Religious Trends No. 2: 2000/2001*, London: Christian Research Association.

Brierley, P. (2001), *Religious Trends No. 3: 2001/2002*, London: Christian Research Association.

Brown, C. (2001), *The Death of Christian Britain*, London: Routledge.

Bruce, S. (1998), *Conservative Protestant Politics*, Oxford: Oxford University Press.

Bruce, S. (1999), *Choice and Religion: A Critique of Rational Choice*, Oxford: Oxford University Press.

Bruce, S. (2002), *God is Dead: The Secularization of the West*, Oxford: Blackwell.

Davie, G. (1994), *Religion in Britain Since 1945: Believing Without Belonging*, Oxford: Blackwell.

Field, C. (2001), ' "The haemorrhage of faith?" Opinion polls as sources of religious practices, beliefs and attitudes in Scotland since the 1970s', *Journal of Contemporary Religion*, 16: 157–75.

Gallagher, T. (1987), *Glasgow: The Uneasy Peace*, Manchester: Manchester University Press.

Handley, J. (1945), *The Irish in Modern Scotland*, Cork: Cork University Press.

Heelas, P. (1996), *The New Age Movement*, Oxford: Blackwell.

Hickman, M. (1995), *Religion, Class and Identity: The State, the Catholic Church and the Education of the Irish in Britain*, Aldershot: Gower.

Iannaccone, L. (1990), 'Religious practice: a human capital approach', *Journal for the Scientific Study of Religion*, 29, pp. 297–314.

Inglehart, R. (1997), *Modernization and Postmodernization: Cultural, Economic and Political Change in 43 Societies*, Princeton, NJ: Princeton University Press.

Kellas, J. (1975), *The Scottish Political System*, Cambridge: Cambridge University Press.

Morgan, V., Smyth, M., Robinson, G. and Fraser, G. (1996), *Mixed Marriages in Northern Ireland*, Coleraine: Centre for the Study of Conflict, University of Ulster.

Paterson, L. (2000), 'The social class of Catholic Scotland', *Journal of the Royal Statistical Society*, A: 163, part 3, pp. 363–79.

Seawright, D. (1999), *An Important Matter of Principle: The Decline of the Scottish Conservative and Unionist Party*, Aldershot: Ashgate.

Voas, D. (2003 forthcoming), 'Intermarriage and the demography of secularisation', *British Journal of Sociology*.

– NOTES –

1. We are not naïve about the limitations on using survey instruments to identify and measure complex social phenomena. As will become clear, what any of the responses mean is often a difficult matter.
2. Non-Christians probably form a slightly larger proportion of the population than this suggests but are generally under-represented in national survey samples. But at 1.2 per cent of our sample any under-representation is not substantial, since various Scottish Executive sources put the ethnic minority population at only 1.6 per cent and of those some will be Christian while others will have no religion.
3. We must remember that these data represent only claimed identities, not active membership. Although the Church of Scotland appears better at retaining its adherents than Protestant sects such as the Free Church and the Free Presbyterian Church, it is clear from membership data that the advantage is confined to retaining nominal attachments. That is, many people who have only a slight connection with organised Protestantism call themselves Church of Scotland. Almost all of those who say they are Baptist or Free Church actually attend regularly. Hence these data are quite compatible with what we know from membership and attendance figures, that is that liberal and mainstream churches have been declining far faster than conservative ones.
4. These observations come from Michael Rosie's analysis of the data; we are grateful to him for allowing us to cite his conclusions.
5. It is worth noting that David Voas (2003), using baptism figures for the Church of England, similarly challenges Brown's dating and locates the main change in or around 1939–45.
6. This argument is debated in articles by Bruce, Gill and Davie in *Journal of Contemporary Religion* 17 (October 2002).
7. For a general description of the Kendal project, see http://www.kendalproject.org.uk.
8. We should recall that at least a quarter and possibly a third of migrants from Ireland were Ulster Protestants. For economic and cultural reasons they were readily integrated. To avoid repetition we will stipulate here that by 'Irish' we generally mean 'Catholic Irish and their heirs'. Similarly, in the historical sections when we refer to Catholics we mean Irish Catholics.
9. Because we suppose that what matters for most of the concerns here is religious identity we have used claimed religious identities rather than some measure of religious practice to identify Catholics and Protestants. In the later section on socio-economic status we have used religion of upbringing to identify the groups because we expect that discrimination, if there is any, will be based on imputed rather than claimed identity.
10. We have performed this analysis just for Labour voting because there are too few cases for meaningful separate analysis of voting for other parties.
11. For now Catholicism is the majority religion of younger Scots but is also in decline.

12. We might add that the only recent well-publicised claims of discrimination were made in the mid-1990s by Protestants objecting to the alleged malfeasance of the Catholic-dominated local council of Coatbridge. A variety of investigations found no substance to the allegations.

13. We recognise that reducing social class to manual versus non-manual is clumsy and loses a lot of analytical detail but it is necessary in order to retain sufficient numbers for comparisons of religion and age, and even then it ignores gender segmentation.

14. Chi-square tests show that the differences in the occupational position of older Protestants and Catholics are statistically significant ($p < 0.01$).

15. We do recognise that there is also significant disadvantage in rural areas of Scotland (for example, Caithness and Sutherland).

16. Although the sample sizes are small, the differences between Catholics and Protestants in table 5.12 are statistically significant.

17. Note the qualification that this assertion refers only to stable affluent societies. The atrocities that accompanied the break-up of the former Yugoslavia remind us that the replacement of large group loyalties by a combination of kinship bonds and universalism is not irreversible.

18. In the USA in 1999 only 3 per cent of marriages are inter-racial.

19. Among all 4,750 respondents to the three Scottish Social Attitudes surveys conducted between 1999 and 2001, less than 1 per cent said they were 'Irish' when asked to choose between British, English, European, Scottish, Irish, Northern Irish, Welsh and 'None of these', and it is likely that they are very recent migrants. We are grateful to David McCrone for supplying the data from the 1999 and 2000 Scottish Attitudes surveys.

20. Conservative Protestants and non-Christians are also more likely to disapprove.

21. Again, the devout from minority churches are more likely to disapprove.

CHAPTER 6

Identity Matters: The Personal and Political Significance of Feeling Scottish

Michael Rosie and Ross Bond

– INTRODUCTION –

In this chapter we aim to gauge the nature, comparative importance, and significance of national identity (or identities) within contemporary, post-devolution Scotland. Surveys have consistently demonstrated that the nature of national identity in Scotland is markedly different from that found in other parts of the United Kingdom. So it is important that we continue to monitor the nature of these identities, not least because of the radically changed political circumstances in which they now operate. For example, it has been suggested that devolution would lead to a heightened sense of Scottishness. But it has also been argued that the establishment of a political institution with the capacity to symbolise and express Scottish values would in fact have the effect that people would feel less need to emphasise their Scottishness (Paterson et al. 2001). By examining contemporary identities and seeing how they might have changed over time we can go some way to establishing which perspective is correct.

While looking at recent trends in the nature of national identities is itself a worthwhile endeavour, it leaves unanswered at least two key questions about the importance and implications of such identities. National sentiments may, for example, be extensive yet shallow, in that they are relatively unimportant compared to other identities. If this were true then we might be tempted to dismiss national identity as interesting yet relatively insignificant. In this chapter we are able to provide what is arguably the most comprehensive analysis to date of how important national identity is in Scotland. We do this by including both well-established and much more novel questions in our survey.

Equally, even were we to conclude that national identity is both prominent and comparatively important, it would still be possible to question its relevance in the absence of any evidence indicating that it had important political or social consequences. In fact, a considerable degree of academic effort has been dedicated to exploring the political significance of national identity in Scotland. Gellner's (1983) assertion that nationalism will be dominated by the principle that each nation should have its own state implies that national identity is likely to have a strong bearing upon certain political beliefs. But empirical investigation of this relationship in Scotland has revealed an interesting and far from straightforward picture. Previous research has suggested that while national identity is associated with left- or right-wing values and can be a moderately good predictor of the *degree* of support for certain political perspectives such as identification with the Conservative party or views on Scottish independence, it is not often found to be related to stark cleavages in opinion. Indeed in certain respects – support for devolution or the Labour party, for example – it may even have quite a weak influence (see, for example, Bennie et al. 1997; Brown et al. 1998, 1999; Paterson et al. 2001; McCrone and Paterson 2002). But at the same time the influence of national identities on attitudes is more evident in Scotland than in England (Brown et al. 1999). So it is important that we continue to monitor the political significance of national identity now that devolution has arrived. Doing so will enable us to assess whether the influence of national identity upon long-standing political issues has changed, the form this influence takes in relation to more novel questions and, in turn, what implications our findings might have for Scotland's political future.

_ NATIONAL IDENTITIES IN SCOTLAND _
AND THE UNITED KINGDOM

In order to put our discussion of the contemporary situation in historical perspective, it is useful to start with a brief examination of the broad pattern of change in national identities in Scotland over the past quarter-century. Respondents have been asked regularly in Scottish surveys to choose the term which 'best' describes their 'nationality', and, as table 6.1 clearly demonstrates, there has been a fairly steady increase in the proportion of respondents who answer 'Scottish', and a steady decline in the proportion answering 'British', since the 1970s. Over three in four now say that they are Scottish compared with no more than two in three in the 1970s.

Table 6.1 Trends in forced choice national identity in Scotland

	1974	1979	1992	1997	1999	2000	2001
	%	%	%	%	%	%	%
Scottish	65	56	72	72	77	80	77
British	31	38	25	20	17	13	16
Other/none	4	6	3	8	6	7	7
Sample size	588	658	957	882	1482	1663	1605

This is one of two key questions asked about national identity in our survey. Respondents are asked whether or not they 'regard themselves as' one or more of a number of listed national identities and invited to choose as many, or as few, as they please. Only thereafter are they asked to choose just one. And it is of interest to examine the answers that were given before they are asked to choose, and to compare the results with those of parallel surveys also carried out in 2001 in England, Wales and Northern Ireland.

Table 6.2 National identities across the UK

% choosing:	Scotland	England	Wales	Northern Ireland
British	50	67	60	45
English	3	63	14	2
Scottish	86	3	1	1
Welsh	–	2	67	–
Northern Irish	1	1	–	27
Irish	2	2	1	30
Sample size	1605	2786	1085	1800

Note: Columns do not add up to 100 because respondents could make up to three choices.

Several points stand out, as shown in table 6.2. Firstly, in each component part of the United Kingdom a multiplicity of national identities is evident; hence it is important to stress that the debate is not so much about national *identity* than about national *identities*. Leading on from this, the figures also demonstrate that this is true not only of each society as a whole but also of the individuals within them. Many people acknowledge more than one identity. In Scotland almost half (48 per cent) do so, with a substantial minority (41 per cent) choosing both Scottish and British. Finally, feeling Scottish is an unusually *widespread* identity. Some 86 per cent of people in Scotland say they are Scottish. This is greater than the proportion of people in Wales who say they are Welsh (67 per cent) and of those in England who claim to be English (63 per cent) or British (67 per cent). It even outstrips the level of feeling British among Northern Ireland's Protestants (73 per cent) and of claims to be Irish amongst Northern Ireland's Catholics (65 per cent).

Our second key question about national identity explicitly acknowledges that many people in the UK make claims to more than one national identity. Often known as the 'Moreno' question,[1] it asks:

Which, if any, of the following best describes how you see yourself?
(Scottish/English/Welsh) not British
More (Scottish/English/Welsh) than British
Equally (Scottish/English/Welsh) and British
More British than (Scottish/English/Welsh)
British not (Scottish/English/Welsh)

Table 6.3 'Moreno' national identity in Great Britain

		'Moreno' national identity					
		x not British	More x than British	Equally x and British	More British than x	British not x	*Sample size*
Scotland	%	36	30	24	3	3	1605
Wales	%	23	22	29	11	11	1085
England	%	17	13	42	9	11	2786

Note: In each case x refers to Scottish, Welsh or English as appropriate.

Table 6.3 shows that when asked this question people in Scotland are much more likely to say they are not British at all than are people in Wales or England. Indeed, twice as many say they are 'Scottish not British' (36 per cent) than claim, in England, to be 'English not British' (17 per cent). Further, of those in Scotland who regard themselves as *both* Scottish and British, more prioritise their sense of feeling Scottish than is true of those in England who regard themselves as both English and British, or in Wales both Welsh and British. Thus while around half of those in Scotland with a mixed Scottish–British identity claim to be 'more Scottish and British', those with mixed identities in Wales and England are much more likely to give equal weight to both identities.

Both our measures of national identity indicate then that feeling Scottish is more pervasive in Scotland than is any other identity elsewhere in Britain. Equally, fewer people in Scotland prioritise a British identity than anywhere else, although a majority at least still regard themselves as in some way British. Moreover, feeling Scottish has become a more popular identity. We have already seen the evidence on this for our first question in table 6.1. So far as our second question is concerned, we find that the proportion who say they are 'Scottish not British' has risen from 19 per cent in 1992 to as much as 36 per cent now.[2]

National identity in Scotland continues then to be distinctive from the rest of Britain while acknowledgement of a British identity appears to be in further decline. However, although these trends are of interest in themselves, our aim here is to explore the wider significance of national identity in Scotland. Our survey provides us with a particularly exciting and valuable opportunity to do this, for two reasons. Firstly, our survey included new questions specifically designed to measure the salience of national identity. Secondly, now that devolution is becoming more firmly established we can consider how far reactions to the new political settlement are being shaped by national identity.

Our discussion is structured into three broad sections. We begin by examining the relative significance of national as opposed to non-national identities. This can go some way to answering a moot point – do national identities matter? We then examine feelings of pride and/or hostility towards key symbols of nationhood, national flags. Finally, we offer an extensive examination of how political attitudes in a devolved Scotland are related to feelings of national identity, and the significance that this may have for the constitutional future of the country.

– ARE NATIONAL IDENTITIES IMPORTANT? –

It is all very well showing that respondents are able to choose a national identity, but do people actually place much importance on their national identity? One way of addressing this is to examine the answers given over a number of years when people in Scotland have been asked whether they feel themselves to have more in common with a fellow Scot from a different class, or an English person from the same class as themselves. Since 1992 at least (though not in 1979), responses to this question have consistently shown that more people feel they have more in common with Scots of a different class than they do with English people from the same class.

Table 6.4 Who do you have most in common with?

% who have more in common with:	1979	1992	1997	1999	2001
English person of same class	35	27	23	23	25
Scottish person of opposite class	30	45	46	41	40
Sample size	608	957	882	1482	1605

This question is however still open to criticism; people in Scotland may have higher levels of 'national' than 'class' solidarity, but *both* might be regarded as relatively unimportant. In order to meet this criticism, our 2001 survey included a new question. Respondents were shown a lengthy list of possible identities[3] and asked to name three they felt were central to their own sense of who they are. The question ran:

Some people say that whether they feel British or Scottish is not as important as other things about them. Other people say their national identity is the key to who they are.

If you had to pick just one thing from this list to describe yourself – something that is very important to you when you think of yourself – what would it be?

And what would the second most important thing be?

And what would the third most important thing be?

Two identities stand out as the most popular first choices. Being a parent is chosen by 24 per cent whilst being Scottish is chosen by 18 per cent. And these identities are still the most common once people make their second and third choices; around half choose being a parent as one of the three most important ways in which they think of themselves, and almost as many choose being Scottish. Being Scottish is more frequently chosen than a number of other identities long seen as central to a person's sense of self, most notably class and gender. Table 6.5 shows the eight most popular identities that were selected.

Table 6.5 'Selected' identities in Scotland

% choosing identity	First choice	Second choice	Third choice	Total
A mother/father	24	16	9	49
Scottish	18	13	15	45
A working person	10	10	10	2
A wife/husband	6	13	9	28
A woman/man	10	8	8	25
Working class	9	8	8	24
Retired	3	4	4	11
British	4	4	3	11

Sample size = 1605

So, a substantial number of people in Scotland say that 'being Scottish' is an important part of how they perceive themselves, and therefore national identity does indeed seem to matter. Yet this leads to a subsequent question – does this make Scotland different from its neighbours? As our new 'multiple identity' question was also asked at the same time in England and Wales, we can also address this issue. Table 6.6 shows the incidence of three non-national identities (being a parent, being a spouse, and gender) as well as of 'British' and the relevant 'national' identities, Scottish, English and Welsh. In each case table 6.6 shows the proportion who opted for that identity as one of three choices.

Table 6.6 'Selected' identities in Britain

% choosing identity	Scotland	England	Wales
A mother/father	49	47	50
A wife/husband	28	26	28
A woman/man	25	29	23
Scottish/English/Welsh	45	19	33
British	11	26	23
Sample size	*1605*	*3287*	*1085*

There is a striking difference in the importance respondents give to national identities in the three countries. While the relevant 'national' identity proves more popular than British identity in both Scotland and Wales, this is more so in Scotland (45 per cent versus 11 per cent) than in Wales (33 per cent versus 23 per cent). Meanwhile, people in England are less likely to choose any kind of national identity, while among those who do, English is chosen less often than British (19 per cent versus 26 per cent). These figures appear to confirm our conclusion so far that national identity operates differently in the different parts of Britain. It has a higher salience in Scotland and Wales than in England. And feeling Scottish is more salient in Scotland than is any other identity elsewhere. More needs to be said, however, about the prevalence of 'being Scottish' in Scotland.

To some extent responses to these questions are limited by there only being three choices, and by the fact that some of the choices that were offered will be inapplicable to some people. For example, an unmarried and childless person is unlikely to see being a spouse or a parent as key to their identity, and is thus faced with fewer potentially relevant categories to choose from. Perhaps people only chose a national identity when there was simply nothing else on our list of possible choices that could possibly apply to them? It is worthwhile, therefore, to examine the responses to these identity questions among some of the sub-groups for whom non-national identities might be expected to be particularly relevant. For example, while we have found that more choose 'being Scottish' (45 per cent) than 'being a man/woman' (25 per cent), might this be because men are less likely than women to regard their gender as key to their identity? Given that it is often thought that 'gender issues' have a *particular* impact on women, might we not reasonably expect to find a higher incidence of gender identity amongst women, perhaps outweighing for them the salience of Scottish identity? In table 6.7 we look at how often some of the key sub-groups in our sample choose a national identity as compared with the category that might be thought to be particularly associated with that sub-group.

Table 6.7 Relative salience of 'national' and 'sub-group' identities

Sub-group	% Choose 'Scottish'	% Choose 'British'	% Choose sub-group identity	Sub-group identity	Sample size
Men	50	15	13	(man)	644
Women	41	8	35	(woman)	960
18–24	57	8	53	(young)	136
75+	35	13	38	(elderly)	195
Married	39	11	48	(wife/husband)	805
Living with their children	43	8	79	(a father/mother)	527
Men living with their children	46	12	68	(a father)	175
Women living with their children	41	5	85	(a mother)	352
Middle class identifier	33	15	17	(middle class)	175
Working class identifier	46	7	43	(working class)	524
Protestant	43	14	11	(Protestant)	764
Catholic	44	6	33	(Catholic)	224
All	45	11	–		1605

Note: Middle class identifier: respondent described themselves as middle class in response to a separate question on class identity (see Chapter 7). Similarly for working class identifier.

We find that in practice 'being Scottish' is rated highly in all of our sub-groups, albeit to varying degrees. So while women are much more likely than men to choose a gender identity and less likely to choose a national identity, more women choose 'being Scottish' than choose 'being a woman'. Likewise, while 'being young' is chosen by over half of those aged 18 to 24, a slightly higher proportion choose 'being Scottish'. Roughly equal proportions of those aged 75 and over choose 'being elderly' and 'being Scottish'. And while being a parent outstrips national identity among those currently living with their children (and especially so for women), over two in five still choose being Scottish.[4]

'Being Scottish' also seems to outweigh class identity, even among those who, when answering a separate question, were willing to describe themselves as middle or working class, though we should also note that those who described themselves as working class were much more likely to choose 'being Scottish' than were those who considered themselves to be middle class. Equally, contrary to the arguments of some commentators that the very idea of a Scottish Catholic 'seems oxymoronic to many' (MacMillan 2000:15), Catholics are just as likely to choose 'being Scottish' as are Presbyterians or the non-religious (see also Chapter 5). Nor are Scotland's Catholics 'different' in possessing such a strongly expressed Catholic identity. While 33 per cent of Catholics in Scotland choose 'being a Catholic' as key to their sense of themselves, so too do 34 per cent of Catholics in England.

It is clear then that across a wide range of social groups[5] people consistently cite 'being Scottish' as a key component of their own sense of themselves. Although there are differences between groups, none of the other identities that we offered were chosen so often and so consistently as 'being Scottish'. We have, then, gone some way to answering the question as to whether national identity matters to the people of Scotland. In terms of their own conception of themselves it would certainly seem that it does. Equally it is also clear that this national identity is 'being Scottish' and *not* 'being British' (nor indeed 'being both').

– National iconography: flagging national pride –

There are many icons that may invoke a nation or state but few have the 'official' status or the immediacy of flags. In Scotland it is common to see both the Saltire (the St Andrew's Cross) and the Union Jack flown on public buildings and in public spaces, thereby to some extent symbolising the dual nature of national identity in Scotland. In our survey we asked people to describe their feelings about these two flags, that is whether they feel proud or hostile when they see them. Strikingly, while a very large proportion of people in Scotland (71 per cent) feel 'very' or 'a bit proud' when they see the Saltire, when it comes to the Union flag a majority (60 per cent) say they 'do not feel much either way' (see table 6.8).

This seems to fit fairly closely with our earlier finding – that people in Scotland have strong Scottish identities, but their sense of feeling British is weaker. Further, the Saltire evokes pride across a range of social groups. For example, between two-thirds and three-quarters of each age group describe themselves as at least 'a bit proud' when they see it. In contrast feelings about the Union Jack do differ across the age groups. Among those aged 18 to 34, only 17 per cent express pride in the UK flag, compared with 63 per cent of those aged 75-plus. Pride in the Union Jack, it seems, could well be largely confined to those who lived through the Second World War. Even so, actual hostility toward the Union flag is difficult to find. Even among those who support Scotland's independence from the rest of the United Kingdom, for example, more actually express pride in the Union Jack (21 per cent) than describe their feelings as hostile (14 per cent).

Table 6.8 Pride in British and Scottish national flags

	Union Jack	Saltire
	%	%
Very proud	11	40
A bit proud	20	31
Do not feel much either way	60	28
A bit hostile	5	1
Very hostile	2	*
Sample size	1605	1605

* Less than 0.5 per cent.

As might be expected, there is a very strong association between how a respondent feels about these flags and how they describe their identity on the 'Moreno' scale of national identity. Table 6.9 shows for each category of that scale the proportion who are at least 'a bit proud' of the Union Jack and equally the proportion who have the same feelings towards the Saltire. Only among the small minority who prioritise their sense of feeling British (that is, those who describe themselves either as 'More British than Scottish' or 'British not Scottish') do a majority express pride in the Union flag and only a minority pride in the Saltire.

Table 6.9 Pride in British and Scottish national flags, by national identity

'Moreno' national identity	%'Very/bit proud' of Union Jack	%'Very/bit proud' of Saltire	Sample size
Scottish not British	24	80	572
More Scottish than British	28	76	490
Equally Scottish and British	39	63	373
More British/British not Scottish	61	41	106

– THE POLITICAL SIGNIFICANCE OF NATIONAL IDENTITIES –

National identities are then clearly and increasingly important to many Scots' sense of themselves. But do people's national identities bear upon their political attitudes? Do they make any difference to the likelihood they support further constitutional change or even full Scottish independence? For example, if the proportion who feel British continues to decline, will this help bring about a serious challenge to the future of the Union?

Previous research has shown that we cannot in fact assume a direct and unproblematic relationship between people's expressed national identity and their support for more autonomous and distinctive Scottish political institutions and organisations. This is true whether we look at support for the establishment of the Scottish Parliament (Brown et al. 1999), support for Scottish independence or support for the principal party that advocates the cause of independence, the SNP (Brown et al. 1998; Bond 2000; Paterson et al. 2001; McCrone 2001). While national identity is associated with both party support and attitudes to the constitution, the political significance of national identity is much more complex than might be supposed.

The results of our survey confirm that picture. For example, in table 6.10 we can show the pattern of national identity among the supporters of Scotland's four main parties. As we might expect, a majority of SNP identifiers, a fairly large minority of Labour identifiers and relatively few Conservative identifiers say they are 'Scottish not British'. Even so, no less than 21 per cent of Conservative supporters are Scottish not British, while no less than 40 per cent of the supporters of the self-proclaimed 'party of Scotland', the SNP, describe themselves as, to some extent, British. In other words, while national identities are associated with party preference, the relationship does not expose a major antagonistic cleavage in Scottish politics.

Table 6.10 Party identification and national identity

'Moreno' national identity	Party identification			
	Conservative	Liberal Democrat	Labour	SNP
	%	%	%	%
Scottish not British	21	23	34	57
More Scottish than British	23	32	34	31
Equally Scottish and British	33	30	25	9
More British/British not Scottish	17	8	4	1
Sample size	164	154	735	253

The same conclusion can be drawn if we examine attitudes towards Scotland's constitutional future (see table 6.11). Support for an independent Scotland is highest amongst those at the most Scottish end of the Moreno scale. Equally the only group showing substantial support for the abolition of the Scottish Parliament are the most strongly British identifiers. Yet even among this group a clear majority support the new *status quo* of devolution, a view that is also the most popular amongst those who are exclusively Scottish.

Table 6.11 Constitutional preference, by national identity (Scotland), 2001

Constitutional preference	Scottish not British	More Scottish than British	Equally Scottish and British	More British/ British not Scottish	All
	'Moreno' national identity				
	%	%	%	%	%
Independence	42	28	11	10	28
Devolution	48	61	72	60	59
No parliament	5	7	14	29	9
Sample size	*572*	*490*	*373*	*106*	*1605*

In fact there is considerable 'non-alignment' in the three-way relationship between national identity, constitutional preference and party identification. Only quite a small minority (17 per cent) of 'exclusive' Scots support *both* independence and the SNP; a much larger proportion (51 per cent) in fact claim to support *neither*. This pattern is even more pronounced amongst those who describe themselves as 'more Scottish than British'; just 10 per cent support both independence and the SNP, while 65 per cent back neither. These figures indicate that the relationship between national identity, constitutional preference and support for the SNP remains as complex in the wake of Scottish devolution as it was before the Scottish Parliament was created (see Bond and Rosie 2002).

If the influence of national identity upon key political attitudes were simple or straightforward, then we would expect a much larger proportion of those who feel exclusively Scottish than we have found here to support both independence and the SNP. We would certainly expect a clear and substantial majority of this group to support at least one of these options. On the other hand, if the influence of national identity were simply weak, then there would be little or no difference in the level of support for independence or the SNP across our various categories of national identity. Clearly, neither of these situations obtains: identity exerts the kind of influence we might expect upon these key political attitudes, but only *to an extent*. Because it does not do so to the *degree* that we would expect, and because there exist substantial sub-groups of people for whom identity appears somewhat at odds with attitudes, we would argue that the interaction between identity and attitudes is best described as complex.

– EVALUATIONS OF DEVOLUTION –

We now turn to exploring the extent to which the relationship between national identity and attitudes towards the experience of devolution is similarly complex, and to considering what implications this might have for future constitutional change. To do so we look first at respondents' evaluations of and aspirations for the level of power and influence enjoyed by the Scottish Parliament. Although we should by now be clear that identity cannot be taken as a proxy for views about Scotland's constitutional status, here we would expect to find that Scottish identifiers are more supportive of increased Scottish parliamentary power than British identifiers. Second, we look at how the Scottish Parliament is assessed in a wider British or UK context, that is how it is thought to have contributed to the governance of the UK and how it fares compared to Westminster. Again, we would expect that more strongly Scottish identifiers look on the new Parliament comparatively favourably. Third, we examine evaluations of the Parliament's performance in key policy areas. Here we might expect that the influence of identity will be more unpredictable because less positive responses may reflect disappointment at perceived failure as much as they do a *desire* to see the Parliament fail. Even so, we would still expect Scottish identifiers to be more positive in their evaluations. Finally, we consider opinions about the *likelihood* of constitutional change in Scotland. This is of course a qualitatively different question than one about *desired* constitutional change. We would probably expect that those who favour change are more likely to foresee such change coming about, and we know that those who favour change are much more likely to be Scottish than British identifiers. But how far this is the case is likely to be tempered by the considerable non-alignment between identity and constitutional preference, as well as the fact that inevitably there will be those who are pessimistic about their hopes of independence being realised.

– *Influence and power* –

We begin by looking at opinions about which political institution *has* most influence over Scottish affairs. It is apparent that national identity has very little impact on perceptions of the Scottish Parliament's influence; in each of our categories of national identity two-thirds believe that Westminster has most influence over Scottish affairs, whereas only between 13 per cent and 18 per cent believe this of the Scottish Parliament. But, as table 6.12 demonstrates, we obtain a very different picture when we examine beliefs about how much influence political institutions *should* have. Strongly

Scottish identifiers are much more likely to believe that the Scottish Parliament should be the most influential political institution; as many as 82 per cent of those who feel exclusively Scottish think this compared with only 51 per cent of more British identifiers. But at the same time, although British identifiers are the most likely to say that the UK government should have most influence, a majority of them are still likely to say that the Scottish Parliament should be the more powerful body. This pattern is replicated if we look at opinion on whether the parliament should be given more powers. 81 per cent of those who say they are exclusively Scottish agree or strongly agree that it should be given more powers, compared with only a minority – but a significantly sized minority – of 35 per cent among those in the more British categories. So while national identity influences aspirations for parliamentary power in what may be thought to be a fairly predictable fashion, the relationship is perhaps also surprisingly complex in that levels of support for the parliament among strong British identifiers are far from negligible.

Table 6.12 Who should have most influence over Scotland, by national identity

	'Moreno' national identity				
	Scottish not British	More Scottish than British	Equally Scottish and British	More British/ British not Scottish	All
	%	%	%	%	%
Who should have most influence over the way Scotland is run:					
Scottish Parliament	82	81	63	51	74
UK government	7	9	24	39	14
'Agree' or 'strongly agree' Scottish Parliament should have more powers	81	74	54	35	68
Sample size	*572*	*490*	*373*	*106*	*1605*

– Scotland's parliament in the United Kingdom –

We now look at how people's views about the contribution that the Scottish Parliament has made to the governance of the UK vary according to their national identity. We will then look at the esteem in which the institution is held in comparison with Westminster.

Only 36 per cent of those who feel exclusively Scottish believe that the way that Britain is governed could not be improved or could only be improved in small ways. This rises to 39 per cent for those who feel more Scottish than they do British, 46 per cent for those who are equally Scottish and British, and 50 per cent for the strongest British identifiers.[6] So, although differences are not huge, there is some evidence to suggest that the more Scottish someone feels the more negatively they evaluate the British system of government. We secure rather weaker differences, however, if we examine attitudes to whether or not the Scottish Parliament has improved the government of Britain as a whole. 33 per cent of those who feel exclusively Scottish believe it has had a positive effect, but so also do 39 per cent of those who feel more Scottish than British, and 35 per cent of those with an equal dual identity. Only amongst those who feel mostly or exclusively British does this figure drop, to 22 per cent. Even so, even amongst this group, slightly more believe the parliament has had a positive impact on the government of Britain than believe it has made things worse.

Again we find that the views of those with relatively strong British identities are at most only somewhat more critical than those of their fellow Scots when we examine how evaluations of the Scottish Parliament compare with those of Westminster. Two pairs of questions in our survey permit us to do this. First, we asked our respondents the extent to which they think MPs in London and MSPs in Edinburgh work together to solve the problems of Britain and Scotland respectively. The answers to these questions largely prove to be uninfluenced by national identity. And as 29 per cent of all respondents believe that Westminster MPs co-operate in this way 'a great deal' or 'a fair amount', but no less than 51 per cent think that MSPs do, this means that even the most strongly British consider MSPs to be more co-operative than MPs.

Meanwhile, the evidence of our second pair of questions is shown in table 6.13. These asked respondents how much they trusted the UK government and the Scottish Parliament to work in Scotland's best long-term interests. Trust in the UK government becomes markedly higher as we move from the Scottish to the British end of the Moreno scale. In contrast, levels of trust in the Scottish Parliament are very similar at all points along the scale. Moreover, even British identifiers are substantially more likely to trust the Scottish Parliament to work in Scotland's best long-term interests than they are the UK government. Once more, then, we see that national identity certainly appears to make some difference to people's political opinions, but not uniformly so, and even when it does make a difference, the nature of the relationships we observe can be complex and even surprising.

Table 6.13 Trust in UK government and Scottish Parliament to work in Scotland's best long-term interests

	'Moreno' national identity				
	Scottish not British	More Scottish than British	Equally Scottish and British	More British/ British not Scottish	All
	%	%	%	%	%
Trust UK government:					
Nearly always or most of the time	14	20	29	40	22
Only some of the time/ almost never	84	78	69	59	76
Trust Scottish Parliament:					
Nearly always or most of the time	62	68	63	64	65
Only some of the time/ almost never	36	30	36	31	33
Sample size	572	90	373	106	1605

The Scottish Parliament: evaluations of performance

We continue our analysis by looking at how evaluations of the Scottish Parliament's performance in some key areas vary according to national identity. Table 6.14 shows the proportions agreeing that the parliament will or has improved Scotland's economy, the NHS in Scotland and the standard of Scottish education. It also includes a measure of whether people believe that the parliament is giving 'ordinary people more say in how Scotland is governed'.

Table 6.14 Expectations and evaluation of the Scottish Parliament, by national identity

	'Moreno' national identity				
% agreeing that it will or has improve(d)	Scottish not British	More Scottish than British	Equally Scottish and British	More British/ British not Scottish	All
Economy	45	45	39	30	43
NHS	51	44	41	31	45
Education	27	29	28	19	27
People's say in government	36	41	36	34	37
Sample size	572	490	373	106	1605

Answers to some of these questions, most notably the economy and the NHS, do appear to be influenced by national identity. Stronger Scottish identifiers are more likely to give a positive response. But on education and 'giving ordinary people more say in how Scotland is governed' the differences are less marked and are not statistically significant. But again we should note that because (as discussed in Chapter 1) relatively few people in any category of national identity think that the Scottish Parliament either has made or is going to make any of these things worse, even among those who have a British identity, more give a positive response than a negative one. Therefore we *cannot* conclude either that national identity uniformly influences evaluations of the parliament's actual or expected impact, or that feeling British is associated with a strongly negative evaluation of the devolved parliament.

– Constitutional futures –

Finally, we consider how views on the constitutional future of Scotland vary by national identity. First we examine how likely respondents believe it is that Scotland will become completely independent from the UK in the next twenty years. We know that more strongly Scottish identifiers are more likely to favour independence. But does this mean they are also more likely to think it actually will happen?

Table 6.15 Perceived likelihood of Scottish independence in the next twenty years

Perceived likelihood of independence	'Moreno' national identity				
	Scottish not British	More Scottish than British	Equally Scottish and British	More British/ British not Scottish	All
	%	%	%	%	%
Very or quite likely	44	39	28	24	37
Quite or very unlikely	53	59	69	73	60
Sample size	*572*	*490*	*373*	*106*	*1605*

Table 6.15 indicates that they are. The more Scottish someone feels the more likely they are to think that independence will happen. However, even among those who feel exclusively Scottish, only a minority believe that independence is likely to be realised in the next twenty years. Scottish identifiers are *relatively* more likely to anticipate independence, but not absolutely so. And while those with a stronger sense of feeling British are significantly less likely to foresee an independent Scotland, nearly a quarter do.[7]

We obtain a similar result if we look at the answers our respondents gave when they were asked whether 'having a Scottish Parliament makes it more likely that Scotland eventually leaves the United Kingdom'. As table 6.16 shows, stronger Scottish identifiers are somewhat more likely to think that the parliament could herald the dissolution of the Union than strengthen it, whereas the opposite is true of their more strongly British counterparts. But the differences are relatively small and the most popular response in every category is that the Scottish Parliament will make no difference.

Table 6.16 Perceived impact of having a Scottish Parliament on Scotland's position in the UK

Scotland more likely to:	'Moreno' national identity				
	Scottish not British	More Scottish than British	Equally Scottish and British	More British/ British not Scottish	All
	%	%	%	%	%
Leave UK	32	28	22	26	28
Stay in UK	21	27	35	34	27
No difference	43	41	38	38	41
Sample size	572	490	373	106	1605

– CONCLUSIONS –

Previous research that has suggested that Scottish national identity has become more salient in Scotland while British identity has faded (and indeed is ageing) is confirmed by the two new measures that were asked for the first time in our survey. People in Scotland are much more likely to say they are proud of the Saltire than the Union Jack, although the relative lack of pride in this symbol of the British state is not coupled with hostility towards it. And according to the answers given when respondents said which three identities are the key to who they are, national identity would seem to matter at a personal level too. Of all the identities offered to respondents only one, 'being Scottish', was found to be consistently and frequently chosen across a wide spectrum of social groups. It is also more popular than 'feeling English' is amongst people in England and 'feeling Welsh' amongst those in Wales. In short, it appears that one particular national identity – 'being Scottish' – is especially, and unusually, salient in Scotland.

But does national identity matter politically? The principal question we addressed here was whether the complexity that is evident in the relationship between national identity, constitutional preference and party support is also found in attitudes towards the performance of devolution *per se*. A complex relationship we suggested was one in which national identity has a clear effect on attitudes towards the performance of devolution that is largely in line with expectations, but that the degree to which it does so varies and such that sometimes the absolute level of support for a particular view amongst those who feel strongly Scottish or strongly British can be rather different from what we might predict.

Our findings lead us to conclude that the most appropriate characterisation of the relationship between national identity and attitudes towards devolution is indeed complex. There are many instances where national identity is strongly or moderately related to attitudes, and these relationships are without exception reasonably predictable. Thus we suggested that those who felt most Scottish would be most likely to want to see the Scottish Parliament have more powers and influence, would be most likely to evaluate its performance positively, and would be more likely to believe that independence would happen in future. And to some degree at least all of these expectations came true, and certainly there are no instances where those views that we suggested would be most likely be held by strongly Scottish identifiers are in fact more common among strongly British identifiers. But that does not mean there are no surprises.

For example, national identity clearly has a strong effect upon opinions about how much power the Scottish Parliament should have. But its impact is not entirely as we would expect because although the opinions of strongly British identifiers are *relatively* negative, in *absolute* terms they are still positive. Meanwhile, the relationship between identity and the relative merits of the Scottish Parliament and Westminster is not as strong as we might have expected. As a result, although British identifiers are more likely to have a positive view of Westminster they still have a more favourable view of the Scottish Parliament than of Westminster. A similar picture is evident so far as the Scottish Parliament's perceived impact in certain policy areas is concerned. Those effects that are observable are consistent with our prior expectations, but national identity only appears to influence opinions about some policy areas and not others. And finally, although strongly Scottish identifiers are most likely to think independence will happen or that having a Scottish Parliament will help it to happen, even among them, a majority believe that independence is unlikely.

So taken together then, we believe these findings indicate that the relationship between national identity and attitudes towards devolution is complex. Although it clearly influences a number of attitudes, and the *direction* of this effect is almost invariably what we would anticipate, the *strength* of this relationship is quite different to what we might expect. The fact that in absolute terms even the most strongly British of identifiers usually take a positive stance on the Scottish Parliament, even in explicit comparison with Westminster, means that there is no polarisation in views between those at opposite ends of the Scottish–British scale. Further, in a number of areas even the relative impact of national identity is small or even insignificant. Thus while national identity does matter in shaping opinions about devolution and Scotland's constitutional future, this is not consistently true to the extent or in the manner that we might expect.

What are the future constitutional implications of our findings? One interpretation is that further increases in feeling Scottish and a decline in feeling British are likely to result in increased demands for greater Scottish autonomy, a more negative body of opinion about government at a British or UK level, and increased expectations of future independence for Scotland. However, one might also argue from our findings that an increased sense of feeling Scottish would boost positive evaluations of the current constitutional arrangements and potentially act as a brake upon radical change. But the final lesson of our findings is that relatively positive evaluations of the Scottish Parliament and desires that it should have more influence are in fact quite evident even among those whose identity accommodates only a relatively weak sense of being Scottish. This seems to indicate that further constitutional change would attract broad support among those of all identities, albeit to differing degrees. This reflects the fact that any disillusionment with the Scottish Parliament and its performance is primarily the result of the limitations on its current power and strength of vision, rather than a desire to see its powers curtailed or abolished.

– REFERENCES –

Bennie, L., Brand, J. and Mitchell, J. (1997), *How Scotland Votes*, Manchester: Manchester University Press.

Bond, R (2000), 'Squaring the circles: demonstrating and explaining the political "non-alignment" of Scottish national identity', *Scottish Affairs*, 32, pp. 15-35.

Bond, R. and Rosie, M. (2002), 'National identities in post-devolution Scotland', *Scottish Affairs*, 40, pp. 34-53.

Brown, A., McCrone, D. and Paterson, L. (1998), *Politics and Society in Scotland*, second edition, Basingstoke: Macmillan.

Brown, A., McCrone, D., Paterson L., and Surridge, P. (1999), *The Scottish Electorate*, Basingstoke: Macmillan.

Gellner, E. (1983), *Nations and Nationalism*, Oxford: Blackwell.

MacMillan, J. (2000), 'Scotland's shame', in T. Devine (ed.), *Scotland's Shame?: Bigotry and Sectarianism in Modern Scotland*, Edinburgh: Mainstream Publishing.

McCrone, D. (2001), *Understanding Scotland: The Sociology of a Nation*, second edition, London: Routledge.

McCrone, D. and Paterson, L. (2002), 'The conundrum of Scottish independence', *Scottish Affairs*, 40, pp. 54–75.

Paterson, L., Brown, A., Curtice, J., Hinds, K., McCrone, D., Park, A., Sproston, K. and Surridge, P. (eds) (2001), *New Scotland, New Politics?*, Edinburgh: Polygon.

– Notes –

1. The 'Moreno' question was developed in Spain and is named (rather misleadingly) after the Spanish sociologist who pioneered its application to Scotland. It was not asked in Northern Ireland because the 'non-state' identity in that part of the UK is highly, and violently, contested.

2. One should, however, exercise care when interpreting these figures. 'Moreno' data can be quite volatile even over very short periods, and there is evidence to suggest that the historical and political context at the time the question is asked may influence response considerably. There are also some opinion poll findings from the 1980s that show levels of feeling exclusively Scottish that are as equally high as those obtained in recent surveys (Bond and Rosie 2002).

3. These were, in order presented to the respondent: Working class; British; Elderly; A woman/man; Not religious; A wife/husband; a Catholic; A country person; A city person; A Protestant; A mother/father; Middle class; Black; Retired; Religious; Scottish; A working person; Young; White; Asian; Unemployed; Other (please say what); None of these.

4. Unfortunately the survey only enables us to identify parents who currently live with their children, rather than all parents in general.

5. While not reported here we also found consistently high levels of 'being Scottish' across occupational class, education, employment status and religiosity.

6. Overall, attitudes on this in Scotland do not appear to be any different to the rest of Britain. According to the 2001 British Social Attitudes survey, 43 per cent of people across Britain as a whole believe that the system 'could not be improved' or could only be improved 'in small ways', compared with 40 per cent in Scotland.

7. If we leave aside national identity for a moment and look directly at the relationship between constitutional preference and beliefs about the likelihood of independence in future, we find that only a bare majority, 53 per cent, of supporters of independence believe that it will happen in the next twenty years. This figure falls to 32 per cent among supporters of the current devolved parliament with tax-varying powers, and 25 per cent among those who would like to see this parliament completely abolished.

CHAPTER 7

A Classless Society?
Social Attitudes and Social Class

Paula Surridge

– INTRODUCTION –

Although far from being new (see, for example, Nisbet 1959), claims by sociologists and politicians that we have witnessed the 'death of class' have become increasingly commonplace over the last two decades (see, for example, Pakulski and Waters 1996). Some point to an apparent decline in class consciousness (Pahl 1996). Others argue that class differences in political behaviour are being replaced by other sources of division (Clark and Lipset 1996).

This latter argument has had particular resonance in Britain in recent years. The country's two main political parties have traditionally been distinguished by a 'left–right' ideological divide. Labour believed government should play a large role in the delivery of services and in the running of the economy – not least in order to achieve greater equality – whilst the Conservatives believed individuals should be given freedom to advance themselves and that a strong economy was a free market economy. This divergence of views was not only reflected in the attitudes of each party's supporters but also in a difference of outlook between people in the working and those in the middle class. However, ever since the election of 'New Labour' in 1997, there has been considerable speculation about whether the party has successfully captured the votes of 'middle England' at the cost of losing support in its traditional working-class heartlands (Evans and Norris 1999). Further fuel was added to this fire at the 2001 general election when turnout was particularly low in Labour's traditional heartlands (Butler and Kavanagh 2001). It seems as though Labour's apparent drift to the right might have succeeded in eliminating the traditional class divide in British politics.

The idea that Labour's more right wing stance might cause it to lose working-class supporters while gaining middle-class ones rests of course on crucial premise – that those belonging to the working class do indeed have different views from those in the middle class on the traditional 'left–right' issues of redistribution, taxation and spending. However, using data from the 1999 British Social Attitudes survey, Evans (2000) argued that there were now only small differences in attitudes between social classes on such topics, and that instead they disagreed more about social and moral issues. But there are some grounds for suspecting that what might be true of Britain as a whole is not necessarily true of Scotland. Analyses of attitudes towards 'left–right' issues show that they are influenced by national identity in such a way that social class differences are exaggerated (Brown et al. 2000: chapter 4). Thus in this chapter our principal aim is to establish whether or not there are still important differences in the social outlook of those in different social classes in Scotland, and whether the existence of such differences means that Scotland is different from England.

– Measuring social class –

Until recently, the measures of social class commonly used by academic sociologists were different from those used in government surveys and in the census. Perhaps the most commonly used academic measure in recent years was the schema invented by John Goldthorpe (Goldthorpe 1987), while the one used most commonly in government surveys was Registrar General's social class. The Goldthorpe schema, however, proved to have at least one key advantage when analysing social and political attitudes in that it alone separates out the self-employed and small-business owners (known together as the 'petty bourgeoisie') who have distinctive right-wing attitudes and are particularly likely to vote Conservative (Heath et al. 1985, 1991).

In 1994, the Office of Population Censuses and Surveys (now part of the Office of National Statistics) commissioned a review of official social classifications, including the Registrar General's social class scheme. This review resulted in a new scheme, the National Statistics Socio-Economic Classification (NS-Sec) being introduced for all official surveys from the 2001 census of population. Although not strictly identical to the Goldthorpe schema, NS-Sec is based on similar principles. As shown in table 7.1, it comes in a number of different versions (as indeed does the Goldthorpe schema), but in this chapter we will use the five class version. Preliminary analysis of our data found little difference in attitudes between those groups that are collapsed to produce this version, while the distinctive attitudes of small employers and own account workers to which we have already alluded means that a three class scheme was inappropriate for our purposes.

Table 7.1 Categories of the NS-Sec

Operational categories	Analytic class schemes			
	Eight category	Seven category	Five category	Three category
L1 Employers in large establishments	1.1 Large employers and higher managerial occupations	1. Higher managerial and professional occupations	1. Managerial and professional occupations	1. Managerial and professional occupations
L2 Higher managerial occupations				
L3 Higher professional occupations	1.2 Higher professional occupations			
L4 Lower professional and higher technical occupations	2. Lower managerial and professional occupations	2. Lower managerial and professional occupations		
L5 Lower managerial occupations				
L6 Higher supervisory occupations				
L7 Intermediate occupations	3. Intermediate occupations	3. Intermediate occupations	2. Intermediate occupations	2. Intermediate occupations
L8 Employers in small establishments	4. Small employers and own account workers	4. Small employers and own account workers	3. Small employers and own account workers	
L9 Own account workers				
L10 Lower supervisory occupations	5. Lower supervisory and technical occupations	5. Lower supervisory and technical occupations	4. Lower supervisory and technical occupations	3. Lower occupations
L11 Lower technical occupations				
L12 Semi-routine occupations	6. Semi-routine occupations	6. Semi-routine occupations	5. Semi-routine and routine occupations	
L13 Routine occupations	7. Routine occupations	7. Routine occupations		

Source: Rose and Pevalin (2001)

The Goldthorpe schema, Registrar General's social class and NS-Sec all share one characteristic in common, as indeed do many other measures of class. This is that they identify the class to which people belong on the basis of their (or their spouse's) occupation. But there is another possible approach. This is to ask people themselves whether they feel they belong to a class and, if so, which. Such 'class identities' were captured in our survey by asking:

Do you ever think of yourself as belonging to any particular class? If Yes: Which class is that?

Those respondents who either said 'No' or said they were something other than middle or working class were then asked a follow-up question to acquire a 'forced' choice class identity, as follows:

*Most people say they belong either to the middle class or the working class. If you **had** to make a choice, would you call yourself middle class or working class?*

Even if people in different kinds of occupations do not have different attitudes, those who feel they belong to different classes might still do so. In this chapter we therefore also look at how attitudes vary by class identity, doing so for the most part by looking at the differences between those who spontaneously assign themselves to the middle or working class on our single 'unforced' measure.

– OCCUPATION AND IDENTITY –

If indeed we have witnessed a decline of class then we might expect to find that relatively few people now have a class identity. Moreover, we might also anticipate that even amongst those who do identify with a class, those who claim membership of any particular class come from a variety of occupational class positions. So we show in table 7.2 for both Scotland and England how many people in each occupational class acknowledge a class identity on our unforced measure.

A majority of people in both Scotland and in England do not in fact consider themselves to belong to a social class. That is also true of each individual occupational class. But amongst those who do claim a class identity, more people in Scotland say they are working class than is the case in England. Nearly one in three people in Scotland say they are working class compared with only just over one in five in England. This difference persists within each occupational class. A possible explanation is put forward by Brown et al. who show that in Scotland those who feel Scottish are more likely to say they are working class, whereas in England a person's sense of national identity does not make any difference to their class identity. And as many people in Scotland say they feel Scottish (see Chapter 6), this means they are more likely to say they are working class (for further details see Brown et al. 1999: chapter 3).

Table 7.2 Occupational class and class identity

Class identity	Managers and professionals	Intermediate	Self-employed	Supervisors and technical	Semi-routine and routine	All
	%	%	%	%	%	%
Scotland						
Middle class	20	10	8	6	7	11
Working class	23	25	27	41	40	31
No class	57	64	65	53	53	56
Other	1	1	–	1	1	1
Sample size	*460*	*170*	*70*	*161*	*587*	*1585*
England						
Middle class	29	19	21	9	10	19
Working class	14	19	17	29	29	21
No class	56	60	61	59	59	58
Other	1	2	1	2	2	2
Sample size	*943*	*364*	*214*	*308*	*865*	*2704*

The failure of so many people on both sides of the border to say that they belong to a class would appear to support the 'death of class' thesis. However, when people are asked the 'forced' choice measure only around 4 per cent of people in both Scotland and England are unwilling to say that they are either middle or working class. So evidently these terms still have some resonance. In any event, even if there are low levels of class identity we cannot assume that people in different occupational classes do not have different attitudes. After all, we can already see from table 7.2 that even on our unforced measure those in the supervisory and technical, and semi-routine and routine occupational classes are far more likely to say they are working class than are those in any of the other three classes. And those who do have a class identity may of course have markedly different views. So in the analyses that follow, we look at the relationship between people's attitudes and both their occupational class and how they responded to our unforced measure of class identity.

– Social class and social attitudes –

Our key question in this chapter is then whether those in different classes in Scotland, either as measured by their occupation or by their self-identity, hold different views, and whether or not class differences in Scotland are greater than they are in England. In so doing we look at three broad sets of attitudes. The first set may be termed 'economic' attitudes. These include redistribution, taxation and spending together with public ownership and constitute the traditional 'left–right' ideological dimension of British politics. The second set comprises social and moral issues such as censorship and drug usage and these constitute the 'liberal–authoritarian' dimension of British politics. The final set are about people's attitudes towards politics and the political system, and in particular whether people feel they have an effective voice in politics, an attribute that is often known as 'political efficacy'. We begin by looking at the 'left–right' divide.

– The 'left–right' divide –

It is often argued that the biggest differences between those in different classes are to be found on the traditional 'left–right' issues of redistribution, taxation and public ownership. This is because it is assumed that people's attitudes are influenced by their self-interest and it would appear that those in the working class would benefit from redistribution and more spending on the welfare state, while the middle classes are harder hit by higher taxation. So we would anticipate that the working class is more in favour of higher spending, redistribution and higher taxation than the middle class.

One possible indication of whether this is so can be found by looking at the answers to the following question:

Suppose the government had to choose between the three options on this card. Which do you think it should choose?
Reduce taxes and spend **less** *on health, education and social benefits.*
Keep taxes and spending on these services at the **same** *level as now.*
Increase taxes and spend **more** *on health, education and social benefits.*

Table 7.3 shows how those in different occupational classes answered this question.

Table 7.3 Attitudes to taxation, by occupational class

	Managers and professionals	Intermediate	Self-employed	Supervisors and technical	Semi-routine and routine	All
	Occupational class					
	%	%	%	%	%	%
Scotland						
Reduce taxes and spend less	3	4	4	3	4	3
Keep taxes and spending the same	27	25	32	31	33	30
Increase taxes and spend more	66	69	59	64	59	63
None of these	3	2	6	2	2	3
Sample size	*460*	*170*	*70*	*161*	*587*	*1585*
England						
Reduce taxes and spend less	2	3	2	4	4	6
Keep taxes and spending the same	33	29	39	38	33	34
Increase taxes and spend more	62	65	57	55	59	60
None	4	3	2	3	3	3
Sample size	*943*	*364*	*214*	*308*	*865*	*2704*

In line with the findings of Evans (2000), the differences of attitude between the social classes on this issue are small. A large majority in each social class would prefer to see increased taxation and more spending on health, education and social benefits. This is more or less equally true on both sides of the border. Moreover, contrary to what we might expect, it is those in managerial and professional, and intermediate occupations who if anything are most in favour of higher taxes and more spending. True, when we look at how attitudes vary by class identity as in table 7.4 it is those who identify themselves as working class who are somewhat more likely to back higher taxes and higher spending, but again what is most notable is the smallness of the difference that we see.

Not only do the classes by and large agree on the need for more taxes and higher spending, but they also largely agree on what the extra money should be spent. In each class, over 50 per cent said that health was their highest priority for more spending while in each case more education spending was the second most popular priority. Recent decisions by the UK Labour government to increase taxes and spend more money on health in particular seem to be exactly in line with public opinion in both Scotland and England.

Table 7.4 Attitudes to taxation, by class identity

| | Class identity | | | All |
	Middle class	Working class	None	
	%	%	%	%
Scotland				
Reduce taxes and spend less	2	2	4	3
Keep taxes and spending the same	36	28	30	30
Increase taxes and spend more	59	66	63	63
None of these	3	3	3	3
Sample Size	*175*	*525*	*885*	*1585*
England				
Reduce taxes and spend less	4	2	3	6
Keep taxes and spending the same	31	31	35	34
Increase taxes and spend more	60	63	59	60
None of these	5	3	3	3
Sample Size	*522*	*601*	*1581*	*2704*

We should, however, perhaps not be surprised at the large measure of agreement that we find in tables 7.3 and 7.4. After all, there seems to be a near universal agreement that even after four years of a Labour government, public services need to be improved. Moreover, the areas on which people want extra spending, the NHS and education, are universal services from which people in all classes benefit rather than those in any one particular class. Other left–right issues such as the merits of public versus private ownership, the role of trade unions and the distribution of wealth might be expected to be more likely to provide evidence of class differences. We look at this possibility so far as occupational class is concerned in table 7.5.

The table shows how our respondents reacted to six statements of relevance to the left–right dimension. Where a statement was worded in a left-wing direction we show the proportion who *agreed* with the statement while where it was worded in a right-wing direction we show the proportion who *disagreed*. Thus the table shows the proportion giving the left-wing response in each case. In addition, the final column presents a measure of class 'polarisation'. This is the simply the difference between the class giving the most left-wing response for that statement and the class displaying the least left-wing attitudes.[1] For two of the statements we are also able to compare the position in Scotland with that in England.

Table 7.5 Left–right attitudes, by occupational class

	Occupational class					
	Managers and professionals	Intermediate	Self-employed	Supervisors and technical	Semi-routine and routine	Class polarisation
% agree:						
It is the government's responsibility to provide a job for everyone who wants one						
Scotland	38	55	43	59	61	23
There is one law for the rich and one for the poor						
Scotland	58	67	63	75	76	18
England	48	58	48	65	64	17
Major public services and industries ought to be in state ownership						
Scotland	45	46	33	51	40	18
% disagree:						
Ordinary working people get their fair share of the nation's wealth						
Scotland	54	70	59	67	60	16
England	53	57	47	66	66	19
Private enterprise is the best way to solve Britain's economic problems						
Scotland	34	39	29	44	39	15
There is no need for strong trade unions to protect employees' working conditions and wages						
Scotland	69	74	64	71	67	10
Sample size						
Scotland	*405*	*155*	*60*	*145*	*490*	
England	*819*	*307*	*182*	*261*	*724*	

Table 7.5 clearly shows that even on these statements there is considerable agreement between the classes. For nearly all of the statements either all of the classes give majority support to the left-wing response or else none of them do. So to that extent at least such differences as we can identify between the social classes are differences of degree rather than of kind. But differences do exist. They are most apparent on whether it is the government's responsibility to provide jobs and whether there is one law for the rich and one for the poor. Thus, for example, more than three in five of those in semi-routine and routine occupations in Scotland believe it is the government's responsibility to provide a job for everyone who wants one, but this is true of less than two in five of those in managerial and professional jobs.

However, no single class emerges as consistently the most or the least left-wing. On the merits of public ownership versus private enterprise, the self-employed appear to be the least 'left-wing', but on the responsibility of government and perceptions of the distribution of wealth it is managers and professionals who occupy that position. These differences are perhaps consistent with what one would expect. The self-employed are engaged in private enterprise and would thus be expected to be most supportive of it. In contrast managers and professionals have the best paid and most secure occupations and thus are least likely to appreciate the merits of greater equality. Meanwhile on some issues those in semi-routine and routine occupations are the most likely to give a left-wing response, while on other statements it is those in lower supervisory and technical positions who do so.

On the two statements where we can also examine attitudes in England, it appears that Scots in any given occupational class are somewhat more likely to adopt a left-wing position than are people in England (see also Chapter 1 and Paterson 2002). For example, 58 per cent of managers and professionals in Scotland believe that there is one law for the rich and one for the poor compared with 48 per cent in England. However, it does not appear that class polarisation is any greater in Scotland than it is in England. Rather, the incidence of left-wing attitudes varies to a modest extent on both sides of the border.

Even so, we might have anticipated that we would find bigger differences in attitudes between those who readily identify themselves as middle or working class than we do in respect of occupational class. After all, these are the people for whom class apparently has some meaning. Yet as table 7.6 reveals this is not the case – in either Scotland or England. Rather the differences in the propensity of middle-class and working-class identifiers to give a left-wing response, as indicated in our measure of class polarisation, are not dissimilar to the polarisation figures for occupational class in table 7.5. Meanwhile, the attitudes of those who do not readily identify themselves as middle or working class lie somewhere in between those of the two sets of identifiers.

Thus we secure the same message irrespective of whether we measure social class by occupation or self-identity. There are some differences between the classes on traditional 'left–right' issues but they are no more than modest ones. Perhaps the advent of New Labour either reflects or has helped bring about a decline in traditional class politics in Scotland in much the same way that previous research has suggested it has done in England. But if that is so can we find any evidence that a new politics might be taking its place?

Table 7.6 Left–right attitudes, by class identity

	Class identity			Class
	Middle class	Working class	None	polarisation
	%	%	%	%
% agree:				
There is one law for the rich and one for the poor				
Scotland	54	77	66	23
England	49	66	55	18
It is the government's responsibility to provide a job for everyone who wants one				
Scotland	46	62	50	16
Major public services ought to be in state ownership				
Scotland	40	53	40	13
% disagree:				
Private enterprise is the best way to solve Britain's economic problems				
Scotland	25	44	36	19
Ordinary working people get their fair share of the nation's wealth				
Scotland	54	70	57	16
England	47	72	57	25
There is no need for strong trade unions to protect employees' working conditions and wages				
Scotland	58	72	62	14
Sample size				
Scotland	157	439	769	
England	459	494	1343	

– LIBERAL–AUTHORITARIAN ATTITUDES –

One widely touted possibility is that traditional left–right issues have been replaced by arguments about social issues. Certainly previous research has indicated that attitudes towards such issues form a separate 'libertarian–authoritarian' ideological dimension (Evans et al. 1996), although others prefer to talk of a 'materialist–post-materialist' one. The claim that this dimension has become more important in recent years is expressed eloquently by Clark and Lipset:

> The classical left–right dimension has been transformed. People still speak of left and right, but the definitions are changing. There are now two lefts, with

distinct social bases. The traditional left is blue-collar based and stresses class-related issues. But a second left is emerging in Western societies (sometimes termed New Politics, New Left, Post-Bourgeois, or Post-Materialist) which increasingly stresses social issues rather than traditional political issues. (Clark and Lipset 1996: 45)

Clark and Lipset assume that attitudes towards social issues do not vary according to social class because people in different classes do not have different interests on these issues. As a result the rising importance of social issues helps explain why class matters less now in determining how people vote. But as we noted earlier, Evans (2000) in contrast has suggested that attitudes towards social issues do vary by class, and indeed that they now do so to a greater extent than do traditional left–right issues. Table 7.7 helps us assess which of those two views is correct by looking at the proportion of people in each occupational class that gives the 'authoritarian' response to a set of statements that capture this second ideological dimension. It also shows a measure of class polarisation analogous to that in table 7.5.

Table 7.7 Liberal–authoritarian attitudes, by occupational class

% agree	Occupational class					Class polarisation
	Managers and professionals	Intermediate	Self-employed	Supervisory and technical	Semi-routine and routine	
For some crimes the death penalty is the most appropriate sentence						
Scotland	40	52	64	71	55	31
England	40	53	59	65	59	25
People who break the law should be given stiffer sentences						
Scotland	66	83	72	83	83	17
England	69	83	83	90	84	21
Schools should teach children to obey authority						
Scotland	73	81	83	88	81	15
England	76	81	87	88	84	12
Censorship of films and magazines is necessary to uphold moral standards						
Scotland	59	73	52	65	63	14
England	58	68	68	63	67	10
Young people today don't have enough respect for traditional British values						
Scotland	59	68	71	70	69	12
England	62	70	71	77	70	15
The law should always be obeyed, even if a particular law is wrong						
Scotland	38	38	37	37	27	11
England	37	38	47	44	44	10
Sample size						
Scotland	405	155	60	145	90	
England	819	307	182	261	724	

We can see that in fact those in different occupational classes do vary in their propensity to agree with these statements. But equally just as the differences on the traditional left–right issues were for the most part modest, so also are the differences here. Thus our measure of class polarisation exhibits similar values to those in table 7.5. And with the exception only of attitudes towards the death penalty, the majority view is the same in every class. Moreover, on all but whether the law should always be obeyed that view is an authoritarian one. The one class that fails to share the majority view on the death penalty is that comprising those in managerial and professional occupations. Indeed the views of this class tend in general to be distinctively relatively liberal. Why this might be so is a subject to which we will return. But for the moment at least we should note that while those in different classes do appear to differ in their views on social issues, at the same time the class that is most likely to support the liberalism of the New Left is not the same class as the one that is most likely to support the traditional position of the Old Left. And in this Scotland again is no different from England.

Table 7.8 Liberal–authoritarian attitudes, by class identity

	Class identity			Class
% agree:	Middle class	Working class	None	polarisation
For some crimes the death penalty is the most appropriate sentence				
Scotland	41	59	50	18
England	38	60	54	22
People who break the law should be given stiffer sentences				
Scotland	63	81	76	15
England	69	86	79	17
Young people today don't have enough respect for traditional British values				
Scotland	58	70	64	12
England	64	72	67	8
The law should always be obeyed, even if a particular law is wrong				
Scotland	30	37	38	7
England	39	41	42	2
Schools should teach children to obey authority				
Scotland	78	81	77	3
England	78	84	78	6
Censorship of films and magazines is necessary to uphold moral standards				
Scotland	64	65	61	1
England	65	61	63	4
Sample size				
Scotland	*157*	*439*	*769*	
England	*459*	*494*	*1343*	

But if those in different occupational classes have somewhat different views on social issues, it does not appear to be the case that whether someone feels middle or working class has an impact on their views. Rather, as table 7.8 shows, those who say they feel middle class have for the most part very similar views to those who say they belong to the working class. Only on the death penalty and whether young people have enough respect for traditional values are there any notable differences at all, with those who say they are middle class being more likely to adopt a liberal view. We should perhaps after all be cautious in concluding that class matters as much on social issues as it does on more traditional left–right ones.

– Political efficacy –

People's trust in politics and their sense that the political system will respond to their demands has declined in recent years (Bromley and Curtice 2002; see also Chapter 1). Indeed it has been argued that this might be the reason why turnout has been so low at recent elections. Turnout has previously been shown to vary by social class (Heath and Taylor 1999), but arguably relatively little attention has been paid to whether those in different social classes have different perceptions of politics and the political process. Here we look at whether this is so, focusing in particular on people's sense of political efficacy, that is whether people feel able to get involved in politics and whether their doing so will make any difference.

Table 7.9 Political efficacy, by occupational class

	Occupational class					
% agree:	Managers and professionals	Intermediate	Self-employed	Supervisory and technical	Semi-routine and routine	Class polarisation
People like me have no say in what government does						
Scotland	54	61	65	75	72	21
England	50	58	62	59	58	12
It doesn't really matter which party is in power, in the end things go on much the same						
Scotland	50	61	58	62	61	12
England	49	65	70	70	71	22
Generally speaking those we elect as MPs lose touch with people pretty quickly						
Scotland	66	65	73	76	76	11
England	66	71	76	78	76	12
Parties are only interested in people's votes, not their opinions						
Scotland	70	68	70	69	79	11
England	69	77	76	77	78	9
Sample size						
Scotland	*460*	*170*	*70*	*161*	*587*	
England	*943*	*364*	*214*	*308*	*865*	

Political efficacy is in general clearly low. A very large majority of all social classes agree that 'people like me have no say in government', 'MPs lose touch with people quickly', 'parties are only interested in votes' and 'it doesn't matter much which party is in power'. But the classes do vary somewhat in the extent of their disillusion. In Scotland at least, the greatest class difference is found on whether 'people like me have no say in government'; three-quarters of those in semi-routine and routine occupations agree with this statement compared with only about half of managers and professionals. Indeed the latter group was the one least likely to give a disillusioned response to the items in table 7.9. However, our measure of class polarisation is for the most part lower than it was in respect of left–right issues, and thus for the most part can only be described as modest indeed. Meanwhile, on this topic too the pattern of attitudes in Scotland for the most part looks very similar to that in England.

Table 7.10 Political efficacy, by class identity

| % agree: | Class identity | | | Class polarisation |
	Middle class	Working class	None	
It doesn't really matter which party is in power, in the end things go on much the same				
Scotland	46	65	64	21
England	55	65	64	10
Generally speaking those we elect as MPs lose touch with people pretty quickly				
Scotland	56	76	72	20
England	64	77	73	13
Parties are only interested in people's votes, not their opinions				
Scotland	57	77	75	20
England	68	79	74	11
People like me have no say in what government does				
Scotland	56	68	66	12
England	58	70	66	12
Sample size				
Scotland	175	525	885	
England	522	601	1581	

These modest differences are confirmed in table 7.10 when we look at class identity. Those who say they feel working class are in general more disillusioned than those who say they belong to the middle class. Intriguingly, middle class identifiers are particularly less likely to feel disillusioned in Scotland, marking them out not only from those who say they are working class but also those who do not claim a class identity.

– Is social class key? –

So far, then, three key points emerge from our analysis. First, there are some modest differences of outlook between those in different classes in Scotland. However, all this simply means is that there are differences in the size of the majority in favour of a particular proposition rather than that a majority of one class takes one view and a majority of another class a different perspective. Indeed, most people in most classes adopt a left-wing stance on traditional left–right issues, uphold an authoritarian view on social issues and exhibit a low level of political efficacy. Second, class differences in Scotland are largely of a similar magnitude to those in England. And third, it seems possible that contrary to Evans (2000), class may still make more difference to people's views on traditional left–right issues than it does on social ones. But it is whether that last statement is really correct that we now pursue further.

All we have done so far is to see whether those in different social classes are more or less likely to agree with various propositions. But demonstrating that those in different classes have different views does not necessarily prove that they hold those different views *because* they belong to different classes. After all, those in different classes also differ on other attributes. Those in managerial and professional occupations for the most part have higher levels of educational attainment than do those in semi-routine and routine occupations. Perhaps some or all of differences of view we have seen are a reflection of differences in education rather than class. In order to establish whether social class really is the key to the differences that we observed, we undertook for Scotland a multivariate analysis of each of the attitudes we have analysed so far. In these analyses we not only examined the influence of both occupational class and class identity, but also that of age, gender, education level, housing tenure, religion and national identity.[2] So the results show the impact of social class after controlling for these other variables. In the following tables we present a summary of the results of each model showing which attributes were statistically significantly related to the attitude in question. (The full results of each model can be found in the Appendix to this chapter.)

Table 7.11 shows the result of these models for six traditional 'left–right' issues. It confirms that even allowing for the other possible influences in the models, those in different classes – either as measured by occupational class and/or class identity – do have significantly different views that cannot simply be ascribed to other social characteristics. At the same time other influences also seem to come into play. The most consistent of these is national identity. As has previously been noted by Brown et al. (1999), those who say they are wholly or mostly Scottish are more likely to adopt a left-wing view than are those who say they are British. We also find that on a number of items those aged 18 to 34 are less likely to adopt a left-wing stance than are their counterparts aged 35 to 64, a result that may suggest that their views have been influenced by having grown up at a time when traditional left-wing attitudes have been less widely espoused by Britain's politicians.

Table 7.11 Models of left–right attitudes

Ordinary people fair share of wealth	One law for rich	No need for strong TUs	Private enterprise best	Major services state owned	Government responsibility to provide jobs
Occupational Class	Occupational Class			Occupational Class	Occupational Class
Class ID	Class ID	Class ID	Class ID	Class ID	
	Education				Education
Age	Age		Age	Age	
	Tenure	Tenure			Tenure
					Religion
National ID	National ID		National ID		National ID

Table 7.12 shows the results of the same modelling exercise for social issues. They confirm our earlier finding that class identity does not make much difference to people's views on this subject. Only in a few cases are there significant differences between those in different occupational classes after we allow for differences in educational level. Instead education is consistently the most important influence on attitudes to social issues, with those who have had a degree-level education being more likely to adopt a liberal position. In addition, those who are younger and those who do not adhere to a religion are also more likely to have a liberal view.

Table 7.12 Models of liberal–authoritarian attitudes

Traditional values	Stiffer sentences	Death penalty	Schools teach obey	Obey law children to wrong	Censorship even if
Occupational class	Occupational class				
		Class ID			
Education	Education	Education		Education	Education
Education					
Age	Age		Age	Age	Age
			Gender		Gender
Tenure	Tenure			Tenure	
Religion		Religion			Religion
	National ID	National ID			National ID
National ID					

So it seems that neither Evans nor Clark and Lipset are correct, at least so far as Scotland is concerned. Contrary to Evans, class does not have as consistent an influence on attitudes towards social issues as it does on attitudes towards more traditional left–right issues. At the same time, however, contrary to Clark and Lipset there are some significant class differences in attitudes towards social issues, differences that cannot simply be put down to variations in levels of educational attainment. Attitudes in Scotland may not be deeply polarised by class but it appears that it is wrong to believe that class is dead.

Table 7.13 Models of political efficacy

No say in government	MPs lose touch	Parties interested in votes	Doesn't matter which party in power
Occupational class	Occupational class	Occupational class	Occupational class
	Class ID	Class ID	
Education			Education
		Gender	
Tenure			Tenure
National ID	National ID	National ID	National ID

Finally, table 7.13 shows the results of our modelling of political efficacy. In each case occupational class proves to be significant while in two cases so also is class identity. So once again it appears that class still matters. Indeed the only other consistent influence is national identity. Those who say they are Scottish and not British are more likely to be disillusioned with the political system, perhaps because some of them would prefer an independent Scotland. In contrast we should note that contrary to much popular commentary (but see Curtice and Jowell 1995), younger people are not significantly more disillusioned with the political system than are their elders.

– Conclusions –

There is then a relatively clear answer to the key question that we have been addressing in this chapter. Scotland has not as yet witnessed the 'death of class'. Those in different classes do have different views. And while these differences may be strongest in respect of traditional left–right issues, they are also differences of view about social issues and about political efficacy. But at the same time we have found that there is nothing particularly Scottish about this finding. Despite the fact that Scotland's distinctive pattern of national identity makes a difference to people's views and despite the existence of a rather different party system, for the most part the differences of view we have found between the classes in Scotland are similar to the differences of view to be found in England.

At the same time we have also discovered that most of the differences we have uncovered are modest. Often those in different classes simply disagree about how much they agree with a proposition rather than take diametrically opposite positions. This would seem to suggest that claims that Labour is in danger of losing working-class votes with its apparent move to the right are misplaced. But to this conclusion there are two important caveats. First, the consensus that emerges on traditional left–right issues proves to be predominantly a left-wing rather than a right-wing one. Moving too far to the right would apparently put Labour in danger of losing votes amongst all classes rather than just the working class, as perhaps the party's decision in the 2001 Budget to raise taxes and spending acknowledged. And second, even though the differences of view between the classes are similar in Scotland to those in England, at the same time those in any given class in Scotland are somewhat more likely to take a left-wing stance than are their counterparts south of the border. In short, moving too far to the right may be particularly a danger for Labour in Scotland, especially given the presence of an alternative centre-left party in the form of the SNP. In adopting a cool response to some of the ideas being promoted by the UK Labour government south of the border for greater use of the market in delivering health and education, Labour in Scotland may well be displaying sound electoral sense.

– Appendix –

The models summarised in tables 7.11, 7.12 and 7.13 are logistic regression models (for further details see the Technical Appendix). In the case of traditional left–right issues each dependent variable was scored such that 1 represented a 'left-wing' view, 0 otherwise. On social issues, 1 represented an 'authoritarian' view, 0 otherwise, while on our political efficacy items, 1 represented a disillusioned response, 0 otherwise. The same set of independent variables was used in each model. The details of each of these is given below, with the reference category in the models shown in brackets.

Occupational class
    Managers and professionals
    Intermediate
    Self-employed
    Lower supervisory and technical
    (Semi-routine and routine)

Class identity
  Middle class
  (Working class)
  None

Age
  18–34
  (35–64)
  65+

Gender
  Female
  (Male)

Educational level
  Degree
  (No Degree)

Tenure
  Owner-occupier
  (Non owner-occupier)

Religion
  Catholic
  Other Christian
  (No religion)

National identity
  Scottish not British
  Scottish more than British
  (Scottish and British equally)
  British more than Scottish
  British not Scottish

The coefficients for each category in all of the models are shown in the following table. Given the way in which the dependent variables are scored, a positive coefficient indicates an increased probability compared with those respondents in the reference category of giving a left-wing, an authoritarian or a disillusioned response, while a negative coefficient represents a reduced chance of giving such a response.

Table 7A.1 Models of left–right attitudes

	Ordinary people fair share of wealth	One law for rich	No need for strong TUs	Private enterprise best	Major services state owned	Government responsibility to provide jobs
Class						
Managerial	-0·075	-0·440*	-0·016	-0·280	0·182	-0·523**
Intermediate	0·537**	-0·217	0·310	0·052	0·396*	-0·161
Self-employed	0·232	-0·729*	-0·226	-0·570	-0·362	-0·570*
Supervisory	0·301	-0·176	0·163	0·105	0·343	0·101
Class ID						
Middle	-0·691**	-0·503*	-0·653**	-0·801*	-0·553**	-0·112
None	-0·542**	-0·460**	-0·264*	-0·185	-0·473**	-0·215
Education						
Degree	0·072	-0·583**	0·089	0·224	0·130	-0·558**
Age						
18–34	-0·403**	-0·531**	-0·031	-0·689**	-0·452**	-0·216
65+	-0·559**	0·059	-0·152	-0·054	0·314*	-0·049
Gender						
Female	0·182	-0·221	0·069	-0·102	-0·131	0·151
Tenure						
Owner	-0·182	-0·365*	0·324*	-0·090	0·094	-0·434**
Religion						
Catholic	-0·147	0·147	0·265	-0·088	0·114	0·583**
Other Christian	-0·204	-0·169	0·134	-0·180	-0·166	0·102
National ID						
Scottish only	0·743**	0·708**	0·029	0·257	0·030	0·255
More Scottish	0·694**	0·123	-0·042	0·101	0·097	0·358*
More British	-0·054	-0·400	-0·293	-0·313	-0·049	0·196
British only	0·284	-0·144	-0·389	-0·802*	0·097	-1·164**

** Coefficient significant at the 1% level.
* Coefficient significant at the 5% level.

Table 7A.2 Models of liberal–authoritarian attitudes

	Traditional values	Stiffer sentences	Death penalty	Schools teach children to obey	Obey law even if wrong	Censorship
Class						
Managerial	-0·462*	-0·568**	-0·262	-0·269	0·207	-0·137
Intermediate	-0·105	0·088	0·135	0·011	-0·009	0·300
Self-employed	-0·271	-0·795*	0·228	0·193	-0·173	-0·435
Supervisory	-0·071	-0·058	0·348	0·538	-0·058	0·250
Class ID						
Middle	-0·196	-0·416	-0·309	0·035	-0·148	0·169
None	-0·153	-0·057	-0·327*	-0·097	0·190	-0·074
Education						
Degree	-0·489	-1·017**	-0·811**	-0·710**	-0·507*	-0·482*
Age						
18–34	-0·841**	-0·763**	-0·204	-0·090	-0·421**	-0·895**
65+	0·802**	0·403	-0·179	0·681**	0·255	0·539**

Gender						
Female	0·014	0·240	-0·767**	0·120	-0·095	0·734**
Tenure						
Owner	0·448**	0·379*	0·007	0·188	-0·109	0·223
Religion						
Catholic	0·232	0·387	-0·183	0·691**	-0·008	0·717**
Other Christian	0·619**	-0·001	-0·104	0·750**	0·270	0·640**
National ID						
Scottish only	0·051	0·455*	0·642**	-0·074	-0·226	0·128
More Scottish	-0·236	0·245	0·180	-0·089	-0·499*	-0·107
More British	0·680	-0·275	0·361	0·423	0·330	1·426**
British only	0·220	-0·248	0·243	0·181	-0·713	0·347

** Coefficient significant at the 1% level.
* Coefficient significant at the 5% level.

Table 7A.3 Models of political efficacy

	No say in govern- ment	MPs lose touch	Parties interested in votes	Doesn't matter which party in power
Class				
Managerial	-0·450**	-0·219	-0·186	-0·466**
Intermediate	-0·441*	-0·443*	-0·541**	-0·363
Self-employed	-0·127	0·017	-0·291	-0·370
Supervisory	0·188	-0·11	-0·405	-0·299
Class ID				
Middle	-0·016	-0·566**	-0·596**	-0·347
None	0·045	-0·086	0·047	0·180
Education				
Degree	-0·524**	-0·187	-0·118	-0·410*
Age				
18–34	-0·053	-0·009	-0·273	-0·217
65+	0·229	0·324*	0·100	0·159
Gender				
Female	0·131	-0·041	0·269*	0·215
Tenure				
Owner	-0·326*	-0·174	-0·261	-0·330*
Religion				
Catholic	-0·116	0·147	-0·004	-0·196
Other Christian	0·014	-0·009	0·084	-0·035
National ID				
Scottish only	0·410*	0·286	0·598**	0·449**
More Scottish	-0·029	0·002	-0·053	-0·146
More British	-0·184	-0·653*	0·091	-0·329
British only	-0·056	0·837*	0·938**	0·043

** Coefficient significant at the 1% level.
* Coefficient significant at the 5% level.

– References –

Bromley, C. and Curtice, J. (2002), 'Where have all the voters gone?', in A. Park, J. Curtice, K. Thomson, L. Jarvis and C. Bromley (eds), *British Social Attitudes: the 19th report*, London: Sage.

Brown, A., McCrone, D., Paterson, L. and Surridge, P. (1999), *The Scottish Electorate: The 1997 General Election and Beyond*, London: Macmillan.

Butler, D. and Kavanagh, D. (2001), *The British General Election of 2001*, London: Palgrave.

Clark, T. and Lipset, S. (1996) 'Are social classes dying?', in D. Lee and B. Turner (eds), *Conflicts about Class*, Harlow: Longman.

Curtice, J. and Jowell, R. (1995), 'The sceptical electorate', in R. Jowell, J. Curtice, A. Park, L. Brook and D. Ahrendt (eds), *British Social Attitudes: the 12th report*, Aldershot: Dartmouth.

Evans, G (2000), 'The working class and New Labour: a parting of the ways', in R. Jowell, J. Curtice, A. Park, K. Thomson, L. Jarvis, C. Bromley and N. Stratford (eds), *British Social Attitudes: the 17th report*, London: Sage.

Evans, G., Heath, A. and Lalljee, M. (1996), 'Measuring left–right and libertarian–authoritarian values in the British electorate', *British Journal of Sociology*, 47, pp. 93–112.

Evans, G. and Norris, P. (eds) (1999), *Critical Elections: British Parties and Voters in Long-term Perspective*, London: Sage.

Goldthorpe, J. (1987), *Social Mobility and Class Structure in Britain*, second edition, Oxford: Clarendon.

Heath, A., Jowell, R. and Curtice, J. (1985), *How Britain Votes*, Oxford: Pergamon.

Heath, A., Jowell, R., Curtice, J., Evans, G., Field, J. and Witherspoon, S. (1991), *Understanding Political Change: The British Voter 1964–1987*, Oxford: Pergamon.

Heath, A. and Taylor, B. (1999), 'New source of abstention?', in G. Evans and P. Norris (eds), *Critical Elections: British Parties and Voters in Long-term Perspective*, London: Sage.

Nisbet, R. (1959), 'The decline and fall of social class', *Pacific Sociological Review*, 2, pp. 11–17.

Pahl, R. (1996), 'Is the emperor naked?', in D. Lee and B. Turner (eds) *Conflicts about Class*, Harlow: Longman.

Pakulski, J. and Waters, M. (1996), *The Death of Class*, London: Sage.

Paterson, L. (2002), 'Governing from the centre: ideology and public policy', in J. Curtice, D. McCrone, A. Park and L. Paterson (eds), *New Scotland, New Society?*, Edinburgh: Polygon.

Rose, D. and Pevalin, D. J. (2001), *The National Statistics Sociolo-economic Classification: Unifying Official and Sociological Approaches to the Conceptualisation of Measurement of Social Class*, Colchester: ISER Working Papers, University of Essex.

– NOTES –

1. This measure will of course produce bigger class differences than if we were to report the difference between the same two classes for each item. However, as the occupational classification is not a strictly hierarchical one there is no clear theoretical basis on which to predict in advance which the most and least 'left wing' classes would be.
2. For full details of the coding of each variable, see the Appendix to this chapter.

CHAPTER 8

Disengaged Individualists?
Young People in Scotland

Alison Park and Kerstin Hinds

– INTRODUCTION –

Previous chapters in this book have looked at the attitudes of the Scottish population as a whole or focused on the many differences that exist between the attitudes and values of particular groups. In so doing, many of them have found that younger and older people often have remarkably divergent views.

In this chapter we examine in detail just what young people in particular think. We focus on their views (rather than, say, those of older groups) because of a desire to shed light on a subject of increasing interest and concern within Scotland – the relationship between young people as citizens and the society within which they live. In particular, concern is frequently voiced about the extent to which young people have become disengaged from a number of traditional civic institutions and practices, particularly political ones (Wilkinson and Mulgan 1995). Moreover, it has been claimed that the young are becoming more individualistic in their outlook, and thus less likely to join organisations aimed at advancing collective interests, the most obvious examples being trade unions and community groups. So our first task will be to examine the ways in which the young are 'connected' within contemporary Scottish civil society. In doing so, we will not only examine their views and behaviour regarding politics, but also their actual or perceived membership of various social, community and cultural groups. And we will look in particular at what, if any, impact the Scottish Parliament has had on young people's views and behaviour.

Our second task will be to examine the views of young people concerning the respective roles of individuals and the state. If, for instance, young people are more individualistic and less collective in their approach, we might expect them to have quite different views from older people about the kind of society in which they would like to live. In particular, we might wonder whether they are more likely to see individuals as being responsible for their own well-being, and more likely to downplay the potential role of the state.

Of course, identifying a difference between young and old does not explain its origins. So, where we find that young and old *do* differ, we will also speculate about the possible reasons for this. There are two broad possibilities. First, young people might have different views precisely *because* they are young. If that is the case, however, then as they get older and, for instance, start paying taxes and bringing up a family, their views will change and become more like those of their elders. These sorts of age differences tend to be referred to as 'lifecycle' differences. But a second possibility exists: that the divergent views of young and old reflect the fact that people's views are shaped while they are young and tend to remain with them as they age. Differences in attitude between young and old reflect differences in the social climate in which they grew up rather than the stage of life at which they currently are, and thus cannot be expected to disappear. These types of difference we will refer to as being 'generational' in origin. Needless to say, disentangling lifecycle and generational differences from one another, especially when everyone's views might also be changing over time about the issue in question, is hard to do. And the absence of comparable past data for Scotland will mean that often we have to restrict our attention to the period from 1997 onwards. However, our analyses should provide us with some clues as to which direction is likely to be the most fruitful when it comes to further inquiry.

Before we start, we need to consider what we mean by 'young people'. In this case, we are interested in what we might call young adults, people aged between 18 and 24 (the Scottish Social Attitudes survey does not interview anyone aged under 18). However, we will also cast our eyes over what we might call the 'older young', those aged between 25 and 34. In both cases, we will compare their views with those of older people, aged 35 or above. Clearly, the latter group encompasses a very wide age range, but as our focus here is upon the views and experience of young people, we will not examine what differences exist among 'older' people.

Not surprisingly, many of the characteristics of our three age groups are very different. Four in ten (39 per cent) of 18- to 24-year-olds still live with a parent, and 19 per cent are in full-time education. Only very small proportions of those aged 25 and over are in this situation. As many as one in six (16 per cent) have a university degree or equivalent qualification, as do a quarter (24 per cent) of 25- to 34-year-olds but only 13 per cent of the 35-plus age group.

– Social and political engagement –

We start by considering what evidence there is that young people in Scotland are 'disengaged' from civil society. In doing so, we will focus on their participation in a range of social activities, from voting in general elections to being members of environmental groups, trade unions or residents' associations. Then, because a person's formal allegiances and activities cannot tell us everything about the extent to which they feel connected to society, we will also focus on other, more nebulous, forms of belonging. To what extent, for example, do young people feel part of a community that is Scottish? Do they identify with other people from the same class backgrounds? Perhaps they might not necessarily *belong* to organisations that express these collective identities but nonetheless still feel them very strongly.

Interest in these types of 'connectedness' has increased markedly over the last few years, not least because of their importance to what is often referred to as 'social capital'. This is roughly defined as the connections that exist between individuals and the benefits that these connections can bring. One crucial alleged benefit of this 'capital' is social trust – the extent to which we have faith in other people and feel that we can call on them in times of need. So this section will conclude with an assessment of the evidence as to whether the young are particularly trusting or mistrusting.

– *Membership of formal groups* –

We begin by looking at the various organisations and groups to which people might belong. Some of these exist to help advance collective interests (such as trade unions, staff associations or political parties), while others are simply a means of meeting and staying in touch with those who have similar interests and beliefs, whether religious, cultural or sporting. In the case of many voluntary organisations, membership might also be taken to demonstrate a desire to give something back to society as a whole.

As table 8.1 shows, in all cases bar one, young people have comparatively low levels of membership. Thus 18- to 24-year-olds are half as likely as the 35-plus age group to be members of a trade union or staff association, and are five times less likely than older people to belong to local community or voluntary organisations. They are also less likely to belong to national and international 'green' organisations, such as Greenpeace, Friends of the

Earth, and the World Wildlife Fund. However, those aged between 18 and 24 are more likely than any other age group to be members of sports clubs or gyms. No less than a third are members, compared with under a quarter of those in other age groups.

Table 8.1 Organisational membership, by age, 2000 and 2001[a]

	Age group			
	18–24	25–34	35+	All
% member of:				
Trade union or staff association (2001)	13	20	25	23
Local community or voluntary group	4	21	24	22
National or international organisation	8	10	17	15
Sports club or gym	32	23	22	23
Cultural group	3	2	7	6
Sample size	*136–44*	*275–95*	*1193–223*	*1605–62*

a. All data are for 2000 unless otherwise stated.

So, when it comes to involvement with various civic groups, it is clear that young people are substantially less engaged than their elders. True, they are more likely to belong to sports clubs or gyms, but in most cases this membership is likely to be based purely on the consumption of certain facilities, rather than active participation in a group's activities. We also know that the young are far less engaged than older groups in religious organisations, a subject explored in more detail in Chapter 5. However, it is by no means clear that these findings herald some impending crisis of civic engagement. Rather, it is far more probable that the lower rates of participation found among young people simply reflect their youth, and that their involvement will increase as they get older. We know, for instance, that one of the best predictors of involvement in local community or voluntary groups is the length of time that a person has lived in a particular area (Johnston and Jowell 2001). As a result, it is likely that young people's participation in such groups will increase as they get older, become more embedded into the communities in which they live, and increasingly recognise the advantages of collective activities. Similar reasons are also likely to account for the lower than average membership of young people in 'green' pressure groups. In addition, the membership fees charged by some of these organisations might be difficult to afford for young people on low salaries or who are not working. Similarly, the lower than average participation of young people in trade unions is likely, at least partly, to reflect their relatively low levels of labour market participation and so, again, we would expect to see membership rates increase as they get older.

Despite these 'lifecycle' differences, it is also possible that some of the membership rates among today's young Scots will never reach those found among older generations. The reason why there might be a 'generational' difference is because of changes in the characteristics of the labour market (in particular, the relative shrinkage of those occupational sectors with traditionally high levels of union activity) and a decline in the tendency, even once this change in the labour market is taken into account, of people to join unions (Bryson 2002). Consequently, unless there are overall societal changes that boost union membership in future, the gap we have found between different age groups will not change as their members age.

– Political engagement –

None of the young people in our sample were members of a political party. However, as only two per cent of our sample overall were paid-up party members, this lack of formal engagement with political parties is hardly unique to the young. But what about engagement with politics more generally? Certainly, concern about low participation rates among the young, most recently in the 2001 general election, has prompted a range of initiatives aimed at persuading the young to get involved in politics, including the Electoral Commission's 'Votes are Power' campaign.

Table 8.2 will certainly prove worrying to those concerned about low levels of political engagement among the young. On every measure we consider, young people are markedly less engaged and interested than their elders. Only one in five, for instance, supports a political party, compared with a half of the 35-plus age group. True, when pushed further and asked whether or not they feel 'closer' to one party than to another, nearly a half of young people say they *do* support or feel close to a party. But so also do a resounding three-quarters of the 35-plus age group. Not surprisingly then, young people are the most likely age group not to have a 'party identification' at all, that is, not to support a party, not to feel closer to one, and not to be able to say for whom they would vote were there an election the following day. No less than one in five falls into this category, double the rate among the 35-plus age group. Given this, it is not surprising to find also that interest in politics rises gradually as we move up the age spectrum. Just one in five young people has 'a great deal' or 'quite a lot' of interest, half the proportion found among the 35-plus age group. Conversely, while a quarter (26 per cent) of 18- to 24-year-olds have no interest in politics at all, this is true of only around one in ten (11 per cent) of those aged 35 or older.

Table 8.2 Political engagement, by age

	Age group			All
	18–24	25–34	35+	
	%	%	%	%
Support a political party	20	34	49	43
No party identification	20	15	9	11
Great deal or quite a lot of interest in politics	16	20	29	26
Sample size	*136*	*275*	*1193*	*1605*

Given these low levels of political interest and support among young people, it is not surprising that 18- to 24-year-olds were by far the least likely age group to report having voted in the 2001 general election. Only 43 per cent said they voted in that election. While this is a similar level to that found among 25- to 34-year-olds (49 per cent), over three-quarters (77 per cent) of those aged 35 voted.[1] This difference between young and old matches that found by both the British Election Study and the Electoral Commission (Electoral Commission 2002).

This lower propensity of young people to vote is matched by a lower than average tendency to think that people have a 'duty' to vote. We asked people to choose between the three statements about voting in general elections as shown in table 8.3. As the table shows, nearly a quarter of 18- to 24-year-olds think it is 'not really worth' voting, and only four in ten see it as being everyone's duty. Among the 35-plus age group, only one in ten thinks there is no point in voting and over three-quarters see it as being every citizen's duty. The 'older young' fall some way between both groups – they are far less likely than their younger counterparts to think that there is no point voting, but are also more likely than their elders to adopt a more 'conditional' view, that is that you should only vote if you care about the outcome.

Table 8.3 Attitudes towards voting, by age

	Age group			All
	18–24	25–34	35+	
	%	%	%	%
It's not really worth voting	23	10	9	11
People should vote only if they care who wins	35	32	14	19
It's everyone's duty to vote	40	57	77	69
Sample size	*136*	*275*	*1193*	*1605*

How can we explain these age differences in both political attitudes and practice? One possibility is that they are linked to variations in political trust or in beliefs about the extent to which the political system is able to respond to its citizens' demands. To assess the former, we asked respondents about the extent to which they trusted 'British governments of any party to place the needs of the nation above the interests of their own political party'.

Only a quarter of all age groups say that they trust governments to do this either 'just about always' or 'most of the time'. So the young are no more distrustful than anyone else. Moreover, when asked whether they agreed or disagreed with the statement 'Generally speaking, those we elect as MPs lose touch with people pretty quickly', 18- to 24-year-olds were actually *less* likely than any other age group to agree, just 53 per cent doing so compared with 75 per cent of the 35-plus age group.

So looking at political trust and efficacy cannot account for the low levels of interest in politics and low levels of participation among the young. Nor should we automatically assume that the fact that young people are less engaged in politics than older groups presages a new period of political disenchantment and disaffection among Scotland's youth. Developing an interest in politics may simply be a gradual but inevitable consequence of people gradually becoming more 'embedded' in society – through work, paying taxes, using government services and so on.

To assess this, we need to look back over time to see whether young people have always been less engaged in politics than their elders and, if so, whether this disaffection appears to be growing. We start by considering turnout. Table 8.4 compares the turnout reported by our three different age groups in the UK general elections of 1992, 1997 and 2001, and the 1999 election to the Scottish Parliament. Two key points emerge. Firstly, turnout has *always* been lower than average among young people. In 1992, for instance, the turnout gap between young and old was some 12 percentage points. Moreover, precisely the same pattern is evident among surveys of British voters as a whole for election years prior to 1992. Secondly, however, the decline in turnout between 1997 and 2001 was steepest of all among the young. As a result the existing gap between young and old widened markedly.[2] Moreover, this widening of the age gap was not apparent in the 1999 elections to the Scottish Parliament. In those elections around six in ten 18- to 24-year-olds voted, compared with around eight in ten in our older group. In 2001, however, the proportion of 18- to 24-year-olds who voted dropped by nearly 20 percentage points (to 43 per cent) while the proportion voting in the 35-plus age group fell by a mere two points.

How can we explain the staggering fall in turnout at the 2001 general election? It was not, of course, peculiar to Scotland (Electoral Commission 2002) and so is unlikely to reflect disproportionate disillusionment among young people with the parliament and its progress since 1999, a subject to which we will return later. In fact, the current gap between young and old is likely to reflect the fact that the 2001 general election particularly failed to enthuse those who were *already* among the least politically motivated, a group which inevitably contains a large proportion of young people (Bromley and Curtice 2002). So, although the differences between young and old do appear to have widened, it is by no means inevitable that this will remain should future elections seem more important and exciting than was true of the 2001 contest.

Table 8.4 Turnout, by age, 1992–2001

Age group	1992	1997	1999	2001	Sample size
		% voting			
18–24	76	70	61	43	85–136
25–34	82	75	55	49	170–275
35+	88	85	79	77	618–1193
All	85	81	72	68	873–1605

If we conduct a similar exercise for political interest, a similar story emerges. Young people have always been less interested in politics than older groups. In fact, if we compare our findings now with those obtained in the mid-1990s, the similarity is striking. In the mid-1990s, for instance, 14 per cent of 18- to 24-year-olds reported having a great deal of interest in politics, compared with 31 per cent of the 35-plus age group. Now the comparable figures are 16 and 29 per cent respectively.

– Attachment to the Scottish Parliament –

So far we have seen clear evidence that the young are not very engaged in politics, and that this is not a particularly new development. So we turn now to consider the attitudes held by young people about one of Scotland's newest institutions, its parliament.

If anything, young people have more confidence in the parliament than their elders. As table 8.5 shows, younger people are slightly more likely to trust the Scottish Parliament to work in Scotland's best interests at least 'most of the time'. As many as 70 per cent trust the parliament at least 'most of the time' compared with 63 per cent of those aged 35 and over. We also asked people to respond to the following statement:

Some people say that it makes no difference which party wins in elections, things go on much the same. Please say how much of a difference you think it makes who wins in elections to the Scottish Parliament.

Young people are substantially more likely than older groups to think that who wins would make a difference. Nearly nine in ten take this view compared with only two in three of the 35-plus age group. Equally, young people are slightly more likely to think that the Scottish Parliament should be given more powers. Although small, these differences are notable because they are not present when we ask similar questions about Westminster, on which there tend not to be any age differences at all.

Table 8.5 Attitudes to the Scottish Parliament, by age

	Age group			
	18–24	25–34	35+	All
	%	%	%	%
Think who wins Scottish Parliament election makes at least some difference	87	72	66	68
Agree that Scottish Parliament should be given more powers	75	75	66	68
Trust Scottish Parliament to work in Scotland's interests at least 'most of the time'	70	68	63	65
Trust UK government to work in Scotland's interests at least 'most of the time'	22	21	22	22
Sample size	136	275	1193	1605

These somewhat more positive views about the parliament among younger people do not appear to arise because younger people are more likely to favour independence for Scotland. Although previous surveys have found that young people were much more likely to be in favour of independence (Paterson et al. 2001), in our latest survey we find little difference between the generations. Just under a third (31 per cent) of 18- to 24-year-olds favour independence, compared with 26 per cent of the 35-plus group. Moreover, there are not any age differences in people's evaluations of the parliament's performance so far. Young people are no more or less likely to think its existence is having a beneficial impact on Scotland's education system, the economy or the NHS. Nor do the differences reflect any greater propensity for younger people to say that they are Scottish.[3]

So it remains unclear precisely why young people are slightly more trusting of the parliament than older people, and are more keen to give it increased powers. Still, this finding does demonstrate that, despite young people's relative lack of engagement with politics in general, there is little to suggest that they are particularly disengaged from the parliament. The small age differences we have found might even point towards a possible way of increasing young people's interest in politics and their participation in the political process in Scotland. Certainly, as we shall see later, young people's lack of engagement in politics does not prevent them from thinking that people should have more say in what the government does.

– Identity and belonging –

The picture painted so far of young people in contemporary Scotland is one of a group who are not notable 'joiners' (except of sports clubs), and who stand in start contrast to older groups in their levels of political engagement. But, of course, connections with wider society are not only about voting or formally belonging to a particular group. In particular, subjective feelings of belonging might be just as important as objective 'membership'. To explore this, we now consider responses to the following question:

Some people say that whether they feel British or Scottish is not as important as other things about them. Other people say their national identity is the key to who they are. If you had to pick just one thing from this list to describe yourself – something that is very important to you when you think of yourself – what would it be?

We presented nearly thirty different options to respondents (including class, national identity, religious identity, parenthood, age, ethnicity, and area of residence) and asked them to pick the three they saw as the most important (see also Chapter 6). As table 8.6 indicates, the answers suggest that national identity is a particularly important means of self-definition for young people. Two-thirds of 18- to 24-year-olds picked being Scottish or British (the two national identity options that we offered to them) as one of their top three self-ascribed identities, with 'Scottish' looming far larger than 'British'. The second most common identity chosen by this group was age, with just over half saying that 'being young' is a key to who they are.

National identity is also a relatively popular choice among our 'older young', but 'lifecycle' factors also come into play for this group, with parenthood and being a husband or wife both popular choices. The importance of these sorts of 'achieved' (rather than ascribed) statuses is even more apparent among our oldest age group, who are also less likely than their younger counterparts to say that their national identity is important to them.

Table 8.6 Self-ascribed identity, by age

	Age group		
	18–24	25–34	35+
% choosing as 1/2/3 choice:			
Scottish	57	51	41
British	9	8	12
Young/old	53	12	10
Working person/retired/unemployed	38	40	42
Male/female	36	36	21
Middle/working class	23	25	30
Parent	15	44	56
Husband/wife	5	25	32
Sample size	*136*	*275*	*1193*

So, although young people clearly are less engaged than older groups on most of the measures we have considered so far, it is clear that they do identify with wider social groups in Scottish society, and particularly with being Scottish and with being young. Unfortunately, as this question was asked for the first time in 2001, we cannot assess the extent to which this might change as people get older. But the fact that lifecycle identities (such as being a husband or wife) become progressively more important in our older age groups strongly suggests that the groups with which people identify will change as they get older and their circumstances change.

– Social trust –

So far, we have considered a range of possible measures that might help us better understand the connections that exist between the young and wider Scottish society. Interest in these types of 'connectedness' has increased markedly over the last few years, because of their alleged importance to what is often referred to as 'social capital'. As we indicated earlier, social capital has been broadly defined as 'connections between individuals – social networks and the norms of reciprocity and trustworthiness that arise from them' (Putnam 2000). The concept is useful because it reminds us that the relationships that exist between people extend far beyond membership of organisations or one's own feelings of identification with particular groups; they also include the myriad of day-to-day interactions that citizens have with one another. Indeed, previous analysis of the data we are looking at here confirms that this relationship between membership and trust exists (Paterson 2001). Therefore, any assessment of the engagement of any particular group with society as a whole should consider the extent to which its members are trusting of others within society, and the degree to which they think they can rely on others.

We consider two different ways of measuring social trust. One attempts to measure it directly, while a second assesses it indirectly by asking respondents how they would respond to particular situations. We begin by considering the indirect approach. This involved asking respondents how comfortable they would be if they had to ask a neighbour for help in a range of different circumstances: with collecting a prescription, with borrowing a sink plunger to clear a blocked sink and with borrowing £5 to pay the milkman (for a further discussion of these questions, see Paterson 2001). On all these measures young people are less comfortable than other groups about asking a neighbour for help. Only four in ten (39 per cent), for instance, say they would feel very comfortable asking a neighbour to collect a prescription for them if they were unwell, compared with nearly two-thirds (64 per cent) of the 35-plus age group.

To some extent, these findings are not particularly surprising. In particular, we know that this kind of 'neighbourhood' trust, like membership of local groups, is closely linked to the amount of time a person has lived within a neighbourhood (Johnston and Jowell 2001). And, although young people might well have grown up in the neighbourhood within which they currently live, their average length of residence in their current neighbourhood is, not surprisingly, far shorter than that reported by older groups. So, to a large degree, once again it is likely that the age differences we have found reflect lifecycle factors. The levels of neighbourhood trust shown by young people, in other words, will in all likelihood tend to increase as they get older and form closer bonds within their local communities.

Of course, had we asked these questions about friends rather than neighbours we might well have obtained a rather different pattern of responses in which the young do not stand out as less able to ask for help. However, we also asked a second set of 'indirect' measures of social trust which do not refer specifically to the neighbourhood within which people live. And here too we find apparently lower levels of trust among young people. For example, when asked how comfortable they would feel asking a passer-by for directions, a half (49 per cent) of the 35-plus age group say they would feel very comfortable, compared with only 40 per cent of 18- to 24-year-olds. Similar differences exist in respect of asking a passer-by to change a five-pound note in order to use a public telephone.

This apparent gap in the levels of social trust held by young and old is further confirmed when we consider responses to our more direct attempt to get at this issue. We included the following two questions:

Generally speaking, would you say that most people can be trusted, or that you can't be too careful in dealing with people?
How often do you think that people would try to take advantage of you if they got the chance and how often would they try to be fair?

As we can see in table 8.7, on both measures young people are substantially less trusting than their elders. Over half, for instance, think that people will try to take advantage either all or most of the time, double the rate found among the 35-plus age group.

Table 8.7 Social trust, by age

	Age group			
	18–24	25–34	35+	All
% say can't be too careful in dealing with people	62	58	51	53
% say people try to take advantage of you all or most of the time	55	44	27	32
Sample size	*132–44*	*268–95*	*1105–1223*	*1505–1663*

How should we interpret these differences? Unfortunately, we do not have any evidence from earlier surveys about levels of social trust in Scotland, so we do not know whether young people have always been less trusting than their elders. However, we have already speculated that at least a part of the difference between young and old will be accounted for by lifecycle influences, such as their length of residence in a particular neighbourhood, for example. Moreover, the close relationship that exists between organisational membership and social trust also suggests that young people's social trust will increase as their formal and informal networks develop and become more complex. But there is an alternative possibility we should not ignore. Our findings may at least be partly generational in origin, reflecting differences in parenting that stem from increasing concern about the 'danger' faced by young children outside the home (Furedi 2001). If this is true, then some of the differences we have found might persist – or at least prove more resistant to change – even once people get older. Moreover, if this speculation is correct, we would also expect to see levels of social trust decline further still in future years as younger generations, currently still children, enter adulthood. For after all, levels of concern about children and 'stranger danger' are more prominent now than ever before.

– THE STATE AND THE INDIVIDUAL –

The differences we have found between the extent to which young and old are engaged within wider society raise obvious questions about what young people's views are of the relationship between individual citizens and the society within which they live. Earlier, for instance, we saw that a significant proportion of young people think people should vote only 'if they care about who wins' rather than believing that it is everyone's *duty* to vote. So we turn now to consider whether this rather individualistic view about voting also applies to their thinking about the role the state can play in people's lives. Are they, for instance, less likely than older groups to think that the state should be responsible for looking after people in retirement? Do their views on state spending differ markedly from those of older age groups?

– *The role of the state* –

A key division within British politics has traditionally been between those favouring state intervention versus those who emphasise the importance of the free market. While the former camp will tend to favour redistribution via taxation and government spending, the latter will focus more upon the benefits of non-interventionist policies and low taxation. And although this division between 'left' and 'right' is no longer as clear cut as it was it remains an important cleavage within British political debate. Consequently, we begin by examining where young people stand on these issues, starting with their attitudes towards the state ownership of public services and industries.

Perhaps the most revealing finding in table 8.8 is simply that, for the first three statements shown, young people are much more likely to sit on the fence than any older group (that is, to respond that they 'neither agree nor disagree' with the statements). For example, over a half of 18- to 24-year-olds take the middle option when asked whether major public services and industries ought to be in state ownership, compared with only four in ten of those aged 25 to 34 and just three in ten of those aged 35 and over. That said, in all three cases, the majority of those young people with a view overwhelmingly favour the 'interventionist' option. Little sign here, then, of a group who favour the free market rather than state involvement in the economy. Moreover, as shown by the answers to the last statement in the table, despite declining levels of unionisation and the fact that – as we saw earlier – young people are less likely than older groups to be union members, young and old have remarkably similar views about the importance of trade unions as a way of protecting workers. Around two-thirds of all groups take a pro-union stance.

Table 8.8 The role of the state, by age

	Age group			All
	18–24	25–34	35+	
	%	%	%	%
Major public services and industries				
ought to be in state ownership				
Agree	31	41	47	44
Neither agree nor disagree	52	40	28	32
Disagree	13	17	22	21
Private enterprise is the best way to				
solve Britain's economic problems				
Agree	8	13	19	17
Neither agree nor disagree	64	54	39	43
Disagree	24	31	40	37
It is the government's responsibility				
to provide a job for everyone				
who wants one				
Agree	48	51	55	54
Neither agree nor disagree	36	24	21	23
Disagree	14	22	22	21
There is no need for strong trade				
unions to protect employees'				
working conditions and wages				
Agree	8	7	14	13
Neither agree nor disagree	23	22	18	19
Disagree	67	69	66	67
Sample size	118	232	1033	1383

How should we interpret the fact that young people are more inclined to sit on the fence on these matters? On the one hand, it might reflect the fact that these issues are highly complex and that young people have simply not had enough time and experience to come to an informed view. If so, then over time we would expect these same young people to begin to take a stance. Alternatively, however, it might be that their relative indecision reflects their having been brought up during a period characterised by a less 'tribal' and clear-cut division between left and right. If this is the case, they may well remain less likely to take sides on these issues as they get older.

However, if we look at the results of earlier surveys in which these questions have been asked, we find that young people have always been more likely to sit on the fence. This lends some credence to the view that they will develop opinions on these sorts of issues as they grow older.

However, there are also signs that the gap between young and old might be widening. This is illustrated in table 8.9 so far as attitudes towards private enterprise are concerned. In 1997, as many as 55 per cent of 18- to 24-year-olds took the middle option, compared with only 36 per cent of the 35-plus age group. In our most recent survey, however, the proportion of young people saying they 'neither agree nor disagree' is 65 per cent, while the proportion of older people taking this view is almost unchanged. So perhaps these are now issues which, although people may still be more likely to develop views about them as they get older, are seen as less clear-cut than was once the case. If so, the uncertainty expressed by current generations of young people may not disappear in the way that it has in the past.

Table 8.9 Views on private enterprise, by age, 1997–2001

% 'neither agree nor disagree' that private enterprise is the best way to solve Britain's problems	1997	1999	2001	*Sample size*
18–24	55	63	65	*72–118*
25–34	45	48	55	*150–232*
35+	36	37	38	*530–1033*

A similar picture emerges when we consider views about the relative roles and responsibilities of the state, individuals (and their families) and employers when it comes to making provision for retirement, long-term sickness and paying for the costs of care of older people in residential homes. True, as table 8.10 shows, young people are slightly more likely than those in older age groups to cite an alternative to the state as being 'mainly' responsible for these things. For instance, one in five 18- to 24-year-olds thinks that individuals and their families should mainly meet the costs of caring for elderly people in retirement homes, double the proportion found among the 35-plus age group. However, the vast majority of *all* age groups think that the government should be mainly responsible for ensuring that people should have enough to live on should they become sick or disabled and for paying for the care of older people in residential homes. Meanwhile in all age groups at least half take this view about ensuring that people have enough money to live on in retirement. So, despite the fact that these issues are likely to have little resonance for young people who have not yet started (or are just starting) their working lives, their views on these issues are in fact markedly similar to those of older people.

Table 8.10 Responsibilities of the state and citizens, by age

Who should be mainly responsible for:	Age group			All
	18–24	25–34	35+	
	%	%	%	%
Ensuring people have enough money to live on in retirement				
Mainly the government	51	54	57	56
Mainly a person's employer	11	7	8	8
Mainly a person themselves and their family	36	37	34	35
Ensuring people have enough to live on if they become sick or disabled for a long time				
Mainly the government	77	82	85	83
Mainly a person's employer	16	12	7	9
Mainly a person themselves and their family	7	5	7	7
Paying for the care needs of elderly people in residential and nursing homes				
Mainly the government	79	89	90	88
Mainly a person themselves and their family	19	9	8	9
Sample size	136	275	1194	1605

– Taxes, spending and priorities –

But are young people willing to pay for the costs of sickness and retirement in their taxes? In fact, as table 8.11 shows, young people are less likely than older people to say that taxes should be increased and more spent on health, education and social benefits. Less than half take this view compared with over two in three of those aged 35 and over. So despite the fact that as we saw earlier young people are more likely to trust the Scottish Parliament, they might be the most resistant to any future attempt to use the body's tax-varying powers.

Table 8.11 Taxation and government spending, by age

If the government had to choose it should:	Age group			All
	18–24	25–34	35+	
	%	%	%	%
Reduce taxes and spend less on health, education and social benefits	4	6	3	3
Keep taxes and spending the same as now	46	37	26	29
Increase taxes and spend more on health, education and social benefits	46	51	69	64
Sample size	136	275	1193	1605

But perhaps young people have always been less supportive of increased spending, with their views then changing as they get older? Table 8.12 shows that young people were also least supportive of increased spending in 1997. However, the gap between the views of young and old widened markedly between the two years – from just nine percentage points in 1997 to twenty-three in 2001. So it is possible that the latest generation of young people is more resistant to higher levels of taxation in a way that will not necessarily fully disappear as they age.

Table 8.12 Taxation and government spending, by age, 1997 and 2001

% say that government should increase taxes and spend more on health, education and social benefits	1997	2001	*Sample size*
Age group			
18–24	65	46	*85–136*
25–34	74	51	*170–275*
35+	74	69	*618–1193*
All	73	63	*873–1605*

But in so far as many young people do think the government should be spending more money, on what do they think it should be spent? What spending areas do the young prioritise? Their two top priorities are in fact the same as everyone else's – health and education. However, compared with those aged 35 and over, 18- to 24-year-olds are more likely to favour spending on education and less likely to favour spending on health. This difference between young and old is not new and seems to reflect an element of self-interest (Park 2001). As we saw earlier many young people are still in education, while older people are more likely to use the health service.

Table 8.13 Priorities for government, by age

| Top priority for government spending | Age group | | | All |
	18–24	25–34	35+	
Health	47	49	58	55
Education	34	28	23	21
Housing	6	5	4	4
Public transport	2	3	3	3
Police and prisons	3	2	3	3
Social security benefit	3	3	3	3
Roads	1	4	2	2
Help for industry	1	3	2	2
Defence	2	1	1	1
Sample size	*136*	*275*	*1194*	*1605*

One of the best known theories of generational change has been put forward by Ronald Inglehart (Inglehart 1977). He argues that the distinctive experiences of those growing up during a particular historical period will lead them to a unique view as to what governments should prioritise. He argues that young people who have been brought up in a post-war period characterised by rising affluence and continuous peace will prioritise self-expression and 'involvement', reflecting what Inglehart calls 'post-materialist' values. By contrast those who were children in less economically and politically stable periods would be expected focus more upon material security (hence 'materialists'). If Inglehart is correct then we might expect to find higher levels of post-materialism among 18- to 24- and 25- to 34-year-olds than we would in the 35-plus group (although obviously much of this group too will have come of age during the post-war period).

The most common question used to assess Inglehart's theory is one which asks respondents to choose two out of four 'priorities for Britain', two of which indicate a materialist approach, and two a post-materialist one. Our answers to this question (see table 8.14) offer only limited support for Inglehart's theory. Young and old alike do not differ in their views about the importance of 'fighting rising prices' (one of the materialist priorities) or of 'protecting freedom of speech' (a post-materialist one). However, young people are more likely than older people to select the post-materialist view that people should have more say in government decisions (75 per cent of 18- to 24-year-olds do so but only 59 per cent of the 35-plus group). Conversely, young people are less likely to choose the materialist option that stresses 'maintaining order in the nation'.

Table 8.14 Priorities for government, by age

% choosing as first or second priority:	Age group			
	18–24	25–34	35+	All
Give people more say in government decisions	75	67	59	62
Maintain order in the nation	44	48	61	57
Fight rising prices	53	49	48	49
Protect freedom of speech	26	34	28	28
Sample size	136	275	1194	1605

The fact that the young are most likely to prioritise giving people more say in government decisions is intriguing, given they are the least likely themselves either to join the collective groups that might facilitate this or, indeed, to vote. It should, however, be encouraging news for those who are concerned about young people's lack of engagement in the political process as it suggests that they may be receptive to moves to further their involvement, albeit perhaps through different channels than their elders.

– CONCLUSIONS –

Young people are clearly less engaged and 'connected' to the institutions and practices that traditionally are seen as part and parcel of civil society. They are less likely to belong to organisations, are less likely to vote or be interested in politics, and are less trusting of others. However, this is not to say that they feel no sense of connection with society as a whole. In particular, majorities identify with 'being Scottish'. Moreover, although we have focused on those types of organisation that have traditionally been seen as important in determining a society's civic 'health', young people may of course be part of social networks that we have not been able to cover.

Moreover, many of these differences between young and old probably reflect the stages they are at in their lives. People's views and behaviour do change as they get older. This, for example, is the most plausible explana-tion for many of the differences in organisational membership and political engagement. But on other issues we found signs of generational differences that are likely to persist over time. This we suggest might be particularly true of trade union membership, some aspects of political engagement and, most speculatively of all, social trust. Consequently, we should not be compla-cent in assuming that the current generation of young people will inevitably end up resembling the generations who preceded them.

We have also seen that young people are among the most trusting and positive about the Scottish Parliament, even though they do not differ from older groups either in their views about how Scotland should ultimately be governed or in their assessments of the impact that the parliament has had so far. So, although the parliament does not appear to have boosted levels of political engagement among young people, potentially it might be a means of increasing young people's involvement and interest in the political process. After all, it is clear that young people, above all other age groups, support people having 'more say' in government decisions; perhaps devolu-tion will offer them this opportunity. Ultimately, the best test of this will be whether young people in Scotland become more politically active than their counterparts in England. At present at least there is little difference between them.

The tendency of young people to be less 'connected' to civil society (whatever the cause of this may be) does not appear to translate into a very different appreciation of the appropriate relationship between citizens and the state. Although, on most of the measures we have considered here, young people are slightly less likely to nominate the state as responsible, the overall pattern of their responses is remarkably similar to those of older people (although they are consistently the most likely to have no view about any particular issue). However, one exception to this comprises attitudes towards taxation and government spending: younger people are markedly less supportive than older ones of increased taxation and spending. Irrespective of whether this reflects lifecycle or generational factors, this suggests that despite young people's higher levels of trust in the Scottish Parliament, they might potentially be the most difficult to bring on board if the parliament wishes to increase taxes in future.

– REFERENCES –

Bromley, C. and Curtice, J. (2002), 'Where have all the voters gone?', in A. Park, J. Curtice, K. Thomson, L. Jarvis and C. Bromley (eds), British Social Attitudes: the 19th report, London: Sage.

Bryson, A. (2002), 'Marching on together? Recent trends in union membership', in A. Park, J. Curtice, K. Thomson, L. Jarvis and C. Bromley (eds), British Social Attitudes: the 19th report, London: Sage.

Electoral Commission (2002), 'Voter engagement and young people', Research Report July 2002, London: The Electoral Commission.

Furedi, F. (2001), Paranoid Parenting: Abandon Your Anxieties and Be A Good Parent, London: Penguin Press.

Inglehart, R. (1977), The Silent Revolution: Changing Values and Political Styles among Western Publics, Princeton, NJ: Princeton University Press.

Johnston, M. and Jowell, R. (2001), 'How robust is British civil society?', in A. Park, J. Curtice, A. Park, K. Thomson, L. Jarvis and C. Bromley (eds), British Social Attitudes: the 18th report, London: Sage.

Park, A. (2001), 'The generation game', in R. Jowell, J. Curtice, A. Park, K. Thomson, L. Jarvis, C. Bromley and N. Stratford (eds), British Social Attitudes: the 17th report, London: Sage.

Paterson, L. (2001), 'Social capital and constitutional reform', J. Curtice, D. McCrone, A. Park and L. Paterson (eds), New Scotland, New Society?, Edinburgh: Polygon.

Paterson, L., Brown, A., Curtice, J., Hinds, K., McCrone, D., Park, A., Sproston, K. and Surridge, P. (eds) (2001), New Scotland, New Politics? Edinburgh: Polygon.

Putnam, R. (2000), Bowling Alone – the Collapse and Revival of American Community, New York: Simon and Schuster.

Wilkinson, H. and Mulgan, G. (1995), Freedom's Children, Demos Paper No. 17, London: Demos.

– Notes –

1. These reported levels overstate turnout in the 2001 elections, both because respondents 'over-report' voting and because those who participate in surveys are also more likely to have voted in elections. For a more detailed account, see Bromley and Curtice, 2002.
2. Similar, but less marked, findings emerge when we use the Scottish Election Study 2001. This found a reported turnout rate of 53 per cent among 18- to 24-year-olds, 62 per cent among 25- to 34-year-olds and 80 per cent among the 35-plus age group. The overall reported turnout for the whole sample was 74 per cent.
3. As measured by the 'Moreno question', discussed in detail in Chapter 6.

Conclusion

The preceding chapters have provided a wealth of evidence on what Scots think about some of the major social and political issues that confront their country as it prepares to vote in the second Scottish election in May 2003. In each case the authors of those chapters have indicated the implications that they think their analyses have for an evaluation of the record of devolution to date and the prospects for its future. Now we attempt to consider what answers are suggested by the findings of this book as a whole to the questions that we posed at the beginning: what has devolution achieved so far and what challenges might it face in future?

Devolution has, it seems, been a disappointment so far for many Scots. Contrary to what many expected, the Scottish Parliament is widely thought to have less influence on what happens in Scotland than does the UK government at Westminster. It is not even thought to have had as much influence as the UK government on the standard of the NHS or the quality of education in Scotland, both of which are now clearly the formal responsibility of the Scottish Executive. Both expectations and evaluations of the parliament's performance are lower than when it took over the reins of power in Scotland in 1999. And judged by how much voters now think it matters who wins a Scottish election, there appears to be a danger that turnout in the 2003 election will be even lower than the modest figure of 59 per cent recorded in 1999.

Yet support for the principle of devolution remains strong. Rather than being disenchanted with the idea of a Scottish Parliament, Scots simply appear to want devolution to work more effectively than it has so far. They want the parliament, not Westminster, to become the centre of the nation's political life. To that end they are prepared to see it take over areas that are currently largely reserved to Westminster, such as taxation and welfare benefits. Moreover, there still appears to be a substantial residue of goodwill towards the parliament. Even those who adhere to a British rather than a Scottish national identity are more likely to trust the parliament to act in the nation's interest than they are UK government at Westminster.

But while there may be considerable public support for a significant rewriting of the current devolution settlement, that does not mean devolution has become a battering ram for independence. Although a considerable minority of Scots still want independence that minority has not grown in the immediate wake of devolution. The symbols of the Union such as the Union Jack may be greeted with indifference but they are not met with hostility. Even amongst those who say they are exclusively Scottish and reject the label 'British', marginally more still favour some form of devolution than back independence. And it appears that what was once a particular enthusiasm for independence amongst younger voters may even have been quelled.

Despite the apparent failure of devolution to meet all the high expectations with which it was invested when Scots voted in 1997 in favour of creating a new parliament, some of the key policies that have been pursued by the Scottish Executive do appear to justify the claim that devolution has helped to provide Scottish answers to Scottish questions. The introduction of 'free' personal care seems to be consistent with a majority view amongst Scots that government should be responsible for paying the cost of community care irrespective of the financial means of its beneficiaries. More surprisingly, perhaps, the abolition of Clause 2A appears to be consistent at least with a majority view that teenagers should be taught about homosexuality in schools. And even the Executive's reluctance to follow the 'lead' of the UK government in introducing specialist schools is in line with a majority view that all secondary children should go to the same kind of school

True, not all these distinctive policies represent examples of the Scottish Parliament following a distinctively Scottish strand of public opinion. Its policy on personal care, for example, is probably more in tune with English public opinion too than that of the UK government. More importantly, however, for each instance where a distinctive Executive policy appears to be consistent with public opinion, it seems possible to find another where the evidence is not so clear. It is far from certain that the Executive's decision to require university students to contribute towards the cost of their tuition only after they start earning is any more popular than the previous policy of requiring them to pay while they are studying – though either policy would seem to be more popular than not charging university students anything at all. With only a little under half saying that young people should be given more information about how to use drugs more safely, and a similar proportion saying that the way to treat drug addicts is to stop them using drugs altogether, the Executive's decision to change its drug harm reduction policy from 'Just Say No' to 'Know the Score' hardly has strong public backing either.

Moreover, the advent of devolution does not necessarily mean an end to policies being introduced in Scotland that are similar to those in England yet are not necessarily in tune with Scottish public opinion. Both the UK government and the Scottish Executive are aiming to reduce if not end the role of local councils as social landlords. Yet council tenants in Scotland at least still appear to have considerable (if declining) loyalty to the idea of renting from a local authority, even though on most criteria housing association tenants give their landlords better marks than do existing council tenants. Similarly the UK government and the Scottish Executive are both committed to the principle of social inclusion. Yet we have discovered that owner-occupiers are reluctant to live in more mixed communities, many people feel uncomfortable at the prospect of living next door to someone with mental illness, while few would countenance someone with learning difficulties sitting on a jury.

None of this is to argue that devolution has brought worse decision-making to Scotland. Indeed, whatever their disappointments about devolution very few Scots believe that to be true either. Instead these examples are perhaps a reminder that governing Scotland is not necessarily a straightforward matter irrespective of whether it is run from London or Edinburgh. But even so, our evidence does suggest one potential flaw in the current devolution settlement. This is that where we have been able to detect at least some difference between Scottish and English public opinion, most notably on attitudes towards inequality, the levers of power often still lie primarily in the hands of the UK government. Behind the demand for a more powerful Scottish Parliament there seems to lie an important truth that Westminster still rules over a number of those matters where Scotland is inclined to take a somewhat different view from England. It has perhaps been somewhat fortuitous that public opinion on one recent high profile example of a UK government domestic decision about a reserved matter – the reclassification of cannabis as a class C rather than a class B drug – is rather similar on both sides of the border.

But if finding Scottish answers to Scottish questions has not proved to be as easy as the advocates of devolution might have hoped, it is not clear that Scotland will be any more difficult to rule in future than it has been in the recent past. Instead of a society scarred by religious antagonism and divided by identity, we have uncovered a country that seems to becoming uniformly secular and Scottish. The traditional signs of religious sectarianism – differences in the educational and occupational attainment of Catholics and Protestants, a reluctance to intermarry, and support for different political parties – may not have disappeared entirely but they appear to be diminishing. More importantly, perhaps, such differences are losing their importance simply because fewer and fewer Scots acknowledge an adherence to any religious denomination let alone attend a religious service. Moreover, most Scots no longer accept the right of religious leaders to pronounce on social and moral issues such as homosexuality while amongst the younger generation of Scots at least relatively few of those who still acknowledge a religious denomination follow their leaders' teachings on such subjects. As a result Scotland can probably be expected to become an even more socially liberal society than it is now.

Meanwhile, although a half of Scots are still willing to acknowledge a British identity, when forced to choose over three-quarters would now say they are Scottish and only one in six that they are British. Such a one-sided distribution in the pattern of national identity means almost inevitably that national identity is not a major source of division in Scotland. In any event we have found that the views of those who still feel British are rarely diametrically opposed to the opinions of the majority who feel Scottish. More debatable, perhaps, is whether such a low level of adherence to the national identity that is associated with the United Kingdom state will eventually undermine the ability of devolution to act as a means of keeping Scotland within the Union. So far at least, the relationship between national identity and support for independence is sufficiently weak that it appears it may not.

Meanwhile, although class differences in social and political attitudes in Scotland may not have disappeared, rarely are those in the middle class and those in the working class on diametrically opposite sides. Certainly class differences are no more marked in Scotland than they are in England. And while Scotland's politicians undoubtedly have a hard time ahead to persuade younger people to become involved in Scotland's political processes, and indeed in Scotland's communal life more generally, it is far from clear that today's young generation will not become more interested and engaged as they get older and have a partner, children and a mortgage to worry about – just indeed as their parents did. And at least it seems they start off with plenty of goodwill towards the Scottish Parliament.

So achieving the aims of devolution has not proven easy. Some Scottish answers have been provided to some Scottish questions. But other questions have perhaps been ignored because they fall within Westminster's remit, while sometimes the answers that have been provided have not necessarily been to Scots' liking. But the biggest failing of devolution so far is that it simply is not thought to have made much of a difference. Whether that perception can be changed within the limits of the current constitutional settlement is perhaps the biggest challenge to face devolution as the Scottish Parliament begins it second term.

Technical Appendix

– Technical aspects of the surveys –

Most data in this book are drawn from the 2001 Scottish Social Attitudes Survey. This was the third year of the study, which started in 1999 with the Scottish Parliamentary Election Survey (Paterson et al. 2001), and was followed up by the 2000 Scottish Social Attitudes survey (Curtice et al. 2002). The series is parallel to the long-established British Social Attitudes Survey (Park et al. 2002). Other surveys from which data have been used are the Scottish Election Surveys of 1979, 1992 and 1997, and the 1997 Scottish Referendum Survey. Data from all these surveys are, or will be, publicly available through the Data Archive at the University of Essex.

– Details of the 2001 Scottish Social Attitudes Survey –

The study was funded from a number of sources. Three modules – attitudes to illegal drug use, religious beliefs, and devolution and constitutional change – were funded through grants from the Economic and Social Research Council (grant numbers R000239295, R000223485 and L219252033 respectively). The community care module was funded by the Scottish Executive; the housing and neighbourhood module by Scottish Homes (now Communities Scotland). The survey involved a face-to-face interview with 1,605 respondents and a self-completion questionnaire completed by 1,383 (86 per cent) of these people. Copies of the question-naires are available from the National Centre for Social Research, web site http://www.natcen.ac.uk.

– Sample design –

The Scottish Social Attitudes Survey was designed to yield a representative sample of adults aged 18 or over in Scotland. People were eligible for the survey if they were aged 18 when the interviewer first made contact with them. The sampling frame for the survey was the Postcode Address File (PAF), a list of addresses (or postal delivery points) compiled by the Post Office.

For practical reasons, the sample was confined to those living in private households. People living in institutions (such as nursing homes or hospitals – though not in private households at such institutions) were excluded, as were households whose addresses were not on the Postcode Address File. The sampling method involved a multi-stage design, with three separate stages of selection – selection of sectors, addresses and individuals:

1. At the first stage, postcode sectors were selected systematically from a list of all postal sectors in Scotland. Before selection, any sectors with fewer than 500 addresses were identified and grouped together with an adjacent sector. Sectors were then stratified on the basis of grouped council areas[1], population density (with variable banding used, in order to create three equal-sized strata per sub-region) and percentage of household heads recorded as employers/managers (from the 1991 census). Ninety-six post-code sectors were selected, with probability proportional to the number of addresses in each sector.
2. Thirty-one addresses were selected at random in each of the ninety-six sectors. In some places more than one accommodation space shares an address. The Multiple Occupancy Indicator (MOI) on the Postcode Address File shows whether this is known to be the case. If the MOI indicated more than one accommodation space at a given address, the chances of the given address being selected from the list of addresses was increased to match the total number of accommodation spaces. As would be expected, the majority of MOIs had a value of one (94 per cent of those where an interview was obtained). The remainder, which ranged between three and eighteen, were incorporated into the weighting procedures (described below). In total the sample comprised 2,976 addresses and each sample point issued to interviewers contained 31 addresses.
3. Interviewers called at each selected address, identified its eligibility, and, where an address was eligible, listed all residents eligible for inclusion in the sample – that is, all persons currently aged 18 or over residing at the selected address. The interviewer then selected one respondent using a computer-generated random selection procedure.

– Weighting –

Data were weighted to take account of the fact that not all the units covered in the survey had the same probability of selection. The weighting reflected the relative selection probabilities of the individual at the three main stages of selection: address, household and individual.

First, because addresses were selected using the Multiple Output Indicator (MOI), weights had to be applied to compensate for the greater probability of an address with an MOI of more than one being selected, compared to an address with an MOI of one. Second, data were weighted to compensate for the fact that dwelling units at an address which contained a large number of dwelling units were less likely to be selected for inclusion in the survey than ones which did not share an address. (We used this procedure because in most cases these two stages will cancel each other out, resulting in more efficient weights.) Third, data were weighted to compensate for the lower selection probabilities of adults living in large households compared with those living in small households. All weights fell within a range between 0.0524 and 4.613. The weighted sample was scaled down to make the number of weighted productive cases exactly equal to the number of unweighted productive cases.

All the percentages presented in this book are based on weighted data; unweighted samples sizes are shown in the tables.

– Fieldwork –

Interviewing was carried out between May and October 2001 (88 per cent of interviews being completed by the end of August). An advance letter telling people living at selected addresses that an interviewer would call was sent out before the interviewers called.

Fieldwork was conducted by interviewers drawn from the National Centre's regular panel and conducted using face-to-face computer-assisted interviewing. (Computer-assisted interviewing involves the use of laptop computers during the interview, with questions appearing on the computer screen and interviewers entering responses directly into the computer.) Interviewers attended a one-day briefing conference to familiarise them with the questionnaires and procedures for selecting addresses and individuals to interview.

The average interview length was 58 minutes. Interviewers achieved an overall response rate of 60.1 per cent. Details are shown in Table A.1.

All respondents were asked to fill in a self-completion questionnaire which, whenever possible, was collected by the interviewer, but in some cases was posted to the National Centre. Up to three postal reminders were sent to obtain the maximum number of self-completion supplements.

A total of 222 respondents (14 per cent of those interviewed) did not return their self-completion questionnaire. We judged that it was not necessary to apply additional weights to correct for this non-response.

Table A.1 Response rates

	Number	%
Addresses issued	2976	
Vacant, derelict and other out of scope[a]	306	10.3
In scope	2670	100.0
Interview achieved	1605	60.1
Interview not achieved	1065	39.9
Refused[b]	732	27.4
Non-contacted[c]	216	8.1
Other non-response	117	4.4

a. 'Deadwood' included empty or holiday homes and businesses or institutions.
b. 'Refusals' comprise refusals before selection of an individual at the address, refusals to the office, refusal by the selected person, 'proxy' refusals (on behalf of the selected respondent) and broken appointments after which the selected person could not be re-contacted.
c. 'Non-contacts' comprise households where no one was contacted and those where the selected person could not be contacted.

– Other surveys used in the book –

– Scottish Election Surveys –

The Scottish Parliamentary Election Survey was carried out in 1999, and full details of its sample design and survey methods – which were very similar to those described above for the 2001 survey – can be found in Paterson et al. (2001). It was funded by the Economic and Social Research Council (ESRC). Scottish Election Surveys have been carried out as part of a series of British Election Surveys undertaken in 1974, 1979, 1992 and 1997. The British Election Surveys, which have been conducted since 1964, take place immediately after each general election.

In this book we use data from the October 1974, 1979, 1992 and 1997 Scottish Election Surveys. Fieldwork and data preparation for the 1992 and 1997 surveys were carried out by the National Centre for Social Research (then called Social and Community Planning Research). The Scottish samples were boosted in each of these years to allow data to be analysed for Scotland independently of Britain. The samples for each study were chosen using random selection modified by stratification and clustering. Up to 1992, the sampling frame was the electoral register (ER); in 1997 it was the Postcode Address File (PAF). Weights can be applied to make the 1997 survey (PAF) comparable with the previous (ER) samples.

Achieved sample sizes for Scotland were:
1979 729 (response rate 61 per cent)
1992 957 (response rate 74 per cent)
1997 882 (response rate 62 per cent)

Weighting of the data was carried out in each year to take account of unequal selection probabilities.

– Scottish Referendum Survey –

The Scottish Referendum Survey (alongside a comparative Welsh Referendum Survey) was undertaken in September–October 1997, funded by the ESRC (grant number M5443/285/001). Fieldwork was carried out by the National Centre for Social Research and interviewing began immediately after the referendum on 11 September 1997.

The sample was designed to be representative of the adult population who were living in private households in Scotland and eligible to vote in the referendum. It was drawn from the PAF and involved stratification and clustering. Weighting of the data was subsequently carried out to correct for variable selection probabilities.

The survey involved a face-to-face interview, administered using a traditional paper questionnaire and a self-completion questionnaire. The number of interviews carried out was 676, a response rate of 68 per cent. Self-completion questionnaires were obtained from 657 respondents (97 per cent of those interviewed).

– British Social Attitudes Survey –

The BSA survey, on which the Scottish Social Attitudes survey is modelled, has been running annually since 1983. It aims to yield a representative sample of adults aged 18 and over living in Britain. Since 1993, the sampling frame has been the Postcode Address File. The sample is selected by methods similar to those used for the Scottish Social Attitudes surveys. The sample size has generally been between 3,000 and 3,500, of which about 300 to 350 are in Scotland. The purpose of the surveys is to go beyond the work of opinion polls to collect information about underlying changes in people's attitudes and values. Further information on the BSA is contained in each of the annual reports on it, for example Park et al. (2002).

– Welsh and Northern Irish Life and Times Surveys –

Some of the questions that were asked by our survey were also carried by parallel surveys conducted in the summer (Wales) and autumn (Northern Ireland) of 2001. The Welsh Life and Times survey, undertaken by the National Centre for Social Research, interviewed a random sample of 1,085 adults. The Northern Ireland Life and Times survey interviewed 1,800 adults and the fieldwork was undertaken by Research and Evaluation Services. Further details of this survey can be found at http://www.ark.ac.uk/nilt.

– CLASSIFICATIONS USED IN ANALYSIS –

– Standard Occupational Classification –

Respondents are classified according to their own occupation, not that of the 'head of household'. Each respondent was asked about their current or last job, so that all respondents except those who had never worked were coded. Additionally, if the respondent was not working but their spouse or partner *was* working, their spouse or partner was similarly classified.

With the 2001 survey, we began coding occupation to the new Standard Occupational Classification 2000 (SOC 2000) instead of the Standard Occupational Classification 1990 (SOC 90). The main socio-economic grouping based on SOC 2000 is the National Statistics Socio-Economic Classification (NS-SEC).

National Statistics Socio-Economic Classification (NS-SEC)

The combination of SOC 2000 and employment status for current or last job generates the following seven NS-SEC analytic classes:

- Employers in large organisations, higher managerial and professional
- Lower professional and managerial; higher technical and supervisory
- Intermediate occupations
- Small employers and own account workers
- Lower supervisory and technical occupations
- Semi-routine occupations
- Routine occupations

The remaining respondents are grouped as 'never had a job' or 'not classifiable'. For some analyses, it may be more appropriate to classify respondents according to their current socio-economic status, which takes into account only their present economic position. In this case, in addition to the seven classes listed above, the remaining respondents not currently in paid work fall into one of the following categories: 'not classifiable'; 'retired'; 'looking after the home'; 'unemployed'; or 'others not in paid occupations'.

– Industry –

All respondents whose occupation could be coded were allocated a Standard Industrial Classification 1992 (SIC 92). Two-digit class codes are used. As with Social Class, SIC may be generated on the basis of the respondent's current occupation only, or on his or her most recently classifiable occupation.

– Party identification –

Respondents were classified as identifying with a particular political party if they considered themselves supporters of that party, or as closer to it than to others, or more likely to support a party in the event of a general election.

– National identity –

The survey uses a scale, known as the Moreno scale, to measure how people relate to being Scottish and being British, if at all. Single identities, either Scottish or British, form the ends of the scale and these identities are equal at the mid-point. At points 2 and 4, one or other is stressed but both are included. The question asks:

Which, if any, of the following best describes how you see yourself?
Scottish, not British
More Scottish than British
Equally Scottish and British
More British than Scottish
British, not Scottish
None of these

A second survey measure also used is a simpler question that asks respondents to select one identity from a list. They are asked:

If you had to choose, which one best describes the way you think of yourself?
British
English
European
Irish
Northern Irish
Scottish
Welsh
None of these

– Attitude scales –

The 2001 Scottish Social Attitudes Survey included two attitude scales relating to political ideology. These were developed to measure where respondents stand on certain underlying value dimensions (Heath et al. 1994). They are a left–right (socialist–laissez faire) scale and a liberal–authoritarian scale. Two versions of these attitudes scales have been in use since the 1986 BSA and 1987 BES. One version has tended to be used in the BSA surveys whereas a slightly different version has been used in election studies (BES). The 1999 and 2001 Scottish Social Attitudes surveys used the BES versions of the left–right scales (see below), whereas the 2000 survey used the BSA version. The 1999 Scottish Social Attitudes survey used the BES version of the libertarian–authoritarian scale, whereas the 2000 and 2001 surveys used the BSA version (see below). For details of the 2000 left–right scale, see Curtice et al. (2001); see Paterson et al. (2001) for details of the 1999 libertarian–authoritarian scale. Each scale consists of an aggregation of individual survey items designed to measure different aspects of the underlying belief system. A useful way of summarising the information from a number of questions of this sort is to construct an additive index (DeVellis 1991; Spector 1992). This approach rests on the assumption that there is an underlying – 'latent' – attitudinal dimension which characterises the answers to all the questions within each scale. If so, scores on the index are likely to be a more reliable indication of the underlying attitude than the answers to any one question.

The items (and their names on the datafile) are:

Left–right scale/socialist–laissez-faire scale
Ordinary working people get their fair share of the nation's wealth [*Wealth1*]

There is one law for the rich and one for the poor [RichLaw]

There is no need for strong trade unions to protect employees' working conditions and wages [TuntNeed]

Private enterprise is the best way to solve Britain's economic problems [PrivEnt]

Major public services and industries ought to be in state ownership [Publcown]

It is the government's responsibility to provide a job for everyone who wants one [GovResp1]

Libertarian–authoritarian scale

Young people today don't have enough respect for Britain's traditional values [TradVals]

People who break the law should be given stiffer sentences [StifSent]

For some crimes, the death penalty is the most appropriate sentence [DeathApp]

Schools should teach children to obey authority [Obey]

The law should always be obeyed, even if a particular law is wrong [WrongLaw]

Censorship of films and magazines is necessary to uphold moral standards [Censor]

Low values on the scales represent the socialist and liberal positions respectively. The scales have been tested for reliability (as measured by Cronbach's alpha). Values of 0.56 were obtained for the left–right scale and 0.70 for the libertarian–authoritarian scale in 2001.

– DATA INTERPRETATION –

– *Statistical significance* –

All the data in the book come from samples of the population, meaning that they are subject to sampling error. However, it is possible to calculate confidence intervals relating to any value from a given sample, creating a range within which we can have a certain level of confidence that the true population value lies. Table A.2 gives an indication of the confidence intervals that apply to different percentage results for different sample sizes. 95 per cent confidence intervals are shown, meaning that we can be 95 per cent sure that the true answer lies within the range shown. For example, for a percentage result of 50 per cent based on a sample of 500, there is a 95 per cent chance that the true result lies within +/- 4 per cent (thus, between 46 per cent and 54 per cent).

These confidence limits assume a simple random sample with no adjustment made for the effects of clustering the sample into a number of sample points. Although such an adjustment would increase the confidence limits slightly, in most cases these would not differ notably from those shown on the table (Paterson 2000: appendix). It should be noted that certain types of variables (those most associated with the area a person lives in) are more affected by clustering than others. For example, Labour identifiers and local authority tenants tend to be concentrated in certain areas and so, when the effect of the sample's clustered design are taken into account, the confidence intervals around such variables are greater than is the case for many other attitudinal variables (see Park et al. 2002 for examples of these kinds of design effects).

Table A.2 Confidence intervals for survey findings

Sample size	Approximate 95% confidence limits for a percentage result of:		
	10% or 90% +/–	30% or 70% +/–	50% +/–
50	8	13	14
100	6	9	10
250	4	6	6
500	3	4	4
1000	2	3	3
2000	1	2	2

Tests of statistical significance take account of the confidence intervals attached to survey findings. They can be carried out using modelling techniques (such as those described below), or by hand. Whenever comments on differences between sub-groups of the sample are made in this book, these differences have been tested and found to be statistically significant at the 95 per cent level or above. Similarly, although standard deviations are mostly not presented alongside mean figures in this book, these have been calculated and used to verify the statistical significance of the differences between mean figures which are commented on.

– Statistical modelling –

For many of the more complex analyses in the book, we have used logistic or linear regression models to assess whether there is reliable evidence that particular variables are associated with each other.

Regression analysis aims to summarise the relationship between a 'dependent' variable and one or more 'independent' explanatory variables. It shows how well we can estimate a respondent's score on the dependent variable from knowledge of their scores on the independent variables. The technique takes into account relationships between the different independent variables (for example, between education and income, or social class and housing tenure). Regression is often undertaken to support a claim that the phenomena measured by the independent variables cause the phenomenon measured by the dependent variable. However, the causal ordering, if any, between the variables cannot be verified or falsified by the technique. Causality can only be inferred through special experimental designs or through assumptions made by the analyst. All regression analysis assumes that the relationship between the dependent and each of the independent variables takes a particular form. In *linear regression*, a common form of regression analysis, it is assumed that the relationship can be adequately summarised by a straight line. This means that a one-point increase in the value of an independent variable is assumed to have the same impact on the value of the dependent variable on average irrespective of the previous values of those variables.

Strictly speaking the technique assumes that both the dependent and the independent variables are measured on an interval level scale, although it may sometimes still be applied even where this is not the case. For example, one can use an ordinal variable (for example, a Likert scale) as a *dependent* variable if one is willing to assume that there is an underlying interval level scale and the difference between the observed ordinal scale and the underlying interval scale is due to random measurement error. Categorical or nominal data can be used as *independent* variables by converting them into dummy or binary variables; these are variables where the only valid scores are 0 and 1, with 1 signifying membership of a particular category and 0 otherwise.

The assumptions of linear regression can cause particular difficulties where the *dependent* variable is binary. The assumption that the relationship between the dependent and the independent variables is a straight line means that it can produce estimated values for the dependent variable of less than 0 or greater than 1. In this case it may be more appropriate to assume that the relationship between the dependent and the independent variables takes the form of an S-curve, where the impact on the dependent variable of a one-point increase in an independent variable becomes progressively less the closer the value of the dependent variable approaches 0 or 1. *Logistic regression* is an alternative form of regression which fits such an S-curve rather than a straight line. The technique can also be adapted to analyse multinomial non-interval level dependent variables, that is, variables which classify respondents into more than two categories.

Full technical details of regression can be found in many textbooks on social statistics, for example Bryman and Cramer (1997).

– REFERENCES –

Bryman, A. and Cramer, D. (1997), *Quantitative Data Analysis*, London: Routledge.

Curtice, J., McCrone, D., Park, A. and Paterson, L. (eds) (2001), *New Scotland, New Society?* , Edinburgh: Polygon.

DeVellis, R. F. (1991), *Scale Development: Theory and Applications*, Newbury Park, CA: Sage.

Heath, A., Evans, G. and Martin, J. (1994), 'The measurement of core beliefs and values', *British Journal of Political Science*, 24, pp. 115–31.

Park, A., Curtice, J., Thomson, K., Jarvis, L. and Bromley, C. (eds) (2002), *British Social Attitudes: the 19th report*, London: Sage.

Paterson, L. (2000), 'The social class of Catholics in Scotland', Statistics in Society, *Journal of the Royal Statistical Society* (Series A), 163, pp. 363–79.

Paterson, L., Brown, A., Curtice, J., Hinds, K., McCrone, D., Park, A., Sproston, K. and Surridge, P. (2001), *New Scotland, New Politics?*, Edinburgh: Edinburgh University Press.

Spector, P. E. (1992), *Summated Rating Scale Construction: An Introduction*, Newbury Park, CA: Sage.

– NOTE –

1. Group 1: Scottish Borders; Dumfries & Galloway; South Ayrshire; East Ayrshire, South Lanarkshire; North Ayrshire.
   Group 2: Inverclyde; West Dumbartonshire; Renfrewshire; East Renfrewshire; Glasgow City; East Dunbartonshire.
   Group 3: North Lanarkshire; Falkirk; West Lothian; Edinburgh; Midlothian; East Lothian.
   Group 4: Argyll and Bute; Stirling; Perth and Kinross; Clackmannanshire; Fife; Angus; Dundee.
   Group 5: Comhairle nan Eilean Siar (Western Isles); Orkney; Shetland; Highland; Moray; Aberdeenshire; Aberdeen.

Index

abortion, 96, 109–10
Act of Union 1707, 1
Advisory Council for the Misuse of
    Drugs, 81
Ancient Order of Hibernians, 110–11
authoritarian attitudes, 147–50

BBC, 95, 96
Bevan, Aneurin, 67
Blair, Tony, 10
Bradley, Joseph, 107
British Election Study, 166
British Election Surveys (BES), 191, 195
British Social Attitudes (BSA) survey,
    4, 9–10, 23, 76, 77, 138, 188, 192,
    195
Britishness *see* national identity
Brown, Callum, 90, 91

cannabis, 82
    legalisation, 75, 76–81, 83–4
    see also drugs
Care Development Group, 40
Catholics, 86, 87, 88, 95, 96, 97, 186
    education, 102–3
    intermarriage, Protestants, 106–7, 110,
      186
    national identity, 107, 119, 124
    party politics, 98, 99, 100–1
    socio-economic status, 101–2, 103–6
    socio-moral values, 109–10
Church of Scotland, 86, 88, 89
Clark, T. and Lipset, S., 147–8
class identity, 140–55, 186
Clause 2A, 2, 108, 184
Comedia, 66
communities

mixed, 51, 66–9, 71, 72, 185
    see also neighbourhoods
community care, 30–47, 185
    funding, 37–47, 184, 185
community empowerment, 49–50, 55, 69–
    70
community ownership, 49–50, 54
community regeneration policy, 72
Community Regeneration Statement, 50,
    51
community values, 61–2; *see also*
    neighbourhoods
Conservative government, 1, 7, 8, 25, 32
Conservative party, 99, 100, 126, 137
constitutional change, 132–3, 135; *see also*
    independence
council housing, 49–50, 53, 54, 55, 56, 57,
    58, 59, 69, 71, 185
council tenants, 54, 56–7, 69, 70, 185

Davie, G., 92
Demos
    'Richness of Cities', 66
Dewar, Donald, 30
discrimination, 101–2
distribution, wealth, 144, 145
distributional justice, 51, 71
drugs, 185
    cannabis, 82, 75, 76–81, 83–4
    ecstasy, 75, 78, 79, 80, 84
    harm reduction, 76, 81–3, 84, 85, 184–
      5
    heroin, 78, 79, 80, 84
    legalisation, 75–81
    methadone, 81, 83
Drugs in Scotland: Meeting the Challenge
    (Ministerial Drugs Task Force), 82